Mirror of a People

ERRATA

On page xv, lines 23—24 should read:

''and robs him of his past. At the same time, a counter obligato is sounded: how wonderful is this great land and what marvelous potential awaits us here.''

On the same page, a new paragraph should start on line 27 with the sentence:

''There is outrage . . . ''

Sheldon Oberman, Elaine Newton, Editors

Mirror of a People

Canadian Jewish Experience in Poetry and Prose

Jewish Educational Publishers of Canada Inc.

Mirror of a People

ISBN 0-920657-00-1

1. Canadian poetry (English) — Jewish authors.*
2. Canadian fiction (English) — Jewish authors.*
3. Jews — Canada — Poetry. 4. Jews — Canada — Fiction. I. Oberman, Sheldon. II. Newton, Elaine.
PS8235.J4M57 1985 C810'.8'0924 C85-091109-5
PR9194.5.J48M57 1985

This book was published with the generous assistance of the Multiculturalism Directorate, Secretary of State, Canada.

Jewish Educational Publishers of Canada Inc.
370 Hargrave Street
Winnipeg, Manitoba R3B 2K1

Contents

Page

Part II: Canadian Born

Page

Part III: Tradition and Faith

Part IV: Holocaust and Israel

Page

Part V: In Search Of Identity

List of Photos

Foreword

From the insular, enclosed world of Eastern Europe, Jews came to the vast, vital spaces of Canada. Accustomed to the time-honoured proscribed ways of an ancient tradition, they encountered the chaos of a young, formless, strident society. Once ghettoized by political oppressors and huddled together by communal choice, the new immigrants were now both lured and betrayed by the promise of mobility and the chance to "make it" within the mainstream. Proudly, tentatively, greedily, skeptically they carved a hyphenated identity for themselves as Canadian-Jews, then sought full assimilation, then reinstated their "ethnicity" as a badge of selfhood within the pluralistic mosaic. The children of uprooted Yiddish-speaking peddlers and garment workers justified the anguish of their parents' immigration by becoming successful dentists and teachers, and lawyers' wives. In one generation, they moved from Estevan to Toronto, from St. Urbain Street to Westmount, and from North Winnipeg to River Heights. And the grandchildren ("slick imposters", Irving Layton has called them) donned tennis whites, gathered wine cellars, studied Plato, toured Europe and recalled with nostalgia and pride the folklore of Minsk and of the Kensington Market, of Lower Town, Ottawa, the St. Lawrence Blvd. cheder, and being the only Jewish family in Espanola, Ontario.

The autobiography of the early Canadian Jewish experience is well-recorded in imaginative literature: a significant body of poetry, fiction and prose narrative written by the Mordecai Richlers, Adele Wisemans, Jack Ludwigs, and A.M. Kleins of Canadian literature. These works convey much of the specific social reality of acculturation and many of the emotional and psychological implications of shifting roles, betrayed expectations, value clashes and fragmented relationships. They provide the feel of an era and the feelings of unfamiliar Canadians - the human dimension. But they also create a sub-genre of literature which is indisputably situated within the Canadian canon itself, partly because of the symbolic importance of the dualistic Jewish experience in a nation which is itself adolescent and identity-seeking, partly because of the tantalizing relationship of all Jewish writing to post-war literary culture, and partly because of the impressively gifted cadre of authors designated as "Canadian-Jewish writers". Although rooted in and nourished by the particularities of the Jewish social, linguistic and religious soil, although influenced by the profound tragedy of the Holocaust and the awesome promise of Israel, Canadian-Jewish poets and novelists provide an artistic vision that extends to the wider Canadian experience and ultimately to the common humanity shared by mankind. At the heart of their writing lies the anxious grey of all modern life, and the celebration of the human potential to cope with and to transcend that situation.

Jewish writing in Canada is a saga of marginality, those crises of selfhood which Quebec-born novelist Saul Bellow has termed "dangling men" and which Miriam Waddington's Danny designates as "English and Jewish". Burdened by old-world attitudes and influences, yet struggling to be accepted by and to accept the not always understood or even desired new culture, the Jew walked a tightrope, balancing the remembered claims of his forefathers and the ambiguous demands of the alien environment. He was the proverbial stranger in a strange and harsh land. And so the first and second generation literature focuses on fathers and sons, on wanderers and outsiders, on strategies of survival, on "where I came from", on adolescents in transition from childhood protection and conformity to adult self-reliance, and on the frustrated, lonely quest for a sense of identity. Again and again, images and anecdotes build a picture of the need to burst out of the narrow, parochial society, of generation conflicts and personal rebellion, of disintegrating customs and rejected mores. But there is also the deep-rooted commitment to preserve the traditions, the memories, and the timeless faith. Repeatedly, there emerges an intense concern with personal and family history and the desire for a moment of particular recognition amid the sprawling milieu which diminishes man, tatters his cherished dreams and robs him of his past. At the same time, a counter awaits us here. The new definitions are unconfident and the paths unrealized, the poet's voice cries of dual estrangement, while the young hero of short story or novel finds that having sloughed off the old, he cannot quite embrace the elusive new. There is outrage and pain, guilt and confusion in the rendered vision. But there is also the awareness of the rich comic potential and the profound capacity for hope, excitement and pleasure. "Without money", writes Fredelle Maynard, "we lived rich." Though the tone is frequently etched in satire or washed by tears, Canadian Jewish writing is rarely cynical and never smug. The future beacons. "We will seize our lives in these scarred hands", insists the patriarch in Adele Wiseman's **The Sacrifice.** Out of the tension and the ferment comes fresh creativity, linguistic virtuosity and an immensely human sensibility. And there is always laughter. The modern Jew is after all, the one who in track shoes, "limps and flies". The Canadian Jewish author has lived raw experience, recollected it and chosen to conserve it. He is most certainly a teller of tales. To the reader, he offers a concerned vision of flawed, foolish, but caring and engaged mankind.

Elaine Newton
York University
Toronto, 1984

Historical Introduction

Question:

What is a Canadian Jew?

Answer:

A Jew who lives in Canada.

— Simple question, simple answer; but perhaps not an altogether accurate one. If the two disparate tags "Canadian" and "Jew" had no closer connection than that, there would be no more reason for this volume than for one, for instance, written by left-handed people from Guelph. The fact that being Canadian has had a real impact on the identities of Jews who settled here, that Jews have both added to and altered the Canadian reality, gives this volume its raison d'être.

The brief history which follows will attempt to give a thumbnail sketch of the origins of Canada's Jewish population and some of the factors which led to its arrival on these northern shores.

JEWISH LIFE IN CANADA — A BRIEF HISTORY

BEFORE CONFEDERATION

In the early days of European migration to what is now Canada there was little opportunity for Jewish settlement. In New France, Louis XIV had specifically barred Jewish or Huguenot incursion.

With the fall of Quebec to the British and the end of the Seven Years' War, the situation changed. A few Jewish merchants entered Canada, among them such brilliant entrepreneurs as Aaron Hart, who founded a "dynasty" which endures to this day. Although many of these first arrivals achieved some fame through their position or power (Aaron Hart was reputed to be the wealthiest landowner in all the British colonies), only a very small number of Jews entered Canada in the century following the British conquest; it has been estimated that in 1881 there were only 2500 in the entire nation, scattered across the country in small groups. Most had come from England or the United States and had settled in southern Ontario and Quebec. During the Fraser gold rush of 1858, a few had immigrated to what later became British Columbia; a few had come down the Red River in the '70's to settle in the new province of Manitoba. Most were cosmopolitan, fairly well-educated and anglophone. They are not represented here. Like the vast majority of Canada's present Jewish population, the writers in this volume are descended from a very different group, formed mostly of the children and grandchildren of Russian-Polish refugees fleeing European oppression. To understand the reasons for their coming, we must refer briefly to European history.

IMMIGRATION AFTER 1881

In 1881 a group of "narodniki" (revolutionary anarchists) assassinated Czar Alexander II of Russia. This action became an excuse for a wave of pogroms which spread throughout southern Russia. These massacres and riots left a trail of devastation and over 100,000 homeless. The suffering Jews of eastern Europe sought a place of refuge.

Help was organized in England. A group known as the Mansion House committee was established to assist in the immigration of Russian Jews to Canada. Alexander Galt, then Canadian High Commissioner in London, lent the committee his advice and wrote Sir John A. Macdonald, proposing Jewish immigration to Canada.

Galt informed Macdonald that he had written Baron Alfred de Rothschild of the famous philanthropic Jewish family about "the feasibility of removing the agricultural Jews to Canada". According to Galt, Canada had "not a bad chance of interesting the Hebrews in our North-West." Sir John expressed a rather cynical attitude towards the Jews, referring to Jewish immigration as the "Old Clo' Cry", (in reference to the stereotypical Jewish rag pedlar,) and suggesting that Jewish immigration into the Northwest would establish a "missing link" between Canada and the Jewish people. Despite his rather off-hand display of prejudice, he was willing to allow Jews their chance in Canada.

Over the next forty years, many Jews did settle in western Canada, either in farm colonies scattered across the three prairie provinces, or in growing Prairie cities like Winnipeg, where they laboured in the factories and lumberyards, opened shoestring businesses, and struggled to survive. Many more found homes in eastern Canada, swelling the large Jewish communities of Montreal's fabled St. Urbain ghetto and Toronto's Spadina Market area, and establishing small enclaves in cities and towns from Glace Bay to Ft. William.

The first section of this book, which deals with the immigrant experience (usually as narrated by their sons and daughters — few of the immigrants themselves were literate in this language . . .), reflects some of the drama of these "greenhorns" first encounter with Canada.

JEWISH LIFE IN THE TWENTIETH CENTURY

In the first decades of the twentieth century, Russian-Polish Jews gradually became the dominant group in Canada's Jewish population. Community activities and organizations were established, and aid societies, by providing language lessons and interest-free loans, helped the new immigrants find their ways in the new world. Pious immigrants founded Orthodox synagogues and ''Talmud Torah'' Hebrew schools to perpetuate Jewish traditions and faith, and to teach their children the Hebrew language. More left-wing newcomers, (many of whom had been forced to flee Russia following the abortive revolution of 1905), established Labour Temples, I.L. Peretz Folk Schules, (schools) and ''Arbeiter Ring'' (Workmen's Circle) associations in an equally fervent attempt to promote the goals of Yiddish culture and Socialist thought.

Meanwhile, in Jewish communities across the nation, a new generation of native-born Canadians was growing up, a generation influenced both by their parents' European sensibility and their own Canadian cultural milieu. Many of the excerpts in the ''Canadian Born'' section of this collection reflect the difficulties of growing up in the interface of these two often antagonistic worlds.

THE THIRTIES AND WORLD WAR II

The comparatively large flow of Jewish immigration that continued through the early years of the twentieth century, slowed to a trickle in the '20's and dried up completely during the Depression and war years. This was a result of a number of factors, besides the obvious belt-tightening necessitated by economic conditions and the dislocation caused by the war. Traditional Canadian preference for Anglo-Saxon and northern European immigrants, Prime Minister Mackenzie King's anxious need to placate anti-Semitic Liberal M.P.'s and power brokers in Quebec, active and committed anti-Semites high in the mandarinate of the Canadian Immigration Department; all these played their parts in thwarting what was for thousands their final hope of escape from the gathering storm in Europe.

Canadian Jews were drastically and personally affected by the rise of Fascism and Nazism. Many of them had relatives and friends trapped in Europe whom they were helpless to assist; many had themselves only just escaped earlier pogroms. They attempted, with growing desperation and almost always in vain, to overcome the Canadian government's indifference to the plight of European Jewry. They watched as their brethren were destroyed and suffered from guilt and helpless rage at their own impotence. Many of the selections in the "Tradition and Faith" and "Holocaust and Israel" sections of this anthology reflect these feelings.

It would be impossible to deal with the history of Canada's Jews without at least some mention of the Holocaust — the destruction of European Jewry by Hitler and his allies during World War II. As a result of the unimaginable horror of Nazi racism, six million Jews were destroyed in the ghettos, slave labour camps and crematoria of the German Reich. Thousands of Jewish communities across Europe were totally obliterated. Poland, which in 1931 had a Jewish population of over three million, has today perhaps a few thousand Jews. Some of the writers included in this volume (A.M. Klein, J.I. Segal) evoke the events of the European nightmare as they happened; others (Leonard Cohen, Mordecai Richler, Irving Layton) visited after the war.

ISRAEL AND CANADA'S JEWS

The scattered remnants of Europe's Jewish community emigrated both to the New World and to British Palestine, where they joined earlier settlers and immigrants from the surrounding Arab states in the struggle to create and perpetuate the new nation of Israel. Many Canadian Jews have strong ties to this young and ancient nation. Zionist organizations, which promote "aliyah" or emigration to Israel, have flourished in Canada since Theodor Herzl founded the movement in the 19th century. Canadian Jews have generously given funds to help in the settlement of Israel and formed organizations which promote Zionist goals. In 1948, Canadian Jews, many of whom were seasoned veterans of World War II, fought and died in the Israeli War of Independence. Many Canadian Jews continue to identify strongly with Israel and her triumphs and difficulties, although the ambiguities shown in Mordecai Richler's wry tale of "The Arabian Nights Hotel", sometimes play a part as well.

THE SITUATION TODAY

Since the War, Canada's Jewish population has evolved and changed both demographically and culturally. Immigrants have arrived from the U.S.S.R., North Africa and even Israel. The second and third generation of Canadian Jews are very different from their parents and grandparents in their education, wealth, and values. Jewish farmers, tailors, factory workers, country storekeepers and pedlars have all but vanished, to be replaced by a new generation of doctors, lawyers, businesspeople, teachers, and university professors. The Yiddish language, which our ancestors spoke for centuries, continues to decline. Dire predictions of assimilation through apathy, intermarriage or simply the complacency of success, continue to be heard. Many worry that within a few short generations, tolerance and acceptance might succeed where Hitler and all his armies failed: Jewish culture might disappear entirely as a distinctive entity within Canadian Society.

There *are* signs which point in the opposite direction. Coincidental with the revival of so-called fundamentalist religions in the Christian world, there has been something of a renaissance in the feeling of young Jewish people towards their own religious observance (see ''Chassidic Song'' or ''The Ritual Hour'' in this anthology). This movement may follow a traditional path or the new wave of ''Aquarian Judaism'' which has its roots in the ''New Age'' philosophies of the 1960's and is open to some influence both from other ideologies and from Jewish Chassidic and mystical thought. Another hopeful development is the Canadian Government's continued push towards multiculturalism. The government, which once actively discouraged ethnic heterogeneity, is now funding a multitude of programs promoting the great variety of languages and cultures that make up the Canadian cultural mosaic. Jewish organizations are contributing fully in this area.

Is this a last efflorescence of activity before an inevitable melding into homogenized North American culture, or is it a sign of renewed and future growth?

The writers represented in this collection do not answer this question. What they do provide us, as we look doubtfully towards the final decades of the twentieth century, is a twofold offering; a testimony to the vitality and creativity provided by Jewish themes and sensibility in Canada yesterday and today, and a vivid picture of some of the contradictions, humour, and pathos inherent in the lives of Canada's Jews as, like Avrum Malus' ''Modern Jew'', they ''limp and fly'' towards an uncertain future.

Murray Goldenberg

Ed. Note: The material in this brief essay was abstracted from Mr. A. Arnold's **Jewish Life in Canada,** and my own **Jews in Manitoba: History and Culture,** as well as other sources.

Mirror of a People

Photo 1: Jewish immigrants from Europe arriving at Halifax c. 1948.

Part One

Immigrant Experience

Immigrant Experience

After the perilous journey from the poverty, insularity and persecution of Eastern Europe's pale, what did Jewish immigrants find in this strange and demanding country? Extremes of climate, vast stretches of untamed land, the clamour of hectic modern cities, the loneliness of isolated prairie towns, the model of Anglo-Canadian manners and attitudes. Struggling to better themselves, they peddled rags and junk, laboured in sweat shops and lumberyards, and learned English. Dispossessed though they were, needing to cling to and preserve memories of the old world, they yet hungrily claimed personal shares of experience, of opportunity, of Canada. Above all, amid mutilations of communal and religious life, they worked to provide a home and an education for their children who would be the 'real Canadians'.

The portraits of the first generation included in this section record the challenges, pathos and humour of the newcomers' existence. Alive to ironies, disillusionments and triumphs of their parents' lives, second generation writers such as Adele Wiseman depict the bewilderment and the determination of the newcomer, trying to impose a sense of order on an alien land where the languages he speaks and the cultural baggage he has brought with him are of little use. Fredelle Bruser Maynard looks affectionately at her idealistic father's attempts to succeed in the uncertain environment of rural Manitoba; Morley Torgov writes wryly of the semi-assimilated burghers of Northern Ontario; Tom Wayman sings of his grandfather's odyssey through India and England to a lonely Canadian grave; and Eli Mandel speaks a wistful eulogy to a Jewish farm community in Saskatchewan.

Adele Wiseman

The Sacrifice

The Sacrifice—An Excerpt
Chapter One begins as Abraham, his wife Sarah and surviving son Isaac approach an unnamed Canadian city after a painful emigration from the Ukraine where they lost two sons to anti-Semitic persecution. This moving story of both sacrifice and hope won the Governor General's Award in 1956.

The train was beginning to slow down again, and Abraham noticed lights in the distance. He shifted his body only slightly so as not to disturb the boy, and sank back into the familiar pattern of throbbing aches inflicted by the wheels below. A dim glow from the corridor outlined the other figures in the day coach as they slept, sprawled in attitudes of discomfort and fatigue. He tried to close his eyes and lose himself in the thick, dream-crowded stillness, but his eyelids, prickly with weariness, sprang open again.

Urgently the train howled the warning of its approach to the city. Facing him, Abraham's wife seemed to seize the same wailful note and draw it out plaintively as she sighed in her sleep. Her body huddled, strained and unnatural, on the faded green plush seat. He could feel the boy, slack and completely pliant, rolling to the motion of the train. The whistle howled again, the carriage jolted, and his son lurched heavily, almost lifelessly, against him.

Enough! With a sudden rush of indignation, as though he had been jerked awake, it came to Abraham that they had fled far enough. The thought took hold in his mind like a command. It came alive in his head and swept through him angrily, in a wave of energy, a rebellious movement of the blood. It was as simple as this. Enough. He must act now.

He sat up carefully, shifting Isaac's limp form into another position, fired in his new determination by the boy's weak protesting mumble. Slowly, he stretched, feeling his joints crackle, willing the cramp out of his body. He looked about him impatiently.

As though summoned, the conductor entered the coach. Abraham turned his head and beckoned imperatively.

''Where are we?'' he asked in Ukrainian, tentatively, his red-rimmed eyes gleaming with excitement, his loud voice muted to a hoarse whisper.

The man stooped, his face polite, questioning, and to Abraham offensively vacant in its noncomprehension. ''I beg your pardon?'' he said in English.

''Where are we stopping, please?'' Abraham asked urgently in Yiddish, speaking slowly and patiently so that the man must understand.

The conductor shook his head. ''No speak, no speak,'' he said, pointing to Abraham's mouth, then to his own, with a deprecating gesture.

Abraham looked at the man with irritation. Was there anyone on the train who could do anything but make faces and smile? ''Why does the train stop?'' he asked suddenly, hopefully, in Polish.

The conductor shook his head helplessly.

Abraham leaned forward and gestured wildly toward the window to where the lights blinked in the distance.

The conductor, as though realizing something, smiled a broad, reassuring smile, shook his head vigorously, patted Abraham lightly on the arm, and made as if to move on.

''The train! stop! why? What city?'' roared the Jew in exasperation, spitting out the words in broken German.

At the sound his son jerked suddenly awake, frightened, and looked blindly about for a moment. Other passengers groaned, stirred their numb bones, and mumbled in protest. The conductor swayed on down the car, shrugging apologetically at drowsy faces.

''Animals here,'' muttered Abraham, subsiding and turning helplessly to his son. ''They can only gibber and gesticulate.''

''What's the matter, Pa?'' Isaac yawned. ''Can't you sleep?''

"*No!*" With a gesture, he flung aside the overcoat he had used as a cover. "The train is stopping. We're getting off."

"But we have two more days."

"Who awaits us?"

There was no answer to this that the boy knew of. Who awaited them? What awaited them? It did not really matter whether they stopped here, blindly, or went blindly on to the other city for which they had bought the tickets. Isaac crouched for another moment and watched his father, who was collecting their bundles. His own limbs were so knotted that it took him a moment to gather the strength to get out from under his warm coat and stretch.

The conductor called out the name of the city.

"No; enough I say," said Abraham. "Fifteen months and eleven days. If I had to spend more days and nights worrying about a new beginning I would not have the strength to begin. Two more days and nights in this position, and this whole human being that you call your father will make sense only to an upholsterer. I do not know where we will sleep tomorrow, but at least our beds will lie flat and we will rock no more."

"But our tickets —" Isaac rubbed his eyes with numb fingers and shook his head to clear his thoughts.

"Ah, our tickets." Abraham scratched the itching skin under his forked beard reflectively. "Well, it's senseless trying to explain anything to that fellow. Listen to him. Me he can't answer a simple question, and now he wakes up the whole train with his shouting up and down. Well, I suppose he can't help himself. Would I have understood him even if he had understood me?"

Strength and humor returned with his decision. He moved around and stretched; his blood began to circulate again. Like a young man entering deliberately into an adventure, he felt excited at making a positive gesture in the ordering of his fate.

"In fact, come to think of it, we'll be saving money. If we get off here we save the rest of our fare, so just in case they're not clamoring for a butcher and I don't get a job here right away, we'll save that much more money to live on in the meantime. That's why it's such a good idea to get off here. You see, your father has not lost his common sense. In fact, it's a wise decision I have made with God's help. And we can see about our tickets in the station."

Lights flashed by; at the other end of the car a young couple were gathering their belongings.

"The important thing now," Abraham continued, "is that we must stop running from death and from every other insult. We will seize our lives in these scarred hands again." He paused to consider his words with pleasure.

"Come, boy, we must wake your mother — but gently. How weary she is."

When the train grunted to a halt Abraham and his family, his wife blinking and shivering with sleep, stood among the few waiting with their bundles in their arms. The conductor, noticing the group assembled to leave, rushed up to them.

"No, no, no!" He shook his head and reached for Abraham's suitcase. "This isn't your stop!"

Abraham brushed his arm away firmly.

"Shalom," he said politely, yet with a certain fierceness that prevented the conductor from persisting. They descended to the platform. The conductor stood shaking his head in exasperation over these immigrants. Abraham cast him a last, forgiving glance. As though it were written, he could see what they must do. First, to find the immigration barracks — to sleep, at last, without the artificial pulse of engines to remind them even in sleep that they were wanderers. Then, with the new day, to settle themselves gingerly on the crust of the city, perhaps someday even to send down a few roots — those roots, pre-numbed and shallow, of the often uprooted. But strong. Abraham felt strength surge up in him, excitement shaking the tiredness out of his body. No matter what is done to the plant, when it falls, again it will send out the tentative roots to the earth and rise upward again to the sky. The boy was young, the boy was blessed, the boy would grow.

Isaac shifted his bundle uncomfortably under curious stares and raised his eyes upward and ahead in imitation of the oblivious purposefulness of his father. He moved stiffly, aware of the difference in dress between these people and himself, and listened, lonely among the strange rhythms about him, for voices of warmth.

That morning they had found a place to live, and now they were bringing their belongings to install in the room. Isaac thought of the new home with trepidation, perhaps not so much in spite of but because of the fact that the landlady had told him happily that she had two daughters just his age. What would two native girls think of him? What if they were like their mother — two garrulous girls with sharp noses, the tips moving like rabbits', incessantly up and down as they talked?

Sarah, Isaac's mother, who had lived for months as in a dream, found herself hypnotized, watching the face of Mrs. Plopler as she talked. When the woman addressed her persuasively, woman to woman, reiterating the merits of this furnished room with its bed, its couch, its bureau, its chair and its big window, she merely nodded up and down, unthinking.

The landlady was a thin, flat-fronted woman with nothing to draw the eye from her hyperactive nose other than a head of tightly grizzled hair that started upward from her head in stiff, small waves. As she talked she examined her prospective roomers and saw that they were no longer young, this straight-backed Jew with his beard thrust forward, as though starched, away from his chest, and his wide-eyed, unresponsive wife. Still talking, she swept her eyes over their pale adolescent son, who stood looking at her in a way which she found vaguely irritating. Her eyes took in their portable belongings. She concluded that they were lucky to get her room, and, reminding them again that they would have the benefit of a furnished room with a bed, a couch, a bureau, a chair, and a big window, as well as kitchen and bathroom facilities, which they would share with her family, she asked for her rent in advance.

Half an hour after they were securely installed and she had their rent pinned away warmly, their landlady was telling a neighbor how she had taken a poor immigrant family into the house, practically right off the train, and how she had made them feel immediately at home. ''Why, they're taking baths already.''

Shortly afterward she met her adolescent daughters at the door with the whispered news that she had rented the room to an immigrant family with a son of about sixteen, who, however, didn't look like much, but that they would nevertheless have to stop running about the house half-naked in the mornings. She added that the tenants had taken baths already, three separate baths, and that she had served them tea in the kitchen and had gleaned that the father was a butcher. At present, she told the girls, they were asleep after their long trip.

Leaving her daughters at home — two overgrown girls who began to wander up and down outside the room, pausing to listen and giggle at the door of their tenants — she went off to shop for supper. At the grocery she mentioned that she had taken an immigrant family into her house, people she knew nothing about, that they had taken baths already, that she had served them tea, that the husband was a butcher, that they were resting at present, and that it was hard for two families to share one bathtub.

When her husband came home she told him that they had finally rented the furnished room to an immigrant family, that the husband was a butcher who didn't have a job yet, though they'd paid rent in advance, that they were at present asleep in their room, that they had taken baths already, and that she wondered how often they intended to take baths during the week, all three of them.

''You have to show them that we have a bathtub right away,'' said her husband, who was a joker and a jolly good fellow at a party but surly, with secret grievances, at home.

''Well, it's by the toilet,'' she defended herself. ''They would have found out anyway. And besides, it's because of the long train ride that they bathed. They're greenhorns; they won't want to bathe very often. You know how filthy these people are apt to be.''

''We have too much hot water for you,'' he grumbled.

''She served them tea, too,'' chimed in Gertie and Goldie eagerly, happy for some diversion after having palpitated around the house all afternoon in vain.

The Ploplers waited to get a glimpse of their tenants, but Abraham and his family slept on until the evening. Then the Ploplers noted that the lights went on and heard their voices murmuring, the man's louder than the rest. But they couldn't catch the words. From the moving about they assumed that the new tenants were unpacking and putting the room in order. Possibly, even, they were eating something from one of their outlandish bundles. Then the lights went out.

''Certainly sleep a lot,'' commented their landlord. ''Why you didn't knock on the door and ask them if they want anything is beyond me. I think I have as much right to see them as you have. I go out in the morning and come back to find half my house rented away, and nobody thinks to introduce me to my new tenants. Nobody thinks fit to ask me if maybe in my opinion they're not suitable for tenants in my house. Who rents a room just like that?''

''Why didn't you tell me when the lights were on to knock on the door?'' said his wife. ''You think they'd come out by themselves to be sociable. They know I have a husband.''

''Maybe they're tired,'' suggested on of the girls.

''I'm tired too,'' said her father. ''So what?''

''What does the son look like?'' asked the other girl, who had heard at least half a dozen times before. They both listened eagerly while their mother described how thin and wretched-looking a boy he was, but not, for all that, entirely ugly. The landlord resigned himself sullenly to waiting till morning.

Maybe they're whispering that we might want some water during the night. Isaac lay, sleepy and thirsty, conjuring up this fanciful hope because he was ashamed to venture out of the room in his bathrobe among all those feminine voices that whispered in the kitchen. It seemed to him that he had not had any water for a long time. The taste of salt herring was in his mouth. He got up and brushed against the chair, making a noise so that the whispering in the kitchen held its breath for a moment. His father's deep, open-mouthed breathing continued to purr and chortle from the bed, and his mother lay silent, curled up under the bedclothes. Isaac found an orange to suck and lay back down on the couch with it.

It was different when they had changed boats and were in England for a short while. There it didn't matter that his clothes were different. He could walk with his hands in his pockets, knowing he'd be leaving soon, and pretend he was a tourist — wealthy, idle, indolent, even perhaps at times a bit supercilious.

He saw himself back in London when he had stood for a long time watching people buy bananas, wondering what was done with them. Yet he had not let on, just cocked his head carelessly to one side and whistled a short snatch of melody, as it were absent-mindedly, as though speculating on some subject far off from these petty transactions.

At last a man and a little boy had bought some of the bananas, and the little boy peeled one of them and began to gobble greedily. So Isaac had bought and peeled to take, tentatively, taste....Pleasant ... Floating in to confront his parents. Mother's gasp. "What are you eating?" Father: "Raw!" ... Isaac, enormously sophisticated, wearing no clothes at all, prowling a strange house with raw girls, whispering, "It's a fruit to gobble greedily in English." Tasting-sipping-drinking deeply. Suddenly, his brothers' heads crowding among the immigrants, Moses: "Like water." "No, like herring." Jacob, the learner, in the darkened room. "Like watered herring" — definitively. "Like water." Moses, the singer, adamant. "Raw water." "Can't get water from a torn bathrobe." — contemptuously.

The orange didn't help much, ventured Isaac. She still wagged her yellow nose. As Isaac slept.

After lunch, when Isaac went to the English-language course that had been organized in the district high school, Abraham left the house with him. Isaac pointed at objects, enunciating carefully the English names.

"Tree. Sky. Cloud. House. Mountain."

Abraham would repeat, fingering the syllables clumsily with his tongue, but with immense satisfaction listening to the sound of his son's apparently adroit mastery. When they parted, the young voice continued to repeat itself in his head, raised, clear, ardent, for to Abraham his son's voice must be ardent. Nothing grows but by desire.

Sky. Houz. He stopped in front of a tree, frowning at it demandingly. Now what did he call this?

His beard jutted out in vexation, and his eyes traveled up the trunk in search of a clue.

Boim. Isaac's voice, speaking cheerfully in Yiddish, came to his mind.

"*Boim,*" said Abraham out loud to the tree with satisfaction and proceeded towards the busy avenue.

The little leaves are falling from the trees. Abraham expanded his scope, carefully enunciating his thought mentally, as though it were an elementary language lesson, thinking in Yiddish, but laboriously, so that he could feel pleasantly as though it were the English equivalent.

He stopped as he reached the avenue and pulled out his little snap purse to look for the address the butcher had given him that morning.

Today I may find work. Then we will go to night school. It may be that there are new thoughts in English. The Russians, too, have very clever sayings.

The chill autumn winds ruffled the hair on his face, outlined his bare cheeks where they met his beard, and crept, clean-smelling, into his nostrils.

Isaac will yet do something fine. He was not spared for nothing.

Mordecai Richler

The Street

"Why do you want to go to university?" the student counsellor asked me.

Without thinking, I replied, "I'm going to be a doctor, I suppose."

A doctor.

One St. Urbain Street day cribs and diapers were cruelly withdrawn and the next we were scrubbed and carted off to kindergarten. Though we didn't know it, we were already in pre-med school. School starting age was six, but fiercely competitive mothers would drag protesting four-year-olds to the registration desk and say, "He's short for his age."

"Birth certificate, please?"

"Lost in a fire."

On St. Urbain Street, a head start was all. Our mothers read us stories from *Life* about pimply astigmatic fourteen-year-olds who had already graduated from Harvard or who were confounding the professors at M.I.T. Reading *Tip-Top Comics* or listening to *The Green Hornet* on the radio was as good as asking for a whack on the head, sometimes administered with a rolled-up copy of *The Canadian Jewish Eagle,* as if that

Photo 2: Highland Regiment parading through St. Urbain in Montréal. (Scene from the movie: ''The Apprenticeship of Duddy Kravitz'').

in itself would be nourishing. We were not supposed to memorise baseball batting averages or dirty limericks. We were expected to improve our Word Power with the *Reader's Digest* and find inspiration in Paul de Kruif's medical biographies. If we didn't make doctors, we were supposed to at least squeeze into dentistry. School marks didn't count as much as rank. One wintry day I came home, nostrils clinging together and ears burning cold, and proud of my report. ''I came rank two, Maw.''

''And who came rank one, may I ask?''

Mrs. Klinger's boy, alas. Already the phone was ringing. ''Yes, yes,'' my mother said to Mrs. Klinger, ''congratulations, and what does the eye doctor say about your Riva, poor kid, to have a complex at her age, will they be able to straighten them . . .''

Parochial school was a mixed pleasure. The old, under-paid men who taught us Hebrew tended to be surly, impatient. Ear-twisters and knuckle-rappers. They didn't like children. But the girls who handled the English- language part of our studies were charming, bracingly modern and concerned — about our future. They told us about *El Campesino,* how John Steinbeck wrote the truth, and read Sacco's speech to the court aloud to us. If one of the younger, unmarried teachers started out the morning looking weary we assured each other that she had done it the night before. Maybe with a soldier. Bareback.

From parochial school, I went on to a place I call Fletcher's Field High in the stories and memoirs that follow. Fletcher's Field High was under the jurisdiction of the Montreal Protestant School Board, but had a student body that was nevertheless almost a hundred per cent Jewish. The school became something of a legend in our area. Everybody, it seemed, had passed through FFHS. Canada's most famous gambler. An atom spy. Boys who went off to fight in the Spanish Civil War. Miracle-making doctors and silver-tongued lawyers. Boxers. Fighters for Israel. All of whom were instructed, as I was, to be staunch and bold, to play the man, and, above all, to

Strive hard and work
With your heart in the doing.
Up play the game,
As you learnt it at Fletcher's.

Again and again we led Quebec province in the junior matriculation results. This was galling to the communists amongst us who held we were the same as everyone else, but to the many more who knew that for all seasons there was nothing like a Yiddish boy, it was an annual cause for celebration. Our class at FFHS, Room 41, was one of the few to boast a true Gentile, an authentic white Protestant. Yugoslavs and Bulgarians, who were as foxy as we were, their potato-filled mothers sitting just as rigid in their corsets at school concerts, fathers equally prone to natty straw hats and cursing in the mother-tongue, did not count. Our very own WASP's name was Whelan, and he was no less than perfect. Actually blond, with real blue eyes, and a tendency to sit with his mouth hanging open. A natural hockey player, a born first-baseman. Envious students came from other classrooms to look him over and put questions to him. Whelan, as was to be expected, was not excessively bright, but he gave Room 41 a certain tone, some badly needed glamour, and in order to keep him with us as we progressed from grade to grade, we wrote essays for him and slipped him answers at examination time. We were enormously proud of Whelan.

Among our young school masters, most of them returned war veterans, there were a number of truly dedicated men as well as some sour and brutish ones, like Shaw, who strapped twelve of us one afternoon, ten on each hand, because we wouldn't say who had farted while his back was turned. The foibles of older teachers were well-known to us, because so many aunts, uncles, cousins and elder brothers had preceded us at FFHS. There was, for instance, one master who initiated first year students with a standing joke. ''Do you know how the Jews make an 's'?''

''No, Sir.''

Then he would make an 's' on the blackboard and draw two strokes through it. The dollar sign.

Among us, at FFHS, were future leaders of the community. Progressive parents. Reform-minded aldermen. Anti-fallout enthusiasts. Collectors of early French Canadian furniture. Boys who would actually grow up to be doctors and lecture on early cancer warnings to ladies' clubs. Girls who would appear in the social pages of the Montreal *Star*, sponsoring concerts in aid of retarded children (regardless of race, colour, or creed) and luncheon hour fashion shows, proceeds to the Hebrew University. Lawyers, Notaries. Professors. And marvelously with-it rabbis, who could not only quote Rabbi Akiba but could also get a kick out of a hockey game. But at the time who would have known that such slouchy, aggressive girls, their very brassieres filled with bluff, would grow up to look so serene, such honeys, seeking apotheosis at the Saidye Bronfman Cultural Centre, posing on curving marble stairwells in their bouffant hair styles and strapless gowns? Or that such nervy boys, each one a hustler, would mature into men who were so damn pleased with what this world has to offer, epiphanous, radiating self-confidence at the curling or country club, at ease even with pot-bellies spilling over their Bermuda shorts? Who would have guessed?

Not me.

Looking back on those raw formative years at FFHS, I must say we were not a promising or engaging bunch. We were scruffy and spiteful, with an eye on the main chance. So I can forgive everybody but the idiot, personally unknown to me, who compiled our criminally dull English reader of prose and poetry. Nothing could have been calculated to make us hate literature more unless it was being ordered, as a punishment, to write *Ode To The West Wind* twenty-five times. And we suffered that too.

Graduation from FFHS meant jobs for most of us, McGill for the anointed few, and the end of an all but self-contained world made up five streets, Clark, St. Urbain, Waverley, Esplanade, and JeanneMance, bounded by the Main, on one side, and Park Avenue, on the other.

By 1948 the drift to the suburbs had begun in earnest. To come home in 1968 was to discover that it wasn't where I had left it — it had been bulldozed away — or had become, as is the case with St. Urbain, a Greek preserve.

Today the original Young Israel synagogue, where we used to chin the bar, is no longer there. A bank stands where my old poolroom used to be. Some of the familiar stores have gone. There have been deaths and bankruptcies. But most of the departed have simply packed up and moved with their old customers to the new shopping centres at Van Horne or Rockland, Westmount or Ville Ste. Laurent.

Up and down the Main you can still pick out many of the old restaurants and steak houses wedged between the sweater factories, poolrooms, cold-water flats, wholesale dry goods stores, and "Your Most Sanitary" barbershops. The places where we used to work in summer as shippers for ten dollars a week are still there. So is Fletcher's Field High, right where it always was. Rabbinical students and boys with sidecurls still pass. These, however, are the latest arrivals from Poland and Rumania and soon their immigrant parents will put pressure on them to study hard and make good. To get out.

But many of our grandparents, the very same people who assured us the Main was only for *bummers* and failures, will not get out. Today when most of the children have made good, now that the sons and daughters have split-level bungalows and minks and West Indian cruises in winter, many of the grandparents still cling to the Main. Their children cannot in many cases persuade them to leave. So you still see them there, drained and used up by the struggle. They sit on kitchen chairs next to the coke freezer in the cigar store, dozing with a fly swatter held in a mottled hand. You find them rolling their own cigarettes and studying the obituary columns in the *Star* on the steps outside the Jewish Library. The women still peel potatoes under the shade of a winding outside staircase. Old men still watch the comings and goings from the balcony above, a blanket spread over their legs and a little bag of polly seeds on their lap. As in the old days the sinking house with the crooked floor is right over the store or the wholesaler's, or maybe next door to the scrap yard. Only today the store and the junk yard are shut down. Signs for Sweet Caporal cigarettes or old election posters have been nailed in over the missing windows. There are spider webs everywhere.

Photo 3: The Atlantic Fur Company, Toronto, early 1940's.

Photo 4: Store and home of Zebulon Frank, Vancouver, c. 1902.

Fredelle Bruser Maynard

The O-Kay Store

The Okay Store—An excerpt from **Raisins and Almonds.**
Fredelle Bruser Maynard grew up in a dozen spots on the Prairies during the twenties and thirties as her father struggled to keep the family fed by running a series of general stores.

Papa's last store was in Grandview, a Manitoba town that looked very much like all the other towns we had tried. "This time," Papa said, "we make a go of it. You'll see." I looked bleakly about me, unconvinced. Older now — at the last auction, we had sold my toys along with the household goods—I viewed the new enterprise with an adolescent's knowing skepticism. The building-store and dwelling combined, an arrangement I had come to dread — was, if anything, more depressing than the last, a great box sheathed in corrugated metal that clattered hideously in bad weather. The house smelled of sour milk, the store of sweat and cheese. In the kitchen, Mama was ripping up old linoleum, moaning softly at the unspeakable discoveries between each layer. I stayed in the store, conducting my own fascinatingly dreadful explorations. The fabric on the bolts was faded, the puffed wheat chocolate bars had worms. The shallow glass display boxes fronting the grocery counter contained substances so ancient, so close to total disintegration, that barley was scarcely to be distinguished from coffee beans. Papa sat on the high stool at his desk, composing. " 'Grand opening of The O-Kay Store,' " he declaimed. " 'It's our birthday, but you get the presents.' Sounds good, eh?"

I feigned enthusiasm. ''Mmm. Terrific.''

''I make it, you see, like a letter to the farmers, signed B. Bruser, manager a whole chain of stores in western Canada.''

''Papa!'' I was shocked. ''How can you say a thing like that? They'll find out we've got just this one store.''

''So? In Gretna haven't I been? In Altona, all the other places? This doesn't make a chain?''

Grandview seemed something less than a bustling metropolis, but then, as the Goodyear traveler pointed out, it was a Saturday night town. Over the sample cases and the wholesale catalogues of rubber footwear, he filled us in. ''You buy right and sell right, Bruser, you got yourself a nice living here. Dead all week — bread, bologna, package of matches. But wait'll you see them wagons come Saturday night. Place really jumps.''

Papa brightened. ''You think maybe I have Saturday specials? Big signs in the window, an ad in the paper maybe?''

The salesman shook his head. ''Nah. That stuff don't go around here. These Polacks pick themselves a store like it's a club, see, and that's it. You get the big boys — Steve Worchuk, say, or Pete Wyrzynowski — and you got it made. They'll bring their whole damn church.''

The big boys, I thought, must be venerable community patriarchs. It was a real surprise when the first of them appeared. I was opening a shipment of penny candy, checking the boxes against the invoice — 2 cinnamon hearts, 1 mint leaves — when a voice demanded, ''Them fresh?'' I looked. The newcomer scooped up a handful of jawbreakers, grinned and spat licorice. He was young and black-haired, arrogantly handsome, with lots of strong white teeth. ''Worchuk.'' The name dropped like a brick. ''Where's the boss?''

Papa was just coming in from the house. Worchuk's pinch — unexpected, unthinkable — caught me as I turned. He winked at my father. ''Say, that's some ripe tomato you've got. Little on the young side, but not bad, not bad.'' Flushed and humiliated, I waited for Papa to wither the offender. But Papa was smiling, hand extended. I fled to the dry goods and there, kneeling safely behind the counter, listened to the compact. Papa's voice vibrated with unfamiliar heartiness. ''You like snuff? Here, take, it costs you nothing. Now, I was saying, you bring your boys in, I fix them up for school — overalls, sweaters, the works. The price is right, I promise. And you don't pay in cash one cent.'' Steve for his part was playing it cool. ''If I deal here, Bruser, it's got to be a fair shake all the way. I bring in butter and eggs, you take 'em, right?'' And senega root. Last fellow had this store, tried to jew me down —" I saw Papa wince. Worchuk bulldozed on. There was to be a flat price on eggs — "I don't go for that candling and grading. I got good eggs" — and a special discount on hundred-pound sacks of flour. Worchuk was at the door already when he looked at me again.

"You got two girls, Bruser?"

"Yes, this is the baby." Papa's smile was proud. "We have also Cecely, in high school."

Worchuk took my measurements dispassionately. "I got a girl, not so fat as yours, little shorter. Any clothes you don't need, we can use. Your old lady too." The door banged.

After that, we saw a lot of the Worchuks. Mrs. Worchuk (her husband never called her anything but "the Cook") was white as a mushroom and Steve, a swarthy man, was terribly proud of her skin. "Look at that," he said, showing her off to Papa the first time. "She's like that *all over.* The Cook looked straight ahead with pale, flat eyes. "I bring eggs," she would announce, or "butter." That was as much as she ever spoke. She communicated through her husband or when he left for the beer parlor, through one of the small brown children who scuffled and clung as she waited for the grocery order. Her butter was unbelievably dreadful, tasting of mice and damp cellars, but Papa accepted it without question. "Why?" he explained. "Because a living I have to make, yes? To Worchuk I don't say 'Your wife makes bad butter.' A temper he has like fire, and friends — the whole district. From such butter one can always make soap."

Whether it was thanks to Worchuk or not, the store prospered. Every Saturday night was a triumph. Even with extra help, we could hardly wait on all the customers who pressed against the front counter, waving their lists. Cecely and I bustled back and forth loading bundles into wagons, Mama manned the cash register. As for Papa, he was everywhere, radiant — greeting, telling his favorite stories, handing out oranges and candy to the children. I suppose he enjoyed the experience of making a little money at last, but his delight went far beyond such mundane satisfactions. He was a community figure, respected and admired; his store had become the meeting place of the district's most prominent farmers; it was *O-Kay*.

With triumph came responsibility. Papa's advice was increasingly sought on financial matters. Mama was consulted on problems domestic and, more surprising, medical. Sometimes I came home from school to find a customer stretched out on the sofa while Mama, frowning, palpated a swollen stomach. Often I was pressed into service to write letters for farmers who signed with an X. There was a steady demand for packaging. One day, just before Christmas, Steve Worchuk appeared with an armload of bundles. "Here, Bruser, wrap these good, They go back to Eaton's." I looked at his purchases. Any one he might have bought at our store, how *could* he ask Papa to handle transactions for a competitor? But Papa's smile was cordial as ever. "You want different merchandise, or I tell them to send you back the money?"

The first Grandview Christmas came, the deep cold Manitoba winter, and then summer. As harvest drew near, a bumper crop seemed certain. Papa started to make plans for improving the store, and Mama put a new coat of whitewash on the privy. "We're staying," I whispered to Cecely. It seemed too good to be true. The very next night we wakened to a great thumping and banging below. I heard Papa's slippers flapping down the stairs, a burst of voices. Then Mama stood by the bed, the kerosene lamp in her hand.

"Freidele? You're not sleeping, dear? Come, help."' Her voice sounded furred and lumpy.

"What's the matter?"

"The Worchuk boy — Alex, the little one. He fell from the tractor — *oy gewald!* — under the wheels. So is now the family downstairs."

I knew Alex — a quick mouse of a boy, always hovering near the cookie bins. I tried to imagine him riding the big tractor, falling, the snap and crunch of wheat stalks all around. Dead. It wasn't real. My face felt stiff, like when the dentist gave me novocaine for a filling.

"But why are they here?"

Mother sighed. It was a sigh that carried with it lament and wonder — wonder at the mysterious ways of the gentile world. "They have tomorrow a big funeral. They come for hats — and yeast."

The hats I understood, but the yeast? Bundling me into my robe, Mama explained. "For a funeral there must be fresh buns. So she makes right away the dough, it should have time to rise."

In the kitchen, Papa was crying. The brandy we kept on hand for sickness stood on the table. Steve Worchuk, his face a furious red, shook his fist and roared. "God damn it, Bruser, that kid could run a tractor since he was born almost! So one day we work a little late, and this happens! I didn't make him! He says, 'Dad, it's plenty light still. You let me finish —' " Seeing me, he broke off. "Here, you, kid. Take the Cook in and get her a hat."

I knew where the funeral hats were stored. Papa made no attempt to keep up with current fashions in headgear; that department he left to Eaton's. But he had always on hand a large carton of featureless dark straws. I pulled it out and began sorting through. A bonnet with under-the-chin ties; that would be for a child. A panama — no, too large; it sunk deep over the Cook's brows. Here now — a big-brimmed garden party sort of hat . . . . Her moon face registered satisfaction. I squinted doubtfully at a bunch of cherries, preposterously large and glossy, pinned to the brim. "You could take those off," I suggested. She shook her head. I followed her back to the kitchen, a strange humping figure, the loose faded housedress hanging just above the oxfords and ankle socks, and the cherry hat riding high.

Farewells were fervent. Papa, I gathered, had made Steve a present of groceries for the funeral feast. He had given, too, a bolt of fine soft muslin for the little shroud. Steve, exuding a warm steamy brandy fragrance, embraced my mother and shook my father's hand. "You're a real white man, Bruser. I won't forget this."

It was shortly after the Worchuk funeral that we heard the first unsettling rumors. There was going to be a new store in Grandview — modern, self-service, just like in the city. Papa pooh-poohed the reports, but I could see he was worried.

"People don't want they should wait on themselves," he said to Worchuk over the grocery counter. "They come to a store, they want service."

"Yah, you're right," Steve said. He reached for an orange and bit into it, skin and all.

"Anyway, to put up a store takes time," Papa went on. "This year for sure they don't build. Already the ground freezes."

"You ain't heard?" There was a hint of teasing in the question. "They bought Johnson's Hardware. Already hammering, too."

It was true. Within weeks, the new store opened for business. Papa and I walked by one evening after the O-Kay was closed and peered through the plate-glass windows. It was a big store, all right, loaded with new goods. Fluorescent lights, plastic counter tops, a row of shiny help-yourself carts lined up at the entrance. I thought of our old brown store and shivered. Papa was cold too. On the way home, he held my hand so hard that the snow on my mitten caked into a hard lump. "Comes Christmas, we show them," he said. "These new fellows got money for fixtures, sure, but display they know from nothing." "That's right." I tried to sound grown-up and knowledgeable. "There isn't anybody can do Christmas decorations like you."

By December I felt less confident. I couldn't face walking past the Bargain Emporium to see for myself, but reports reached us daily. The new store had put up a giant tree with lights and glass balls (a dazzling novelty in rural Manitoba), and underneath was a pile of surprise boxes labeled with customers' names. Every regular customer got a box. They had an immense cardboard Santa riding across the roof in a sparkling sleigh; they were giving out tickets on a free Christmas turkey. It seemed to me, as we hung our accordion-pleated paper bells and streamers, that the colors were getting a bit thin. Papa had made a new window display — a toy circus — but there were fewer oglers this year. People rushed by, shouting and laughing. There were plenty of clear spaces at the grocery counter. ''I think,'' Papa said, ''we let go the extra help. A man has such a family, who needs strangers?''

The last Saturday before Christmas was always a big day in the store. I woke very early and tiptoed down the back stairs. The old black stove was already roaring in the kitchen; Mama had set the table with platters of sweet-smelling cinnamon toast and dishes of sparkling jelly. Papa wiped his lips with a linen napkin and pushed back his chair.

''Boris, sit a while,'' Mama said. ''The customers don't break down the doors.''

Papa smiled. ''But if they should, I must be there, no?''

There was a tiny silence, and then Mama said, quite carefully. ''Steve Worchuk, I don't see him these days. He's been in?''

''The roads are bad — and so much sickness everywhere. Today for sure he brings in the Christmas order.''

''I see in the *Jewish Post,* '' Mama said, as though this were a logical continuation, ''is for sale in Churchill a nice little business.'' ''Churchill!'' I was interrupting, but I couldn't help it. I had seen Churchill on the map, a dot poised on the edge of the great blue gash of Hudson's Bay. I imagined us setting out by dog sled to forge a new link in the chain of stores — Eskimos — sealskins — the frozen North . . . . ''Oh, Mama, *no!*''

''Rona, what kind of an idea?'' Papa spoke reassuringly. ''In Grandview we make always a living. So we don't get rich. You lie on the ground, you can't fall down. Come, I want we should be ready before the rush.''

But there was no rush. Shoppers floated in and out, picking up small items, and Papa greeted them with torrential enthusiasm. ''Package of needles? Sure thing, Mrs. Olsen. The best. You got plenty of thread? Buttons? A nice piece percale, maybe, on special? Here, some candy for the little ones. Christmas toys you don't need?''

Watching Mrs. Olsen escape with her needles, I was ashamed of my shame. He was doing this for us. These people had never seen Papa's face, still and grave and beautiful, when he listened to Jan Pierce singing *Kol Nidre*. They had heard his jokes, but not the tender little stories with which he used to put us to sleep. ''Then the bad fairy said, 'Let me have your youngest child, the baby, and I give to you a mountain all of gold.' And the Papa said, 'What good is a mountain all of gold and I have not my heart.' '' They had never known his joy and pride at the Passover service — ''Oh Lord, Thou hast preserved us and sustained us and brought us to this day'' — and his radiant prayer, ''Next year in Jerusalem!''

Papa had plenty of time, that day, to straighten piles of sweaters that didn't need straightening. It was late afternoon when I saw Steve Worchuk. He was walking on the opposite side of the street, laden with packages, his face turned away. Papa saw him at the same moment. He put down the turkey-feather duster.

''Let him go, Papa,'' I said. ''He can shop at the Emporium. We don't need him.''

Papa shook his head. ''This I don't believe. Steve is always my friend. Something is wrong, a mistake. I go to see.''

I watched him cross the road, in the chinchilla coat that had lost its plush, the ear flaps of his hat drawn down against the cold. The two men talked a minute, Steve stamping his feet and blowing on his fingers as he shifted the heavy bags.

''He'll be in,'' Papa said, shaking the snow off his coat. ''He goes to get the family.'' Sure enough, a few minutes later, there was Steve, followed now by the Cook, hatless, and the two older girls. He carried a single, crumpled bag.

''Well, now,'' Papa's voice was a shade too hearty. ''Christmas so soon, and so much always to get. What will it be, Steve?''

Steve walked past the dry goods, past the ladies wear and the hardware and the toys. He stood at the grocery counter. ''Five pounds of sugar,'' he said flatly. ''And a plug of chewing tobacco.''

''That's everything?'' I couldn't look at Papa's face.

''Well, no, not quite. I got a exchange here.'' Steve was fishing in the paper bag. Then he drew something out. ''The Cook don't like this hat.''

The funeral hat lay on the counter. The black straw, dust color now, was raveling at the brim; the few straggly cherries were split and faded.

Papa seemed bewildered. ''You joke.''

''No, by God, I'm not joking. This ain't the kind of hat she wanted, and she got no use for it. I want my money back.''

''The hat you *charged,* Steve. And how can I take back merchandise has been worn already?''

''*Worn?* I say she ain't never worn that hat, and she ain't never *going* to wear it. Call me a liar, will you — *you lousy kike!''*

Papa's face split in a clown's tragic smile. Then he walked slowly, like a cripple or a man whose back has been broken, to the cash register and rang up No Sale. ''Here,'' he said, taking out two dollar bills and smoothing them flat on his palm. ''Now I owe you nothing. The hat she can keep.'' The Cook's pale flipperlike hand reached out. Steve was too fast for her. He snatched the hat from the counter, strode over to the potbellied stove, banged open the door, and threw the hat into the flames. I thought I heard the cherries pop.

We stood still a long moment, watching them climb into the wagon, the Cook blubbering, the children huddled together, and Steve furiously whipping the horses on. Papa put his arm around me. ''So who needs them?'' he asked of no one in particular. ''Money we can't eat, our health we have. And next year —'' He looked outside, where our old sign creaked and swung in the bitter wind. ''Next year in Churchill, yes?''

Morley Torgov

Queen Street

Queen Street—An Excerpt from **A Good Place to Come From.**
Queen Street is the main street of Sault Ste. Marie, Ontario which is the setting of the small Jewish community in which Torgov grew up during the late thirties and early forties.

Queen Street is the main street of Sault Ste. Marie. It runs east and west, roughly paralleling the St. Mary's River, for a distance of about five miles.

Today, Queen Street is lined with signs telling you it is a one-way thoroughfare heading west. You get onto Queen Street at, say, Pim, and you drive past Brock, Spring, March, Elgin, Bruce, Dennis, Tancred, Gore, travelling westward past the new International Bridge, following the setting sun all the way. Now you are as far as James Street in the heart of Little Italy. A few blocks more and you are into Steel Plant Country: Bayview, the wrong side of the tracks - smoke, dust, the grinding noises of trains and cranes, the overpowering, deep-seeping smells of sulphur and coal-tar. You obey the road signs, and you go west.

Yesterday - in the nineteen-thirties and early forties - Queen Street was a one-way thoroughfare heading east. There were no signs that told you this, only an instinct, a compelling sense of direction. You got onto Queen Street, at, say, Huron, and you passed about two dozen streets as you travelled eastward, stopping - if you were a Gentile - at Simpson Street where the stately red brick houses and the green lawns were; not stopping - if you were a Jew - until you had gone as far east as you could go: east along Highway 17 and eventually along Highway 11 passing through Sudbury and North Bay and Huntsville, until the road signs said "City of Toronto" some 500 miles later. Then, and only then, did you stop.

For the smalltown Jew, and especially for the children of the smalltown Jew, Queen Street was a one-way street heading eastward to Toronto. There could be no stops in between.

The people of whom I write - the thirty to forty families who made up the local Jewish community - occupied stores and apartments and houses within a relatively small area in the central part of Sault Ste. Marie. The intersection of Queen and Bruce Streets formed the hub of this area, and most of the Jewish business establishments and homes lay no more than a block or two from that point. Despite this apparent concentration, it is impossible to characterize the inhabitants as ghetto-dwellers, nor was this a shtetl environment in the European sense of the term. As you walked along Queen Street, you saw, true enough, signs that read "Himmel's Ladies' Wear," "Friedman's Department Store," "Fishman's Men's Wear." You heard two neighbouring merchants call to each other on the sidewalk, "Hello, Joe," "Hello, Isaac." You heard Mr. Cohen and Mr. Mintz greeting each other in Yiddish outside the Royal Bank. Yet you were not conscious of being in the midst of a Jewish world. It was as if the Jews - even those who owned their own properties - were no more than temporary tenants who borrowed time and space on Queen Street during daylight hours in order to make their living. To the Gentile population we were a mysterious subterranean breed, a race who surfaced daily from 8:00 A.M. to 6:00 P.M. (midnight on Saturdays) to sell merchandise, and disappeared into the ground after hours to do God-knew-what. There were no Jewish theatres, delicatessens, butcher shops, corner confectionaries; none of the storefront street-level institutions one associates with the ghetto. Until the mid-1940's there was no synagogue.

If there was little resemblance to the big-city ghetto, there was even less resemblance to the shtetl. Having been blown across Europe by a hundred different winds of turmoil, and having vomited their way across seas and oceans to North America, our fathers were far too worldly to live the life of simple villagers. They had shaved off beards and sidelocks, discarded skullcaps, eaten pork when it meant the difference between living or starving, battled with the English language and called down plagues upon its unfamiliar spellings and pronunciations.

They worked on the Sabbath, indeed worked harder and longer on the Sabbath than on any other day of the week, for that was the one day of the week when the Gentiles were most often in a spending mood. To nothing - save the inescapable curse of old age - did they resign themselves. Before no one did they bend or cower. The rabbi was always no more than a few minutes away, ready to be consulted when the spirit was low or the conscience was tortured. But somehow he could never be the symbol of rigid, orthodox discipline that his shtetl counterpart had been in Europe; rather, he could only be one of them. Granted he hadn't shed the trappings of his religion as they had done; nevertheless, the same gales that had carried them like pollen from one continent to another, had carried him as well. He and they were comrades, shipmates, fellow-tenants.

Not ghetto Jews, not shtetl Jews. What then were they?

Upside-down weeds ... that perhaps is the best way to describe them. Weeds that had planted themselves in strange ground, weeds that grew with with their foliage - the fruit of their labours - submerged in the earth and their roots exposed to air and sky. They spent their lives this way, scratching, scraping, building up, tearing down, conniving and surviving. Always there was the struggle to invert themselves, to establish root and leaf in proper order, to become more than mere weeds; to become indigenous plants.

They never entirely succeeded.

My father demobilized himself from the Russian army late one night in the summer of 1917. Reluctantly he had spent two years and eight months in the service of the Czar and his lack of enthusiasm for military life only deepened when the Czar was eliminated and the Bolsheviks moved into the royal palaces. The southern part of Russia, near Odessa, where my father had been born and raised, was famous for producing great watermelons and violinists, both of which products my father loved, but these attractions were not powerful enough to draw him back to a land which was also famous for producing misery and cruelty. Taking liberty without leave, he headed in the direction of Roumania and never saw Russia again. Nine years later, his tour of the Western World came to an end in a small, northern Ontario town, the name of which he could barely pronounce - Sault Ste. Marie.

In the interval between his self-demobilization and his descent in the Soo's railway station, he had dabbled profitably in the currency market in Roumania, earned the price of a steerage ticket to "Kanada," harvested wheat in Saskatchewan, taught Hebrew in Winnipeg where he married the older sister of one of his pupils - a prize catch because she had been born in England and her father was a man of property who had once been reeve of West Kildonan. After Winnipeg, it was peddling made-to-measure suits to miners in Timmins, doing business out of the back of a horse-drawn wagon. For engaging in this enterprise without a transient licence, he was arrested and fined $50.00. That experience crystallized his thinking. It was high time to stop being a transient.

But where to settle: In the financial circles frequented at the time by my father (i.e., the roving bands of fellow peddlers and other here-today-gone-tomorrow types), word was spreading about the golden promise of a town with a crazy French name which they pronounced ''Sahlt-stee-maria.'' The Algoma Steel plant there was taking on hundreds of immigrants from Italy and the Slavic countries. The town held potential riches for a clothing man who didn't mind working eight days a week, could communicate in the foreigners' lingo, and was fast with a tape measure.

Sault Ste. Marie society little noted nor long remembered the day my father and mother, anchored by a large steamer trunk, disembarked at the railway station at the head of the street appropriately named ''Pilgrim Street.'' To the by-standers on the station platform who eyed them with only casual interest, this was simply another greenhorn and his wife come to town to hustle yard goods and ribbons. But to the handful of Jews already there, the new couple would be welcome company. Would this mean a fresh source of competition? Yes. Sometimes, however, in this semi-wilderness, it was better to lose a dollar here and there and gain a landsman, a neighbour from your part of the old country, someone who spoke Yiddish, could perhaps quote a bit of Talmud, someone who slurped tea from a glass through a sugarcube held between the front teeth, and remembered what the watermelons were like in the south of Russia.

Before long, the town began to yield some of its golden promise: a small shop on Queen Street, a self-contained flat over the shop, a Model T, and for the first time, a feeling of permanence. The young Russian Jew, still sporting the pencil-slim moustache he had affected years before in the Russian Army, and the quiet Winnipeg girl who worked at his side day and night in the shop despite the fact that she was now very pregnant, were here to stay.

Like most of his fellow merchants, my father was everything in the business - merchandise-buyer, window-trimmer, window-washer, cashier, stock- controller, salesman, even seamstress on occasion. And like most of his colleagues in the trade, he depended heavily upon his wife, who assisted him in nearly all of these diverse functions. But there was one ritual in which he relied entirely upon her. That was when the "Inspector-Generals" made the rounds. The Inspector-Generals were women who customarily travelled in pairs, visiting one store after another along Queen Street. They would finger their way through long racks of dresses and try on every hat in the place, whispering furtively to each other in Italian or Ukrainian or Finnish, never committing themselves one way or the other, but examining each garment critically at arm's length. Truly an outsider at such moments, the merchant could do nothing but stand idly by, wondering whether the Inspector-Generals were planning a purchase or plotting a pogrom. At last, one of the women would speak up: "Where Missus?" That was the signal for the merchant's wife to come forth. If "Missus" neither spoke nor understood these foreign languages, she was at least fluent in the international language of hemlines and bodices; therefore, "Missus" usually clinched the sale, turning the tricky, final stage of the transaction - the price haggling - back to her less gentle husband.

When it came to male trade, it was a different story. Here the merchant himself took over exclusively because this aspect of the business involved a fine art known as "sidewalking." My father would position himself on the sidewalk directly in front of his emporium, standing well out towards the curb so that he had a commanding view of the eastern and western approaches. His competitors up and down the street stationed themselves similarly on the sidewalk in front of their establishments. All of them pretended not to notice each other. Then, from a distance, the merchants could spot the first contingent of spenders. They might be steel workers just finished the night shift, still grimy and sweaty, carrying their empty lunchpails and bearing those most important fortnightly pay cheques in their wallets. Or they might be lumberjacks just arrived in town on the Algoma Central from the "bush", desperately needing hot baths and fresh clothes, their pockets bulging with a winter's pay. Whether or not the steel worker or lumberjack had a familiar face was immaterial. As soon as the fellow was within hooking range, my father would call out to him, "Hey Mike! (It was always assumed that the man's name was Mike) . . . . Mike, come on in, I got some real good buys for you today. Gotta nice suit for you for Easter. C'mon, Mike!" The next thing Mike knew, he was standing before a full-length mirror draped in the latest blue serge or black pinstripe. The fitting of such a garment involved a degree of ingenuity and virtuosity never dreamed of in Savile Row. These smalltown Jewish merchants had learned the art of fitting in the ''tuck-and-pull'' school where a suit was literally yanked, stretched, jammed and cajoled into shape in an exercise that amounted to an outright assault upon the customer's sagging body. The physical effort was accompanied by grunts, sign language, quips in the customer's native tongue, Yiddish oaths. Finally, sighs of relief from both vendor and purchaser as the last pin was pressed into place in the trouser cuffs. When the ordeal was over, the merchant would stand back to admire his handiwork. ''Mike,'' he would assure the fellow in the mirror, ''you'll be the talk of Queen Street on Easter Sunday, believe me.'' Before Mike had time to agree or disagree, he was choosing a shirt, matching tie, socks, shoes. The split-second Mike was out the door, having left behind him a fair chunk of his pay, the shopkeeper was back once again at his sidewalk stand, calling out to the next available steel worker or lumberjack, ''Hey Mike, c'mere . . . .''

The social life of the Jewish community revolved around a suite of two rooms rented in the second storey of a building near the corner of Queen and Bruce. Located within easy reach of nearly all the Jewish stores and homes, the shul had the advantage of convenience. But that was all.

The smaller of the two rooms was occupied as a cheder for the children as well as a place for memorial services. Here the young were instructed and the dead remembered, all in an atmosphere of mustiness and overcrowding. The room constantly reeked of cigarette smoke and ancient mildewy prayer books. Even when the windows were opened wide, fresh air refused to venture within; instead it hung outside in the bright sun, beckoning children to come out and play. The men, swaying idly to and fro as the rabbi murmured and chanted, stared longingly out of the windows and daydreamed of sitting in rowboats, fishing and munching hardboiled eggs.

The larger of the two rooms was much too large for the average community function. Therefore, it was used very little, mostly for special occasions - High Holiday services, Bar Mitzvahs, weddings, benefits. Long wooden benches ran along the walls of this chamber, leaving a vast empty space in the middle. Thus it was quite impossible to make an entrance or exit without the entire congregation's eyes falling upon you and without attracting comment. ''Look at that, he just got here and already he's running back to the store'' . . . . ''Look at Queen Esther, if you please, sneaking in a minute before the service is over so God should think she was here all day'' . . . . On Yom Kippur, late entries and hasty exits were dead giveaways: ''Aha, the bastard's just come from breakfast'' . . . . ''There she goes, couldn't wait like the rest of us until the rabbi blows the shofar''... It was a seating arrangement designed for conspicuous prayer only; private sacrilege was quite out of the question.

The worst feature of the larger room was that it lacked exclusivity, since it was also the local headquarters for the Independent Order of Foresters. Indeed, the Foresters had the main claim to the premises and filled the walls with their regalia. There were photographs of officials all posing stiffly and sternly as if guaranteeing posterity that the Foresters would always be independent and stand for order. Huge framed charters, adorned with red wax seals and gold ribbons, proclaimed the legitimacy of the local branch. Shields were mounted in recognition of noble collective efforts and plaques honoured all sorts of individual acts of self-sacrifice. Only a dull cabinet that cried for a coat of varnish belonged to us. It stood against the east wall of the room and housed the two Torahs during High Holiday services and Passover. All the rest was Foresters' property in Foresters' territory.

The two rooms were connected by a dimly-lit corridor where the boys gathered to exchange dirty jokes and tease the girls, and where everyone gathered occasionally as a diversion from religious devotions, to listen to a Finnish husband and wife who occupied an apartment on the same floor, screaming at each other in their native cacophony.

In 1946, after years of fund-raising, planning, debating (put ten Jews together and you immediately had ten architects), the first synagogue was consecrated. At last the congregation possessed its own building, a modest red brick structure on a modest plot of land - on where else? - Bruce Street, not far from its intersection with Queen.

I wonder: in all the years preceding the opening of the new synagogue, how many little Jewish kids were convinced, as I was, that God was actually a member of the Sault Ste. Marie Lodge of the Independent Order of Foresters?

Why did we, the children of the smalltown Jews, leave home? Why this perpetual motion eastward?

There are a thousand and one reasons, but they all boil down to a single reason: we left because our parents counselled us to leave, begged and pleaded with us to leave, even ordered us to leave. Only yonder in the big city, they insisted, could one be a truly big person; here in this town one could be no more than a large fish in a tiny pond.

Better to be the tail of a lion in a great city, than the head of a jackal in Sault Ste. Marie.

We, the children, resisted at first. Life seemed so simple, so attractive in the small town.

There was little, if any, overt discrimination against the pocket-size Jewish community. Happily for us, the Gentile population was too engrossed in a civil war of its own to pay us much attention. It was a cold war, waged between the Anglo-Saxons of the East End and the Italians of the West End. The latter group, who numbered many thousands, were beginning to look eastward from the Latin Quarter towards Simpson Street. Dr. Mancini, recently graduated, preferred to live in the same fashionable part of town as old Dr. Macmillan. Old Dr. Macmillan was prepared to tolerate Dr. Mancini at meetings of the local medical society but having Dr. Mancini and all the little Mancinis residing next door to the Macmillans was another matter. So totally did this conflict occupy the two principal racial establishments that somehow we Jews were able to slip out from between the two sides and maintain a state of neutrality. Besides, a handful of Jews such as we could scarcely pose any threat even if we *had* become partisans in the struggle. So we kept our feelings to ourselves, smiled compatibly at both major factions, and simply carried on selling them non-combat merchandise — clothing, furniture, scrap metal — in return for which they were gracious enough to pay their bills and leave us in peace.

And what of the eternal quest to earn a decent livelihood — wasn't it easier in the small town? Our fathers had planted the saplings for us, had endured the depression, had prospered through the war years; now all that remained for us to do was to nourish the orchards and harvest the fruits. Every afternoon there was lunch at home and a short nap. In the summer, you could close your store at six and be sitting down to supper at your cottage at Pointe-aux-Pins by six thirty. Wednesday afternoons there was fishing at Garden River or Echo Bay, a few miles down Highway 17. Who needed fancy college degrees? Who needed the urban rat race? Who needed suburbia?

On the surface, it was an effortless, uncomplicated existence.

But our fathers and mothers knew otherwise. Beneath the paper-thin crust of their serenity, volcanoes were boiling. Gone were the days of "sidewalking," now there were petty jealousies and, sometimes, bitter competition as business rivals strove to consolidate the gains of the war years and expand their tidy fortunes. Fathers and mothers stewed privately and publicly about the love affairs of their sons and daughters: how could young David ever find and settle down with a Jewish girl if, instead of venturing forth to Detroit or Toronto, he stayed put on Queen Street and took out shiksas on Saturday nights? What could be done to prevent young Miriam from becoming too involved with that shaygetz from Pim Hill, the fellow with the Irish surname who kept taking her to Hi-Y dances and Boat Club regattas? The same people saw each other all the time. They did the same things all the time. The men played cards around the dining-room table, while the women sat in a circle in the living room and gave each other recipes (often deliberately omitting a key ingredient or a crucial measurement, a favourite bit of one- upmanship). Old-timers who knew each other intimately, too intimately in fact, were getting on each other's nerves. The neighbourly pat on the back was beginning to leave claw marks.

How ironic it is that the years from 1939 to 1945 — in many ways the best years of their lives — had left these smalltown Jews stale and worn out, fiercely determined on the one hand to hang onto the narrow but secure patches of life they had cultivated for themselves, but equally determined that their children should cultivate far different patches in far-away metropolises.

Thus, my father, surveying all he had accumulated, did not turn to me and proclaim, "Some day all this will be yours." Rather, he looked about him at the racks of suits and dresses that were in style today and out of style tomorrow; at the Inspector-Generals who still managed to make their rounds despite their arthritis and fallen arches; at the bleak, black silence of Queen Street on a February night when it seemed that the only thing stirring in the whole world was a solitary snow plough. And all he said was, "Get out, get out before it's too late".

And I did. I got out before it was too late.

Tom Wayman

Where I Come From: Grandfather

A dead man. A dead person,
who ran away from the London Jews and joined
the Royal Sussex Regiment, shipping east
in an old three-decker to India, his pay-book
stamped *Church of England,* under his new
English name. The Regiment
taught him grammar and arithmetic
while he garrisoned the North West Frontier,
had the collar of his uniform shot off,
and was promoted to corporal, but one night
an officer returned to camp drunk
without the proper challenge, so every NCO on duty
— including him — got reduced to the ranks.

Back in England, they say he and his brother
stood in Trafalgar Square and tossed
to decide who would go to Canada and who to South Africa.
Thus my grandfather was awarded Toronto
and a job as a machine operator
for Tip Top Tailors, a wife, a family,
a death, and another wife,
a house on Borden Street eleven-and-a-half feet wide
in a street of Jews, with Jews living upstairs.
He also got a strike, in the midst of the Depression
and only went back to his machine during
another war. In 1945 he was chosen
Inner Guard of the Mozirir Sick and Burial Society
— a social and self-help club for ex-Russian Jews
which he was too, if you went back far enough
though locally he was known for his speech and military bearing
as ''the Mayor of Borden Street'' or ''the Englishman''.

In his last years, he refused to give up the house
though he was sick a number of times, and though
the street began to fill with south Italians.
A kid from the neighborhood prepared a meal for him most days
in return for a little money. And his room
began to hold all the clutter and dust of the single elderly poor:
faded snapshots and photographs, a calendar, the same few dishes
used every day, a television continually muttering
and mumbling to itself, the bed rumpled and half-made.

When he died, few on the street knew him.
He had to be carried into death by
a step-cousin's band of musicians
who had attended the funeral out of courtesy
and stayed to bear the old man to the grave.
They lifted him into a small shed at the edge of the cemetery
and came out and stood around, while shards of porcelain were put
on his ears, eyes, nose and mouth
to show that in the grave nothing is heard,
nothing seen, nothing smelled, nothing tasted
and nothing said. The first handful of sand from the grave
earth to the earth.

                                        And standing at the open gravesite
the young rabbi with the red band in his hat
who never knew any of us in life or death
but managed anyway to make up a little message about my grandfather
which actually could have been about anybody
now led my father in the halting, word-for-word
repetition of the Kaddish.
Then they turned on the machine for lowering the coffin
and flung a mat of synthetic grass
over the slowly descending box, as inside
what was left of what had been my grandfather went down
wrapped in the step-cousin's shawl.

Seven days the candle burned for him: seven days
seven years ago now. And from my grandfather
I got my father, my name,
the ring they took off his body that he had been given
when he made Inner Guard, and I got
a cheap disposable yarmulka handed out from a tray
at the funeral, a skullcap I still have
scrunched up in one pocket of a coat in a closet
kept in case I ever need it again.

Michael Usiskin

How Come Jews Want to be Farmers?

Uncle Mike's Edenbridge is a recently translated (1983) book of memoirs originally published in the Yiddish language in 1945 under the title, **Oksen Un Motoren.** The selection excerpted below recounts Mr. Usiskin's visit to a neighbouring farm to buy some provisions. (Trans. by Marcia Usiskin Basman.)

No sooner had we entered the house when the dog leapt on me like a caged wild beast. A few sharp words from its mistress, in her native Norwegian, and the dog put its tail between its legs and slinked away, ashamed of its behaviour. ''Now,'' she said, ''the dog will never bother you even if we aren't at home.''

We sat down at the kitchen table and she introduced me to her younger son who lived at the farm with her. Suddenly she turned to me and asked: ''What are you? Jewish?''

''Yes,'' I said. ''I'm Jewish.''

''And you want to be a farmer?''

''Yes, I want to be a farmer.''

''A Jewish farmer?'' she asked in disbelief. ''A Jewish farmer just can't be.''

''Why can't a Jew be a farmer?'' I asked her.

''I'll bet you ten to one that Jews won't make good farmers,'' she assured me with great confidence.

''And homesteaders, at that! It's a far cry from being just a farmer to being a homesteader. Homesteading is such hard work. We've always worked the land, but you Jews have always refused to be farmers.''

I asked her if she'd heard of Jews refusing to work the land in Norway.

''No'' she said, ''not in Norway, but in Russia they did. When we lived in the States,'' she continued, ''a priest told us that in Russia, the Tsar, being concerned for the well-being of his people, inquired of all his citizens (and there were many races) who would like to farm and who would like to engage in trade and live in the city. All the Jews refused to live in the country and work the land. They all chose to have little businesses in the towns and cities. Whenever you come across a Jew, you will find he's a business man of one sort or another and lives in town. And, you know, business men aren't always honest.''

I said that I had never heard of a ruler being that interested in the well-being of the common folk, especially the Russian Tsar. I asked her if she thought all Jews were dishonest. ''No, I'm not saying that,'' she said, ''I'm just saying that all Jews are businessmen and business isn't always 'kosher.' You can see how long it takes for a farmer to eke out a living, and yet within a year, a businessman gets fat and is bedecked with gold. Harry, however, never made a success of it. And do you know why? Because Harry is an honest man.''

''Who is Harry?'' I wanted to know.

''Harry is a Jewish young man who was a pedlar. Whenever he came to visit us, we'd have a real celebration. We'd gather together a houseful of farmers and listen to his tales. He'd tell us which countries were at war, and who was benefitting from the war, and who was suffering. He would tell us why there were strikes at the factories, why the rich were rich, and why there were so many poor people. He told us how prices were fixed for products that farmers produced and that the farmers had no say in these prices. He told us what the children were taught in the schools and how the teachers were told what to teach. He'd tell us how a poor man could be sent to prison for stealing a loaf of bread for his hungry children, but that a large contractor could swindle hundreds of people out of their money and still be as free as a bird. He told us of the world-wide struggle between the rich and the poor.''

The old woman began telling me of a rich shopkeeper who wanted to have Harry arrested as a 'red agent.' Her townspeople couldn't believe that a Jew would turn on one of his own people. But Harry was right; there were just two classes in the world, be they Jew or Turk. ''Our townspeople,'' she went on, ''stood up for Harry. We told our storekeeper if he pressed charges against Harry, not one of us would set foot in his shop. And this action helped."

I suddenly remembered my poor colleagues back at my farm and their empty stomachs. And here was I sitting in this pleasant kitchen enjoying myself with this old woman. I suggested to her that we postpone our conversation for now, and that I'd best collect some food supplies as was the original purpose of my visit. She went off to the storeroom and soon returned with a good supply of bread, potatoes, honey and eggs. When I asked her how much I owed her, she came up with the grand total of sixty cents. When I asked her why she was asking so little, she said that she wouldn't have gotten any more for it (perhaps less) from the storekeeper, and she didn't want to make undue profits from a neighbour.

Our friendship with these neighbours continues to this day. The old lady is dead now, but we have been friends with her children these thirty-three years. And no one knows better than we farmers how important the friendship of good neighbours is here in the wilderness.

There should have been an artist there to capture the looks on the faces of my friends when they caught sight of me laden down with provisions. I can still hear the sounds of that night ringing in my ears. We all crowded into the shack, huddled ourselves under the blankets, and sang. Our songs rang out into the bush well into the night, and for miles around our music filled the air.

Photo 5: Jewish farm, Lipton, Sask. 1916.

Eli Mandel

Rabbi Berner's Farm

record our searching for the place
the years of childhood blown across
has scattered like the jews of Hirsch
wherever secondary highways lead
through renewed green fields roads
passing cattle sheds
                                        his first wife
one son friends inhabit land lying
here or close to other townships
or the dead   he is alone
an island now
under warm rains and cedar

not even ruins here

Norman Levine

Lower Town—Ottawa

At the start they knew nothing about fruit, vegetables, rags, or horses. They were shopkeepers, small business men, scholars. They came at the beginning of the century, driven out by persecution, from Poland and from the provincial towns and villages of Eastern Europe. From the very beginning it was a question of survival. It did not take much money to buy a secondhand horse, a secondhand harness, a wagon, from one of the dairies or bakeries. Then in the market a couple of bags of potatoes from a farmer and whatever fruit was in season. And you rode through the city streets not knowing the language, knocking on doors with your basket of samples; or else just shouted out one's presence.

And they remained pedlars. They were kept down by the indifference of the outside community and by their own inability to make contact with it. Instead of self-pity, they joked, they cursed, they rode their wagons through the streets playing schoolboy games amongst themselves, making bets who would be first home or at a certain cafe, or raced through the streets with their empty wagons at night. And they had their religion. Most of them were Jewish, a few Catholic. Religion did not end in the bare synagogue with the small badly painted Zodiac around the front of the women's balcony. It was there in the drab houses, the rich food, the smells, the candles, and also in the street. I remember a service by the river. Twenty men standing in a late autumn afternoon in the park, by the shore, silhouetted against the sky. The muddy water passed by and under the Black Bridge, the Hebrew Chant, the sound of birds and frogs, bulrushes, leaves, sky. As a child one did not understand or as yet question; but this felt right. And then at Corpus Christi the Catholic procession through the streets. The men and women on the sidewalk kneeling and crossing themselves as the white canopy with the golden embroidered edges was carried by, the cross held underneath. And in front and behind the small girls in communion dresses, their Hail Marys going through them like a wind through a wheatfield. While those on the wooden verandas, behind the lace curtains, watched in silence.

There was no pretence about them. They had little ambition. They lived life instinctively. They didn't belong to Ottawa or to Canada; they never fitted in. It was Lower Town and Murray Street where their lives were; the place was like a village. But I doubt if there was anyone in the city who knew the streets of Ottawa physically as well as these men. They were out in all weather. I remember seeing my father's hands in winter; the skin was hard and split open in several places by the cold.

But their wives were different. It was she who was bored staying behind at home looking at the street through lace curtains. It was she who nagged, who worried about the practical side of life. And it was the wife who goaded on the man to give up the horse and wagon for a truck; to make money, to move away from Murray Street to a better district. And the men reacted instinctively to this by taking longer to go through the streets, coming later home. Then they ran away from home and got together in a room and played cards.

The sleigh changed to the wagon and back again. A horse died. It was replaced by another secondhand one. While they waited for their children to grow up. But their sons and daughters betrayed them. It began at school, where learning took a secondary place to that of moulding one to want to belong to "the outside"; not to Lower Town, or Sandy Hill, or New Edinburgh, but to something larger and anonymous. And this was repeated in the newspapers, in the films, on the radio and in school. I can still remember those afternoons when we had to go up to the front of the class in turn, and pretend we were selling something; a car, a washing machine, a house, while our teacher criticized our technique. To "get on" meant turning one's back on Lower Town and the values it represented.

And the sons and daughters moved away from Murray Street and began to cover up their tracks. They changed their names. They charmed. They imitated. Lower Town was failure. Their parents were failures. And their own success was doomed by the reminder of failure that they carried with them.

Letter from Israel: For me the most striking thing about Murray Street was the manner in which our Jewishness managed to isolate and insulate us from the usual qualities of a lower-class, near-slum neighbourhood. The drunkenness, wife-beating, poverty, illness, drabness, the lack of meaningful ceremonial, of cultural artifacts — we felt and heard these things in the dimmest and most fragmentary of ways. Our identification was simply not with the non-Jewish aspects of the street: on the contrary, it was the patriarchial set-up of our tight-knit Jewish family pattern, the religion, festival, synagogue which emphasized our apartness, gave us our values, sensitized us to our isolation and to the cultural values by which we could overcome the street. If *Hashomer Hatzair* was a cry against our families, it was also a positive shout against a society which our Jewishness primarily prevented us from identifying with. It wasn't our poverty (and we really weren't so badly off) that separated us from the community; it was our Jewishness. For me at any rate this seems to be the determining factor in my relations not only with the Street but with life in general.

Now. A pair of eyes look out from behind double windows, lace curtains, at the empty street, out of habit. For there are no horses, no sleighs. The few old men who still live here look sick and tired. They sit on the wooden verandas bundled up in heavy coats and scarves and caps, or else inside by the stove in the kitchen, asleep. Most of them still have to work. Too weak to peddle they go on as nightwatchmen, or else sweep up store floors after closing. What I admired about them, their gaiety, their jokes, their obscenities, their ability to lash out instinctively at life, their gesture of going against the grain, was gone. And it left in its place a doddering uncertainty. They mumbled about the success that their children were having. But you could see by their insistence, the repetition of the same words — ''wonderful job'', ''getting ahead'', ''doing well'', that they didn't understand. A community that human injustice had thrown together was breaking up: by dying out. And those who replace them — the immigrants since 1945 — come to Lower Town better equipped. They are old hands at survival. The black market, the camps, have done their work. Murray Street is only a stopping- off place for them; one of many. In a few years they will have forgotten that they were ever here. And it is also made easier for them by the rootlessness and the restlessness, which has drained the Lower Town of its young and left behind these husks of men and women. They have lost something. Something that one, too late, understood and valued. And now, from here, it is gone.

Part Two

Canadian Born

Photo 6: Balfour Day parade, Winnipeg, 1918.

Canadian Born

Armed with the hopes of their parents and their own vitality and visions, the children of the immigrants jostled their way into medical school, thriving businesses and middle class lifestyles. A generation removed from the realities of Europe with its firmly ordered Jewish traditions, lured by the possibility of acculturation, they were tightrope walkers. With humour, ambiguity and a tinge of sadness, the writers in this section chronicle their coming of age in Canada, and the attempt to understand and bridge the widening social and cultural chasm between their views and the values of their parents. Ted Allan's Montreal child grappling with anti-Semitism, death, and paternal conflict; Jack Ludwig's high school smartalecks amid the poverty of Winnipeg's North End, Miriam Waddington's unfortunate Danny, Mordecai Richler's street-wise young toughs; all portray the resourcefulness, the energy and the heart needed for the climb up and out. With skill and speed, this generation learned the bruising lessons of self-betterment; and in the process, with wit and compassion they wrote poems and stories about their struggle.

Photo 7: *Prospectors' Store, Timmins, Ont., 1912.*

Ted Allan

Lies My Father Told Me

My grandfather stood six feet three in his worn-out bedroom slippers. He had a long grey beard with streaks of white running through it. When he prayed, his voice boomed like a choir as he turned the pages of his prayerbook with one hand and stroked his beard with the other. His hands were bony and looked like tree-roots; they were powerful. My grandpa had been a farmer in the old country. In Montreal he conducted what he called "a second-hand business".

In his youth, I was told, Grandpa had been something of a wild man, drinking and playing with the village wenches until my grandmother took him in hand. In his old age, when I knew him, he had become a very religious man. He prayed three times a day on week-days and all day on Saturday. In between prayers he rode around on a wagon which, as I look back, rolled on despite all the laws of physics and mechanics. Its four wheels always seemed to be going in every direction but forwards. The horse that pulled the wagon was called Ferdeleh. He was my pet and it was only much later, when I had seen many other horses, that I realized that Ferdeleh was not everything a horse could have been. His belly hung very low, almost touching the street when he walked. His head went back and forth in jerky motions in complete disharmony with the rest of him. He moved slowly, almost painfully, apparently realizing that he was capable of only one speed and determined to go no faster or slower than the rate he had established some time back. Next to Grandpa I loved Ferdeleh best, with the possible exception of God, or my mother when she gave me candy.

On Sundays, when it didn't rain, Grandpa, Ferdeleh and myself would go riding through the back lanes of Montreal. The lanes then were not paved as they are now, and after a rainy Saturday, the mud would be inches deep and the wagon heaved and shook like a barge in a stormy sea. Ferdeleh's pace remained, as always, the same. He liked the mud. It was easy on his feet.

When the sun shone through my windows on Sunday morning I would jump out of bed, wash, dress, run into the kitchen where Grandpa and I said our morning prayers, and then we'd both go to harness and feed Ferdeleh. On Sundays Ferdeleh would whinny like a happy child. He knew it was an extra special day for all of us. By the time he had finished his oats and hay Grandpa and I would be finished with our breakfast which Grandma and Mother had prepared for us.

Then we'd go through what Grandpa called "the women's Sunday song". It went like this: "Don't let him hold the reins crossing streets. Be sure to come back if it starts to rain. Be sure not to let him hold the reins crossing streets. Be sure to come back if it starts to rain." They would repeat this about three hundred times until Grandpa and I were weary from nodding our heads and saying, "Yes". We could hear it until we turned the corner and went up the lane of the next street.

Then began the most wonderful of days as we drove through the dirt lanes of Montreal, skirting the garbage cans, jolting and bouncing through the mud and dust, calling every cat by name and every cat meowing its hello, and Grandpa and I holding our hands to our ears and shouting out at the top ot our lungs, "Regs, cloze, botels! Regs, cloze, botels!"

What a wonderful game that was! I would run up the back stairs and return with all kinds of fascinating things, old dresses, suits, pants, rags, newspapers, all shapes of bottles, all shapes of trash, everything you can think of, until the wagon was filled.

Sometimes a woman would ask me to send Grandpa up to give her a price on what she had, and Grandpa would shout up from downstairs, "My feet ache. The boy will give you a price." I knew what he offered for an old suit, for an old dress, and I would shout down describing the items in question and the state of deterioration. For clothes that were nothing better than rags we offered a standard price, "Fifteen cents, take it or leave it." Clothes that might be repaired I would hold out for Grandpa to see and he'd appraise them. And so we'd go through the lanes of the city.

Sometimes the women would not be satisfied with the money Grandpa had given me for them. Grandpa would always say, "Eleshka, women always want more than they get. Remember that. Give them a finger and they want the whole hand."

My Sunday rides were the happiest times I spent. Sometimes Grandpa would let me wear his derby hat which came down over my ears, and people would look at me and laugh and I'd feel even happier feeling how happy everyone was on Sunday.

Sometimes strange, wonderful smells would come over the city, muffling the smell of the garbage cans. When this happened we would stop Ferdeleh and breathe deeply. It smelled of sea and of oak trees and flowers. Then we knew we were near the mountain in the centre of the city and that the wind from the river was bringing the perfumes of the mountain and spraying it over the city. Often we would ride out of the back lanes and up the mountain road. We couldn't go too far up because it was a strain on Ferdeleh. As far as we went, surrounded on each side by tall poplars and evergreens, Grandpa would tell me about the old country, about the rivers and the farms, and sometimes he'd get off the wagon and pick up some black earth in his hands. He'd squat, letting the earth fall between his fingers, and I'd squat beside him doing the same thing.

When we came to the mountain Grandpa's mood would change and he would talk to me of the great land that Canada was, and of the great things the young people growing up were going to do in this great land. Ferdeleh would walk to the edge of the road and eat the thick grass on the sides. Grandpa was at home among the trees and black earth and thick grass and on our way down the mountain road he would sing songs that weren't prayers, but happy songs in Russian. Sometimes he'd clap his hands to the song as I held the reins and Ferdeleh would look back at him and shake his head with pleasure. One Sunday on our ride home through the mountain a group of young boys and girls threw stones at us and shouted in French: "Juif . . . . Juif . . . .!" Grandpa held his strong arm around me, cursed back muttering "anti-Semites" under his breath. When I asked him what he said he answered, "It is something I hope you never learn." The boys and girls laughed and got tired of throwing stones. That was the last Sunday we went to the mountain.

If it rained on Sunday my mother wouldn't let me go out, so every Saturday evening I prayed for the sun to shine on Sunday. Once I almost lost faith in God and in the power of prayer but Grandpa fixed it. For three Sundays in succession it rained. In my desperation I took it out on God. What was the use of praying to Him if He didn't listen to you? I complained to Grandpa.

"Perhaps you don't pray right," he suggested.

"But I do. I say, Our God in heaven, hallowed by Thy name, Thy will on earth as it is in heaven. Please don't let it rain tomorrow."

"Ah! In English you pray?" my grandfather exclaimed triumphantly.

"Yes," I answered.

"But God only answers prayers in Hebrew. I will teach you how to say that prayer in Hebrew. And, if God doesn't answer, it's your own fault. He's angry because you didn't use the Holy Language." But God wasn't angry because next Sunday the sun shone its brightest and the three of us went for our Sunday ride.

On weekdays, Grandpa and I rose early, a little after daybreak, and said our morning prayers. I would mimic his sing-song lamentations, sounding as if my heart were breaking and wondering why we both had to sound so sad. I must have put everything I had into it because Grandpa assured me that one day I would become a great cantor and a leader of the Hebrews. "You will sing so that the ocean will open up a path before you and you will lead our people to a new paradise."

I was six then and he was the only man I ever understood even when I didn't understand his words. I learned a lot from him. If he didn't learn a lot from me, he made me feel he did.

I remember once saying, "You know, sometimes I think I'm the son of God. Is it possible?"

"It is possible," he answered, "but don't rely on it. Many of us are sons of God. The important thing is not to rely too much upon it. The harder we work, the harder we study, the more we accomplish, the surer we are that we are sons of God."

At the synagogue on Saturday his old, white-bearded friends would surround me and ask me questions. Grandpa would stand by and burst with pride. I strutted like a peacock.

"Who is David?" the old men would ask me.

''He's the man with the beard, the man with the bearded words.'' And they laughed.

''And who is God?'' they would ask me.

''King and Creator of the Universe, the All-Powerful One, the Almighty One, more powerful even than Grandpa.'' They laughed again and I thought I was pretty smart. So did Grandpa. So did my grandmother and my mother.

So did everyone, except my father. I didn't like my father. He said things to me like, ''For God's sake, you're smart, but not as smart as you think. Nobody is that smart.'' He was jealous of me and he told me lies. He told me lies about Ferdeleh.

''Ferdeleh is one part horse, one part camel, and one part chicken,'' he told me. Grandpa told me that was a lie, Ferdeleh was all horse. ''If he is part anything, he is part human,'' said Grandpa. I agreed with him. Ferdeleh understood everything we said to him. No matter what part of the city he was in, he could find his way home, even in the dark.

''Ferdeleh is going to collapse one day in one heap,'' my father said. ''Ferdeleh is carrying twins.'' ''Ferdeleh is going to keel over one day and die.'' ''He should be shot now or he'll collapse under you one of these days,'' my father would say. Neither I nor Grandpa had much use for the opinions of my father.

On top of everything, my father had no beard, didn't pray, didn't go to the synagogue on the Sabbath, read English books and never read the prayer books, played piano on the Sabbath and sometimes would draw my mother into his villainies by making her sing while he played. On the Sabbath this was an abomination to both Grandpa and me.

One day I told my father, ''Papa, you have forsaken your forefathers.'' He burst out laughing and kissed me and then my mother kissed me, which infuriated me all the more.

I could forgive my father these indignities, his not treating me as an equal, but I couldn't forgive his telling lies about Ferdeleh. Once he said that Ferdeleh ''smelled up'' the whole house, and demanded that Grandpa move the stable. It was true that the kitchen, being next to the stable, which was in the back shed, did sometimes smell of hay and manure but, as Grandpa said, ''What is wrong with such a smell? It is a good healthy smell.''

It was a house divided, with my grandmother, mother and father on one side, and Grandpa, Ferdeleh and me on the other. One day a man came to the house and said he was from the Board of Health and that the neighbours had complained about the stable. Grandpa and I knew we were beaten then. You could get around the Board of Health, Grandpa informed me, if you could grease the palms of the officials. I suggested the obvious but Grandpa explained that this type of ''grease'' was made of gold. The stable would have to be moved. But where?

As it turned out, Grandpa didn't have to worry about it. The whole matter was taken out of his hands a few weeks later.

Next Sunday the sun shone brightly and I ran to the kitchen to say my prayers with Grandpa. But Grandpa wasn't there. I found my grandmother there instead — weeping. Grandpa was in his room ill. He had a sickness they call diabetes and at that time the only thing you could do about diabetes was weep. I fed Ferdeleh and soothed him because I knew how disappointed he was.

That week I was taken to an aunt of mine. There was no explanation given. My parents thought I was too young to need any explanations. On Saturday next I was brought home, too late to see Grandpa that evening, but I felt good knowing that I would spend the next day with him and Ferdeleh again.

When I came to the kitchen Sunday morning Grandpa was not there. Ferdeleh was not in the stable. I thought they were playing a joke on me so I rushed to the front of the house expecting to see Grandpa sitting atop the wagon waiting for me.

But there wasn't any wagon. My father came up behind me and put his hand on my head. I looked up questioningly and he said, ''Grandpa and Ferdeleh have gone to heaven . . . .''

When he told me they were *never* coming back, I moved away from him and went to my room. I lay down on my bed and cried, not for Grandpa and Ferdeleh, because I knew they would never do such a thing to me, but about my father, because he had told me such a horrible lie.

Jack Ludwig

Requiem for Bibul

Once upon a time — if we counted time not by calendars but by assimilated history and scientific change, I'd be tempted to say four or five thousand years ago — before total war and all-out war, before death camps, Nagasaki, before fusion and fission, jets, moon shots, astronauts, luniks in orbit, before antibiotics, polio vaccine, open-heart surgery, before TV, garburetors, and other wonders of automation, before dead-faced hoods on motorcycles, dead-faced beatniks on maldecycles; once upon *that* kind of time lived a boy and his horse. The year was 1939. The boy and the horse are both dead.

This is no pastoral tale.

Twenty years late, counting time by the calendar, I write you of this boy Bibul and his horse Malkeh, of Bibul's ambition and his sad, sad end. In time-sorrowed perspective I record for you the imprint Bibul left on my mind and feeling: his tic-like blink, his coal-black hair in bangs over his forehead, his emery-cloth shaver's shadow, his ink-stained mouth, his immutable clothes that wouldn't conform to style or the seasons — always black denim relief-style pants whitened by wear and washing, always a brown pebbled cardigan coiled at the wrists and elbows with unraveled wool, always a leather cap with bent visor, split seams, matching the color and texture of Bibul's hair. And old ruined Malkeh, scorned before lamented, making her daily round under Bibul's urging, dragging his creak of a fruit peddler's wagon through Winnipeg's "island" slum north of the Canadian Pacific Railway yards.

Bibul peddled while my time burned: in 1939 all of us high school boys were owlish with sixteen-and seventeen-year-old speculation and almost missed seeing this Bibul, all foxy with world-weary finagling. We were out to save the world; Bibul, a buck. Hip deep in reality, trying to beat tricky suppliers, weaselly competitors, haggling customers, Bibul couldn't believe in us vaguesters. Peddling had forced him to see, hear, and judge everything. By his practical measure, we were simply unreal. We'd speculate; Bibul would respond with *"Yeh-yeh,"* the Yiddish double affirmative that makes a negative. He didn't have to say a word, or raise that skeptical eyebrow, or even frown with that tic. His smell alone argued a reality out of reach of our politely neutral, Lux, Lifebuoy, Vitalis middle-class sweetness: "effluvium Bibul" we called that mixture of squashed berries, bad turnips, dank pine apple-crates, straw, chickens, sad old horsy Malkeh. Bibul had a grand gesture to sweep away our irrelevance, a sudden movement of the hand like a farmwife's throwing feed to chickens, his nose sniffing disgust, his sour mouth giving out a squelching sound, *"Aaaa."* Sometimes he sounded like a goat, other times a baby lamb; just *"Aaaa,"* but enough to murder our pushy pretensions.

We were a roomful of competitive sharks — math sharks, physics sharks, English, Latin, history sharks — secretly, often openly sure that we surpassed our teachers in brains and know-how. Joyfully arrogant, we shook off the restricting label of "high school student," considering ourselves pros — mathematicians, scientists, writers, artists. In our own minds we had already graduated from the university, had passed through Toronto or Oxford, were entangled in public controversies with the great names in our respective fields, ending right but humble, modestly triumphant. But where was Bibul in this league? As loudly as we pros hollered, Bibul heard nothing. He only yawned, slouched, even snoozed, gave out with that killing *"Yeh-yeh,"* poked his grayish nose into his peddler's notebook red with reality's ooze of tomato.

"Bibul," we'd try to break in on him, "aren't you interested in semantics? Don't you care for the coming intellectual revolution? Once and for all, are you for Count Korzybski or are you against him?"

"Aaaa," was Bibul's response, and that chicken-feeding gesture

waved us back to our ivory towers. Bibul turned to reality with a lick of his indelible-pencil's tip and a purple inscription in his book of life.

''You nuddin' bud gids,'' he'd say impatiently if we insisted on disturbing his audit. ''A 'ell of a lod you guys know about live.''

We'd jeer and mock, which made no impression on Bibul, nor did much for us. Weren't we the kings of St. John's High School? Even if Bibul wasn't very active, he was still one of us on the top floor, dominating with us the giants and dwarfs living the underground life and blazing forges and screeching lathes in the school basement, second-generation Canadians joyously illiterate, English having to fend for itself in their houses, a poor second to Ukrainian or Polish or German; or the salt-of-the-earth commercial students, blond and blue-eyed, clearly dedicated to the sensible life, who heard our loud violent arguments and shuddered in silence and good taste.

We might have been kings, but how could anybody crown Bibul? We ran the yearbook, but it, sad for Bibul's talents, was printed neither in Yiddish nor Hebrew, and on Bibul's ''island'' who had mastered English? We wanted him to debate, but peddling had made him overexcited; wrought up, he stammered, angry, he slobbered — hindrances to the winning of arguments. Tone-deaf, he was no candidate for the glee club; a business man through and through, he had no time for politics. At sports he was terrible; he couldn't swim a stroke, or skate, was flubby-knuckled at baseball, slashingly pigeon- toed at soccer, kamikaze going over a hurdle. He had no time for women in his life. Malkeh and the ladies who bought from him were the only females Bibul knew; these customers whom he called with a little, if not much, affection, *schnorrers,* pigs.

In recognition of his great talent, we made him room treasurer. After school, while we theoreticians sprawled on boulevards and took pleasure from the long-limbed, large-breasted twelfth-grade girls giving the lie to an educator's pious wish that the serge tunic neutralize the female form, Bibul hurried off to Malkeh, that wagon open-pored and gaping for paint, the running of a gauntlet of schnorrers avid for a beet or turnip to fill an empty pot. And early on a morning, when we theoreticians-turned- lovers, wearied after a long night of girls, sat in the Street Railway waiting house knocking ourselves out over my noisy reading of Panurge's adventure with the Lady of Paris, Bibul, up and dressed at 4 a.m., waited with Malkeh for the fruit row to open and the struggle for possession of the bruised fruit and battered vegetables he'd have to wrest from ancient wizened trickster peddlers and their muscular sons so that his schnorrers would have something concrete to haggle over later in the day.

Lost in abstraction, and me, I thought little of Bibul in those days. He was a clown. A mark. A butt. The Peddling was part of the sad, desperate struggle for money every family in the Depression knew. Bibul was the oldest of four children, his widowed ma supporting them on what she could make out of a tiny grocery store, doing the best she could, the dear lady, and known throughout the island as the ''Golden Thumb'' and the ''Adder,'' the latter reference ambiguous, meaning either snakes or computation, Bibul's ma being famous for a mathematical theorem that said 5 + 6 = 12, or 13, whichever was higher.

Not till the year of our graduation did I discover why Bibul peddled with such dedication, why he rode out like a teen-age Don Quixote to do battle with those abusive, haggling, thieving schnorrers.

What a riding out that was! His paintless wagon listed like a sinking ship, moved with the sound of fiddles scraped rosinless in a concert by deaf mutes, its wheels' circles successfully squared, a few spokes missing from each, its seat a tatter of leatherette bulged at the ends like a horsehair cream puff, its wilted greens and culled fruit lorded over by Bibul's faultless-in-his-favor scales, rusted fistlike weights, a battered tin scoop more dented than a defeated World War I veteran's helmet. For such a wagon, what was more fitting than a progress through the island under the leadership of a nag like Malkeh!

As beat up as Don Quixote's Rosinante would look next to elegant Pegasus, that's how Malkeh would look next to Rosinante: she was U-shaped in side view, as if she'd been ridden by the fattest knight in heaviest armor; she sagged like a collapsed sofa with its stuffing hanging low. She was bare as buffed mohair, her shoulders tanned from the rub of reins, her color an unbelievable combination of rust, maroon, purple, brown, found elsewhere only in ancient sun-drenched velvets. Her tail was a worn discarded feather boa picked almost clean. Like a badly carpentered table, all four of her legs were of assorted lengths, which made her move by shuffling, like a pair of aged soft-shoe dancers making a final farewell. Her hoofs were fringed with fuzzy hairs like a frayed fiddle bow abandoned to rain and sun, her horseshoes were thin as dimes, rusty as the metal hinges on her wagon's tail gate.

Her faded yellow horse collar and harness once sat on a czarist artillery horse, but now, padless, dry, broken, reknotted, supported Malkeh in poor style, fitting much like the suits handed up by Bibul's competitors' muscular sons to their tiny fathers. To encourage her to see out of her old eyes, Bibul flatteringly covered them at the sides with a pair of snappy black racing-horse blinkers trimmed with shiny silver rivets, a touch to Malkeh's decor like a monocle in the eye of a Bowery bum.

Out of loyalty to this Malkeh, Bibul let his wagon go to ruin: a wagon could be covered over with paint or varnish, but poor mortal Malkeh, where was the therapy or camouflage to hide from the world what *she* really was?

She was the horse version of *The Dying Gaul.* While Malkeh lived on her island she wasn't subject to the reality of horse hierarchy, but on a main thoroughfare like Salter Street her submarginal, subproletariat position was exposed. High-stepping T. Eaton Company horses, glossy-flanked, curried, combed, middle-class cousins of aristocratic thoroughbreds seen only on race tracks and in stables, spurned Malkeh as they sped past, their harnesses shiny with saddle soap, their hoofs steel-ringing, their heads up, their traces white as snow, their tails prinked out with red ribbons, their wagons elegant as chariots, freshly painted, glowing blue-black, red, white, and gold where it counted, their drivers uniform and uniformed, not like sloppy Bibul. Horses like these had blankets, slept in fancy T. Eaton stables, ate oats from an unfaded green feed bag, not the ripped postman's pouch Bibul filled with bad lettuce, carrot tops, shriveled beets wisped over with a sign of hay. Their snubbing was a denial that Malkeh was a horse. Even the heavy, powerful working-class Percherons, inexorably destined for life to the smell of the garbage scows they pulled through the city, refused to acknowledge kinship with Malkeh, speeding up without any urging, turning into a can-ridden back lane with relief, much as a person at a high-toned party successfully hides from a waiter who turns out to be a close relative.

I saw her only once, when Bibul brought her to school. A crowd gathered, some to gawk, some to cluck, some to find cause for letters to the editor. The principal happened to look out. Malkeh died a long time ago, but her memory is gnomically preserved in a memorial tablet that went up early next day and says clearly "No Parking at Any Time."

That was the first and last time Bibul brought Malkeh to school.

Not that the island was without hazards. Perhaps Bibul had put blinders on Malkeh to keep the old animal from seeing reality too clearly with whatever sight she still had left in her eyes. Those schnorrers, bare feet stuck hurriedly into their husbands' felt house slippers, wearing nightgowns at four in the afternoon, their hair uncombed, their hands deep in housecoat and apron pockets in a gesture like stick-up men's, pennies and silver tightly clenched, prizes Bibul could get with bargains, fast talk, tempting, threats, guile. Singly they watched for him, in concert they plotted unbeatable stratagems, their motto simple: Pay little, get much. To the victor went the spoiled spoils.

''Giddy ahb, Malgeh,'' Bibul would holler from his high seat, and the schnorrers knew that war was on.

Into the lists Malkeh dragged the keening wagon, onto the island in ruins like a medieval town (Canadian history is short, but our buildings add spice by getting older faster). Foundationless houses sagged, leaned at angles to astound Pisa, some north, some south, giving an effect of pure craziness, what kids might have built with assorted-sized decks of cards. Gates tipsy as Malkeh's wagon swung on one hinge from a last lost post; dry, cracking wood fences leaned in surrender toward the ground, begging like old men in sight of a grave to be allowed to fall the rest of the way; windows were tar-paper patched, like pirates' eyes, and ominous as the blackness left in the streets by uninsured fires.

Behind every window or screen opaque with dust, behind every door splintered from kids' kicking waited the schnorrers, trying to make Bibul anxious, make him sweat a little, a cinch for persistent hagglers.

''Ebbles, ebbles, den boundz f'a quadder!'' Bibul shouted.

The schnorrers didn't move.

Unflustered, unfooled, Bibul used his phony war time well, popping into his mouth the only three unspotted cherries in his entire stock. Malkeh, for her bit, sighing and groaning, panting but pulling, dragged the exposed tin rims of the wheels off the street and into the frost heaves and crevices of the muddy back lane which Bibul and his customers had silently agreed was the Compleat Battlefield, Bibul because the cloudlike stench of chicken droppings and horse dung hanging over the lane was unbeatable camouflage for whatever imperfection time and decay might bring his produce, his schnorrers because the cramped quarters of a narrow lane made scale tampering easier for their anxious old hands, detection difficult, filching not so.

''Whoa beg, whoa der, Malgeh,'' Bibul ordered, and there among ripped mattresses resembling enormous wads of steel wool, in a bone yard of Model T Fords, Malkeh finally halted. Dogs came yapping from all directions, cats hissed from rust-streaked iron roof tops, frightened pigeons whirred into the air, wheeling high over sun-beaten stables, returning to their places like grandstand fans anxious to be close to the scene of scuffle.

Bibul's ticlike blink was a cover for all expression. He looked blanker than the Sphinx. He faked a brow-furrowing entry into his book, peeled an orange, scratched himself variously and thoroughly. The schnorrers couldn't stand the suspense. Dead was their united front. A few broke ranks and, already cursing Bibul's bad prices, shuffled out in a gait to match Malkeh's.

Horseflies, the pickings so sparse they had to drop their high standards and declare Malkeh a possible host, left the poor banquet of the uncovered garbage cans — each lid long commandeered to serve as targe in the minor-league jousts of the schnorrers' knightly kids — and, under cover of the schnorrers sneakily advancing to do Bibul battle, launched assault on Malkeh's weak flank. In a second, both boy and horse were under siege.

The attack came swiftly: stealthily, deftly, a red-haired old woman flipped two-cent oranges into the one-cent bins, her rasp of a voice trying to get Bibul to look up at the sky and predict weather; her accomplice meanwhile made a great display of finding a terrific buy.

''Boyaboyaboy, f'a change you god good tings in this stinkin' wagon,'' she said shamelessly.

Bibul's ticlike blink was a camera shutter ready for mischief, and snapped the entire action.

''Give over here dat bag,'' he said gruffly. ''Mizzuz, *yoisher,* show a liddle resdraind,'' he scolded the only innocents watching the oranges fall back into the proper bin.

A pair of raspberry hands crunched lettuce greens. ''How much you give off f' damaged goods?'' the criminal hollered, while still wiping lettuce juice off on her apron.

The red-haired old woman was set on getting oranges. ''Robber, black-hearted robber,'' she cried out, shaking a fist under Bibul's disapproving nose. ''Perls d' fruit man, a father who supports eight growin' kids and a sister in Russia, Perls charges two coppers cheaper for fresher and firmer, so ha come, ha? Ha come?''

''My oniges are Sundgizd, Blue Gooze,'' came back Bibul, a sucker for brand names. ''Berl's oniges grow on ebble drees.''

With a slamming of doors and a shuffle of feet the schnorrers came now in full force, wave after wave, surrounding Bibul's wagon, pressing fruit, squeezing, poking, tapping, filling the air with shrieks and curses that urged the pigeonhearted pigeons high to the sky. Like a bucket brigade, the ladies passed fruit the length of the wagon, each nose a compulsory inspection station. Some — baseball fans, no doubt — tried the hidden-ball trick with Bibul's apples; others, proud of what teeth they had left, showed off a little by nipping fruit as it passed by.

For each bite Bibul took his due.

''Schnorrers dad youz are,'' he yelled, imposing and collecting his fine, ''you god no gare vor my brovids? You eadin' ub all my brovids!''

''Don' be s'independent,'' said the red-haired one, fruitlessly after a fistful of cherries, ''don' hold yourself big. You' fadder ain' no doctor, he ain' no mayor!''

Bibul was a lone guard defending his fortress from desperate pillagers; ubiquitous as Churchill, many-handed as Shiva, he had to be compassionate as Schweitzer. Though I didn't know what Bibul's dedication to peddling was all about, the schnorrers did: Bibul was saving up to become a rabbi. Bibul immersed himself in the practical, pedestrian, material life because of a Great Cause — the Yeshiva in New York, eventual immersion in a spiritual life dedicated to suffering mankind.

How the schnorrers used that Great Cause in their war with Bibul! It was all double: in sincerity they poured out their hearts to him; an educated boy, soon to be a rabbi, maybe he'd understand *their* side — the husband who had taken off and never come back, the bad-hearted rich relatives, the ungrateful kids, the treacherous friends, root, trunk, branch of a Jewish Seven Deadly Sins. They dizzied him with complicated stories, unsettled his strong stomach with demonstrations of human frailty — missing teeth, crossed eyes, wens, tumors, needed operations.

As a bonus to sincerity they hoped the tales would divert Bibul long enough for their aprons to fill with filched fruit.

Crying real tears, Bibul would free an apricot from a fist already stained with cherry.

''A religious you call yourself?'' the caught thief howled. ''God should strike me dead if I stole ever in my life one thing!''

Glancing up at the sky, she moved closer to the other ladies: who knew what kind of pull with God a boy to be a rabbi had?

''Bibul, *boychik,*'' cooed this Mrs. Fenson, bleached a little but not yet forty, without a man since her husband disappeared into the harvest lands of Saskatchewan years before. ''Give off ten cents on this here dozen, eh, doll? I can show plenty good appreciation.''

Bibul shuddered a No. There were some things in this material world even the Great Cause did not justify.

For their part, his schnorrers prayed God to give Bibul good enough ears to hear out their incriminating bill of particulars against the human race, bad eyes to miss seeing what their energetic hands were doing; and they cursed fate when Bibul's unaffected eyes snapped them filching. After a day of listening to lamentation, was there anything Bibul could hear that would amaze him?

''My brudder's second wibe's kid wid da hump in back god already her tird miscarriage, Bibul,'' he'd hear, and a second later, ''Ha c'n ya cha'ge two cends a pond f'a busted wadermelon?'' —this to the accompanying sound of a melon being smartly cracked against the side of the wagon.

''Bay ub, bay ub.'' Bibul would rise to his full height on the wagon's seat, like a soapbox orator trying to sway these masses.

That's when the curses changed from rain to hail, the moment for desperation measures — pinching, throwing a kiss, snatching a potato, gulping a cherry, pit and all. But Bibul was through. A loving kick woke Malkeh, a swish of the broken whip banished her horseflies. The swaying tin scoop clattered retreat, the creaking wagon mocked the defeated schnorrers cursing boy and horse down through all possible generations.

Was it any wonder, then, that when we sharks, all hot for culture, oozing ideology, long on judgments, short on facts, turned our abstract faces toward Bibul, he responded with that *''Aaaa''*? What was there in our books and ideas to compete with a schnorrer's lament? Now I know what that *''Aaaa''* meant in part: *''Aaaa''* translated ''When I was a child I spake as a child'' (may Bibul forgive me for invoking St. Paul!) or ''You nuddin' bud gids.'' *''Aaaa''* said, ''vanity of vanities; all is vanity'' and, in explanation of Bibul's giving himself to Mammon for a term so that he might give the rest to Abraham, Isaac, and Jacob, ''To everything there is a season, and a time to every purpose under the heaven.''

The sharks vaguely yearned for the Higher Life; Bibul alone had a concrete goal, a building in a specific city, New York. Every knightly thrust and parry with an unqueenly schnorrer, every cull of orange he sold, every bruised apple brought him that much closer to the Yeshiva.

On graduation day at St. John's, Bibul was already half a rabbi. Gone were the familiar cardigan and accompanying accessories. Bibul wore a brand- new serge suit. His sideburns were religious enough to be called side curls, the emery-cloth shadow was lengthened. His eyes shone with a fervor no schnorrer had ever seen. He looked beautiful, incredibly happy.

''Damorrow,'' he said in a low secretive voice, ''I go d' Yeshiva in New Yorg. I wanna say goo'by, Joe.''

''New York?'' I said. ''A city that big? Aren't you a little afraid?''

''Aaaa.'' Bibul gave me that wave of his. ''Wadz t' be sgared?''

''You're a stranger. Winnipeg's a village compared with New York.''

"*Aaaa*. Zame ding. Beoble is beoble."

"What about Malkeh?"

"Berls da beddler robbed me. I gave Malgeh away t' him. Da groog knew I was goin' d' New Yorg."

"Bibul," I said enthusiastically, "good luck to you. Be a good rabbi!"

"*Aaaa*," he said with the usual flourish, his last word to me then or ever.

That fall we sharks entered the university, and Canada the war. Winnipeg was transformed, full of air crew trainees from places known to me before only through postage stamps; yellow skins, black, red, brown, Maori tribesmen from New Zealand, Bushmen from Australia, strange-sounding South Africans, sculpture-faced Indians thronged the city's streets and beer parlors. But far off in New York, Bibul, who'd known war with his schnorrers since his thirteenth year, paid no attention to this latest struggle, his mind committed to the study of Torah and Talmud, his spare time involved in a fruit-selling job among the East Side schnorrers around New York's Essex Street market. His old customers, a little cash to speculate with now that the Depression seemed ended, haggled halfheartedly with old man Perls and old Malkeh, the one mercifully deaf, the other almost totally blind.

Once in a long while I checked in at Bibul's mother's store and, gleaning news of Bibul, let her weigh me up a light pound of corned beef. She wore her hair Buster Brown, carried a huge buxom body on little feet tucked into gray-white tennis shoes.

She shoved a letter at me.

"Look how a educated boy writes," she said, pugnaciously proud. "Who but a rabbi could understand such hard words?"

She pulled it back before I could give an opinion.

"See him only, look, look." She pushed a picture at my eyes.

Bibul huddled against a bare Williamsburg wall, grinning the same grin as three other Bibuls in the picture, all of them bearded and wild as Russians, in black beaver hats bought with money they had earned tutoring the Americanized grandchildren of rich Hasidim.

"Some boy, my Bibul," his mother called to me as I was leaving.

Winter passed; the war grew grimmer. Spring was beautiful; the war more dreadful. Summer was very hot in New York, where Bibul divided his time between the Yeshiva and Essex Street's schnorrers. For days, the temperature was in the high humid nineties. Bibul had never known such heat. He couldn't study, sleep, sell. In desperation he took himself one evening to the Y, forgetting, in the heat, that he had never learned to swim.

An attendant, going off duty, warned Bibul away, told him not to enter the pool. Who can be blind to Bibul's response?

"*Aaaa,*" and that gesture.

He drowned.

His schnorrers, being told, wept and lamented. We sharks, even in the midst of the war's casualties, were moved and stricken.

Bibul was the first of us to die.

I cannot find Bibul's like in Winnipeg today.

Somebody waved a T-square wand over the old island, and the ninety-degree angle, unknown a few thousand years ago, in Bibul's time, has made its appearance there. Progress pretends Bibul's island never existed: the back lanes are paved, paint has been sloshed all over the bare wood fences. When the green gave out, the painters, unflustered, turned to brown. Bibul's world has left signs of itself: a clothesline pole, exhausted from long years of supporting soggy fleece-lined underwear, seems ready to give up the ghost; an outside staircase, impermanent as a hangman's scaffold, still mocks the fire commissioner who asked for safety and got greater danger.

Malkeh is dead. The wagon fell to pieces. Motorized peddlers in trucks like Brink's cars zoom through the island late at night with the remnants of produce picked over by ringed and braceleted upper-middle-class hands on the day route: River Heights, Silver Heights, Garden City; places of Togetherness, Betterness, Spotlessness, the answers Comfort has given the questions of Civilization.

"Apples, apples, two pounds for a quarter," cry the peddlers, but not too loudly, and the women once poor enough to be schnorrers — few are left — and the women living in the rebuilt T-squared houses look over the produce, ironically like Bibul's old rejects because of prior pawing, buy a little, haggle not at all, or withdraw with a snub at peddlers, a bow in favor of the superior refrigeration of the supermarkets.

Throughout Bibul's city, cars pass in unending gaggle, the drivers great speedsters with no goal for their horsepower. The mayor tells the people to "Think big" and hang many flags and buntings. Slums like Bibul's island and the city hall are doomed; Winnipeg is obviously a better place in which to live; who doesn't salute the coming of prosperity?

But the fact remains, I cannot find Bibul's like in Winnipeg today. And that is why, here and now, in this, his and my city, I write you this requiem for Bibul, for his face, for his Cause, his tic, his wave, his "*Aaaa.*" In love and the joy of remembering, I sing you this Bibul and all that's past and passing but not to come.

When the city hall is torn down they will build Winnipeg a new one, but where, oh, where shall we find more Bibuls?

Leonard Cohen

The Favourite Game

Mother—An excerpt from *The Favourite Game.*
Lawrence Breavman, the central character, is strongly drawn from Cohen's own adolescence in Montreal's Westmount. Breavman, brilliant, privileged and deeply alienated, breaks away from one relationship after another as he searches for his own vision of life. The selections are taken from the early part of the novel.

Mother

The heavy gold frame of his father's picture was the first thing he noticed. It seemed like another window.

"You're wasting your life in bed, you're turning night into day," his mother shouted outside the door.

"Will you leave me alone? I just got up."

He stared for a long while at his bookshelf, watching the sun move from the leather Chaucer to the leather Wordsworth. Good sun, in harmony with history. Comforting thought for early morning. Except that it is the middle of the afternoon.

"How can you waste your life in bed? How can you do this to me?"

"I'm on a different cycle. I go to bed late. Please go away."

"The beautiful sun. You're ruining your health."

"I still sleep my seven hours, it's just that I sleep them at a different time than you sleep yours."

"The beautiful sun," she wailed, "the park, you could be walking."

What am I doing arguing with her?

"But mother, I walked in the park last night. It was still the park then, in the night."

"You turn night into day, you're using up your time, your beautiful health."

"Leave me alone!"

She's in bad shape, she just wants to talk, she'll use any maternal duty as an occasion for lengthy debate.

He rested his elbows on the window sill and let the landscape develop in his thought. Park. Lilacs. Nurses in white talking together beside the green branches or pushing dark carriages. Children launching their white sailboats from the concrete shore of the blue pool, praying for wind, safe journeys or spectacular wrecks.

"What do you want for your brunch? Eggs, scrambled, salmon, there's a lovely piece of steak, I'll tell her to make you a salad, what do you want in it, Russian dressing, how do you want your eggs, there's coffee-cake, fresh, the refrigerator is full, in this house there is always something to eat, nobody goes hungry, thank God, there are oranges imported from California, do you want juice?"

He opened the door and spoke carefully.

"I'm aware how fortunate we are. I'll take some juice when I feel like it. Don't disturb the maid or anybody."

But she was already at the banister, shouting, "Mary, Mary, prepare Mr. Lawrence some orange juice, squeeze three oranges. How do you want your eggs, Lawrence?"

She slipped the last question to him like a trick.

"Will you stop shoving food down my throat? You can make a person sick with your damn food!"

He slammed his door.

"He slams a door at a mother," she reported bitterly from the hall.

What a mess! His clothes were everywhere. His desk was a confusion of manuscripts, books, underwear, fragments of Eskimo sculpture. He tried to shove a half-finished sestina into the drawer but it was jammed with accumulated scraps, hoarded envelopes, abandoned diaries.

What this room needs is a good, clean *fire.* He couldn't find his kimono so he covered himself with *The New York Times* and ran across the hall into the bathroom.

"Very pretty. He wears a newspaper."

He managed to creep downstairs, but his mother ambushed him in the kitchen.

''Is that all you're having, orange juice, with the house filled with food, half the world fighting for leftovers?''

''Don't start, Mother.''

She threw open the door of the refrigerator.

''Look,'' she challenged. ''Look at all this, eggs that you didn't want, look at the size of them, cheese, Gruyere, Oka, Danish, Camembert, some cheese and crackers, and who's going to drink all the wine, that's a shame, Lawrence, look at them, feel the weight of this grapefruit, we're so lucky, and meat, three kinds, I'll make it myself, feel the weight . . . . ''

Try and see the poem, Breavman, the beautiful catalogue.

'' — here, feel the weight . . . .''

He heaved the raw slab of steak at her feet, splitting the wax-paper on the linoleum.

''Haven't you got anything better to do with your life than stuff food down my face? I'm not starving.''

''This is the way a son talks to his mother,'' she informed the world. ''Will you leave me alone now?''

''This is a son talking, your father should see you, he should be here to see you throwing down meat, meat on the floor, what tyrant does that, only someone rotten, to do this to a mother . . . .''

He followed her out of the kitchen.

''I just asked to be left alone, to wake up by myself.''

''Rotten, a rat wouldn't treat a mother, rotten as if you were a stranger, would anybody throw meat and my ankles are swollen, beat you, your father would beat you, a rotten son . . . .''

He followed her up the stairs.

''You can make someone sick with your screaming.''

She slammed her closet door. He stood beside it and listened to her opening and shutting the big drawers.

''Get away! A son talks to a mother, a son can kill a mother, I knew everything, what I have to hear, a traitor not a son, to talk to me, nobody who remembers me to talk . . .''

He heard her slide open the dress compartment. First she tore the sleeves from some old housecoats. She tripped over a tangle of hangers. Then she began on an expensive black one she had bought in New York.

''What good are they, what good are they, when a son is killing a mother . . . .''

He heard every sound, his cheek pressed against the wood.

Miriam Waddington

A Place of Witches

The summer Danny was five his friends on the street began to ask him, "Hey, Danny, what are you anyways, English or Jewish?" Danny knew there was something different about his family. After thinking about it for a while, he said: "Well, you see, it's like this. My Daddy is English, my Mommy is English, and I'm Jewish."

This answer, slowly and deliberately delivered, seemed to satisfy everyone. It satisfied Lewis, who was Jewish and went to a Hebrew school, and it did equally well for Johnny who wasn't Jewish, because at Christmas his mother hung a green holly wreath outside their door. Most of all, Danny knew that Johnny couldn't be Jewish because he went to Lynstead School, while Danny had to go to Camden School, along with Anne, Judy and Gerald, all of whom he figured must be Jewish too.

It was a deep grief to Danny that he couldn't go to Lynstead School, and it puzzled him because he knew that their street was right in the part of Montreal everyone called Lynstead. His house was just across the street from Johnny's house and right next door to Karen's - and both Karen and Johnny went to Lynstead.

What made it all the more sorrowful was that Lynstead was such a fine big school with a playground and skating rink and a big auditorium where they showed movies on Friday nights. When his mother had taken him there on the first day of school to write his name down for kindergarten, he had seen that the floor was covered with linoleum which shone like a mirror, and the teacher had on a pretty orange smock. He looked around the newly painted shelves in the kindergarten room, and let his eyes range over the toys. Some of them were so new they still had brown paper wrappings around them!

While his mother sat down to talk to the teacher, Danny wandered around and looked at everything. He thought how good it would be to have his friend Karen sitting beside him in kindergarten.

His mother at last finished writing, and was handing the paper to the teacher. The teacher said something to his mother and he saw her face take on the look that meant she was angry. Then he heard the teacher speak again, quite loudly this time, loud enough for him to hear.

"I'm very sorry, but we do not take Jewish children in Lynstead School."

Suddenly he didn't want to hear anymore. He knew it was something about him, something bad, and he got down on his hands and knees and crawled into the little white doll-house that stood over in the corner. He hoped he wouldn't be able to hear any more, but the voices of his mother and the teacher were loud and angry. They came right through the windows of the little house.

He could hear his mother arguing and talking about public school, saying she had never heard of anything like this. Pretty soon the voices stopped and he could hear his mother's resolute steps walking towards the doll-house, towards him, until there she was, looking in through the window.

With a determined gaiety that didn't fool him at all, she said, "Danny, wait for me here. I'm going to talk to the principal; I'll be right back."

He didn't want to wait there. He was scared to stay alone with the teacher who didn't look pretty anymore. He huddled down on the floor of the doll-house and made himself as small as he could. He tried hard not to tremble, but he was scared. Maybe the teacher was going to punish him. He must be very bad if she wouldn't let him come to her kindergarten. He kept thinking and thinking, trying to decide how he was bad, what was wrong with him, and he just couldn't puzzle it out.

Finally he hit on it. He was Jewish. Of course!

He didn't know what to do. He was getting ready to cry. It was no use asking his mother why they couldn't be English and go to church like Karen's family. She would only get mad. He got up the courage and rose to look outside the window of the doll-house. He saw two or three mothers come in with their children, write out their papers, and he felt full of envy as he watched the teacher taking the new children by the hand and smiling to them.

He was glad to see his mother enter the room. She came straight to the doll-house, took him by the hand and led him out. On the stairs outside the school the sun was warm, and little brown sparrows were hopping about. Danny did not feel merry. To his mother he said,

"Mummy, my heart is so sad."

His mother bent down to kiss him, and answered gently, "I know, darling. But don't worry. There is no room for you here, but after lunch we'll go and write you down for Camden School."

Danny knew his mother was lying. He knew there was room at Lynstead. He knew the real reason why he couldn't go to Lynstead. All the same it was hard to find an answer to Johnny's loud greeting when he and his mother approached their house.

"Hi, Danny, are you going to Lynstead?"

And when Karen ran out on her porch and yelled to ask if he was going to Lynstead, he snapped at her.

That afternoon his mother took him to Camden School. He didn't want to go, and kicked and yelled, but nothing worked. His mother took him by the hand and made him come.

From the first minute he laid eyes on Camden School, he hated it. He scorned its smallness, its cement playground. The halls were old and dark. They smelled stale. He had no friends here. He was mad at the school, mad at the new teacher, and mad at his mother, to whom he said petulantly, "You made me come here but I'm not going to walk home alone, oh no! You'll have to call for me, or I'll make myself lost!"

Danny gradually got used to going to Camden. At home he complained that there were so many children in class that he never got a turn on the bicycle, and the teacher made him play drums in the orchestra when he wanted the tambourine. Yet some of his days were happy, and some were even touched with pride. He loved the days when he brought home large colored drawings for his mother to see.

And his mother, who would be watching for his homecoming at the front window would gaze at the procession of children as they drifted past, colored papers floating in the wind like the flags of many nations. It was touching and beautiful to see the children coming home, and she was saddened to think how on this one street, the children had to attend two different schools. Meanwhile the street itself changed. It was no longer a friendly collection of families in a housing project. Even the children had become subtly transformed. When Johnny saw Danny starting out for school he frequently yelled:

"Yah, yah, kindergarten baby, stick your head in gravy, baby, baby."

Danny found the walk to Camden slow and tiresome. Along the way he often met groups of older children, who came from the mysterious area of the vast city that lay on the other side of the street-car tracks which boundaried his world. The girls, large and rosy-faced in their white blouses and dark tunics, looked ominous. The boys, fair and proud as they carried their school bags carelessly over their shoulders, aimed clods of earth at the birds, who spread like ink stains over the sky. These boys from Lynstead School would often halt their games in order to threaten Danny and other small children. They would begin to sing derisively:

"Camden bums, suck your thumbs, carry valises on your bums!" and the little children would scatter in terrified flight.

Once three girls in tunics got off their bicycles in front of Camden School to tease the children who were loitering outside.

"Look at your school," one fat girl yelled, "it's nothing but a fire-trap."

"Hah, hah!" jeered another, "do you call that a school? I don't call that a school! It's nothing but a matchbox, a fire-trap, a mouse-trap!"

Danny stood among the children in the schoolyard. As he listened to this shameful chorus of reproach, a narrowness passed in on him, crowded him and squeezed anger out of him. If only he were older! He was glad when a boy from grade three came forward and stuck his tongue out at the girls and began dancing up and down, singing out his reprisal,

"Lynstead bums, suck your thumbs."

Soon the whole yard took up the refrain until it was a deafening chorus accompanied by a shower of gravel and small stones which quickly made the girls take off on their bicycles.

These high points, these times when he was on the winning side, were rare in Danny's life. His days were beset by dangers. There were the goblins, first of all. They lived in the empty building lots that he had to pass on his way to school. True, like Cinderella's magic charioteers, the goblins turned into dry withered leaves when he came close to them, but he knew they were just obeying the spell, it was temporary. Then there was the old witch. She hid behind the great pile of new bricks which stood walled up with straw against the winter. Danny knew he must be very careful passing those bricks, or the witch might fly out at him, broom and all. It was a scary thought. Even the memory of it was enough to send him burrowing deep under the covers at night.

So usually he hurried right home after school, looking neither to the left nor to the right. He trotted as fast as his legs would carry him, past the park, and then the empty fields where the building lots had been marked off into subdivisions, and where sometimes men would be at work digging and hammering.

On this day he was thinking of goblins and witches and how he didn't want to meet them, when he heard the familiar voice of Karen calling behind him.

"Oh, look, there's Danny! And look at his coat, it's all torn."

There was an answering jeer from her companion, an older girl whom Danny did not know,

"Yah, look at that dirty old coat on him!"

Danny paused and looked around. He looked down at his coat and all he could see was a tiny rip where he had caught it on the coat hook at school. He didn't say anything but stared solemnly at the two little girls.

"Look at him," continued the older girl to Karen, "I guess that's the uniform at Camden, hah, hah, hah, didn't you know the Jews are rag peddlers?"

Still Danny did not speak. He continued to walk backwards, staring at his tormentors. He saw Karen poke her friend and whisper something to her. He watched them both as they guffawed with laughter. Then the bigger girl said in a cajoling tone,

"You're a Jew, aren't you Danny?"

As he did not reply, she called more roughly,

"Sure, you're a Jew. All the Jews go to Camden because they're not allowed in Lynstead School, hah, hah, hah!"

And Karen, who used to be his friend, to whom he had always lent his bicycle and given the orange-flavored lollypop, this same Karen now took up the cry,

"You're a Jew, a Jew, a Jew, a Jew, yah, yah, yah!"

Danny never saw the truck that hit him as he stepped backwards off the curb. All he heard were the heavy wheels grinding out a thick rubbery refrain which splintered his consciousness into a million muddy little diamonds like the pattern on the tires, and each diamond shrieked and yelled, ''Jew'' at him, ''Jew, Jew, Jew.''

In the months that followed, when Danny's mother was nursing him back to health, she tried to find out how it was he had happened to get run over. Her questions to Karen met with a blank innocent stare.

What could have made Danny so careless? He must have seen the truck, or at least heard its approach. Why? A thousand times she looked into the dark pupils of her son's eyes and plumbed the luscent agate that surrounded them for an answer. Each time she was met by a look of wonder, astonishment and secrecy, the depth of which terrified her.

In her heart she knew that there was now something in Danny's life which would remain closed to her forever.

Miriam Waddington

Second Generation

Child of a lonely traveller
in a strange country
I live towards my doom
closed in a small tight room.

Closed in a small tight room
where whitehaired quiet ladies
claw the walls conspire in lies
and wicked things to come.

Closed in this small tight room
there is a warm illimitable
thing inside me keeps me
alive and proud and sane.

Had my father known what
his children would suffer
through the oiled words
and dull circumstance,

had my father dreamed the cunning
of this anglo-saxon conference,
he had never ventured beyond
the plains of home bloody and

cruel and violent as life was,
he would never have brought us
to this small tight room
to this bite-your-tongue-off doom.

Mordecai Richler

Pinky's Squealer

One bright, cloudless morning in July 1941, Noah, Gas and Hershey arranged to meet on the balcony of Old Annie's candy store in Prevost, a village in the Laurentians, where their families had taken cottages for tne summer. They were determined to climb the mountain behind the Nine Cottages to get to Lac Gondon, where the *goyim* were.

Hershey turned up first.

Old Annie, who was a tiny, grey-haired widow with black, mournful eyes, looked the boy up and down suspiciously. A first-aid kit and a scout knife were strapped to his belt. "What is," she asked, "a revolution?"

Hershey grimaced. "He who hears no evil, speaks no evil."

Old Annie's store was a squat sinking yellow shack all but covered with signs advertising Kik and Sweet Caporal cigarettes. She wasn't called Old Annie because she was sixty-two. Long ago, in Lithuania, the first three children born to her parents had not survived their infancy. So the village miracle-maker had suggested that if another child was born to them they should call her *alte* (old) instantly, and God would understand.

Gas arrived next. He had a BB gun and a package of crumbly egg and onion sandwiches.

''Knock, knock,'' he said.

''Who's there?'' Hershey asked.

''Ago.''

''Ago who?''

''Aw, go tell your mother she wants you.''

Behind Old Annie's store was the scorched, spiky field that was used as a market. Early every Friday morning the French Canadian farmers arrived with poultry, vegetables and fruit. They were a skeptical bunch, with hard, seamed faces, but the St. Urbain Street wives were more than a match for them and by late afternoon the farmers were drained and grateful to get away. The women, who were ruthless bargainers, spoke a mixture of French, English and Yiddish with the farmers. ''So *fiel,* Monsieur, for dis *kliene* chicken? *Vous* crazy?''

Pinky's Squealer saw the two boys sitting on the stoop, waiting for Noah. He approached them diffidently. ''Where you goin'?'' he asked.

''To China,'' Gas said.

When the Squealer's mother wanted him to go to the toilet she would step out on her balcony and yell, ''Dollink, time to water the teapot.'' Pinky, who was the Squealer's cousin, was seventeen years old, and his proper name was Milton Fishman. He was rather pious and conducted services at Camp Machia. The Squealer was his informer.

''I've got a quarter,'' Pinky's Squealer said.

''Grease it well,'' Gas replied.

Habitually, those families who lived on Clark, St. Urbain, Rachel and City Hall clubbed together and took cottages in Prevost for the summer. How they raised the money, what sacrifices they made, were comparatively unimportant — the children required sun. Prevost had an exceedingly small native population and most of the lopsided cottages were owned by French Canadians who lived in Shawbridge, just up the hill. The C.P.R. railway station was in Shawbridge. Prevost, at the foot of the hill, was separated from Shawbridge by that bridge reputedly built by a man named Shaw. It was a crazy-quilt of clapboard shacks and cottages strewn over hills and fields and laced by bumpy dirt roads and an elaborate system of paths. The centre of the village was the foot of the bridge. Here were Zimmerman's, Blatt's, The Riverside Inn, Stein the butcher, and — on the winding dirt road to the right — the synagogue and the beach. In 1941 Zimmerman and Blatt still ran staunchly competitive general stores on opposite sides of the highway. Both stores were sprawling dumpy buildings badly in need of a paint job and had dance halls and huge balconies — where you could also dance — attached. But Zimmerman had a helper named Zelda and that gave him the edge over Blatt. Zelda's signs were posted all over Zimmerman's.

Over the fruit stall:

AN ORANGE ISN'T A BASEBALL. DON'T HANDLE WHAT YOU DON'T WANT. THINK OF THE NEXT CUSTOMER.

Over the cash:

IF YOU CAN GET IT CHEAPER BY THAT GANGSTER ACROSS THE HIGHWAY YOU CAN HAVE IT FOR NOTHING

However, if you could get it cheaper at Blatt's, Zelda always proved that what you had bought was not as fresh or of a cheaper quality.

The beach was a field of spiky grass and tree stumps. Plump, middle-aged ladies, their flesh boiled pink, spread out blankets and squatted in their bras and bloomers, playing poker, smoking and sipping cokes. The vacationing cutters and pressers seldom wore bathing suits either. They didn't swim. They set up card tables and chairs and played pinochle solemnly, sucking foul cigars and cursing the sun. The children dashed in and out among them playing tag or tossing a ball about. Boys staggered between sprawling sun-bathers, lugging pails packed with ice and shouting:

"Ice-cold drinks, Chawk-lit bahs. Cig'rettes!"

Occasionally, a woman, her wide-brimmed straw flapping as she waddled from table to table, her smile as big as her aspirations, gold teeth glittering, would intrude on the card players, asking — nobody's forcing, mind you — if they would like to buy a raffle in aid of the Mizrachi Fresh Air Fund or the J.N.F. Naked babies bawled. Plums, peaches, watermelons were consumed, pits and peels tossed indiscriminately on the grass. The slow yellow river was unfailingly condemned by the Health Board during the last three weeks of August, when the polio scare was at its height. But the children paid no attention. They shrieked with delight whenever one of their huge mothers descended into the water briefly to duck herself — once, twice — warn the children against swimming out too far — then, return, refreshed, to her poker game. The French Canadians were too shocked to complain, but the priests sometimes preached sermons about the indecency of the Jews. Mort Shub said, "Liss'n, it's their job. A priest's gotta make a living too."

At night most people crowded into the dancehalls at Zimmerman's and Blatt's. The kids, like Noah, Gas, and Hershey, climbed up the windows and, peashooters in their mouths, took careful aim at the dancers' legs before firing. Fridays, the wives worked extremely hard cleaning and cooking for the Sabbath. Everybody got dressed up in the afternoon in anticipation of the arrival of the fathers, who were met in Shawbridge, most of them having arrived on the 6:15 excursion train. Then the procession through Shawbridge, down the hill and across the bridge, began; an event that always horrified the residents of the village. Who were these outlandish, cigar-chomping men, burdened with watermelons and Kik bottles, salamis and baskets of peaches, yelling at their children, whacking their wives' behinds and — worst of all — waving merrily at the sombre Scots who sat petrified on their balconies?

Noah showed up last.

"Pinky's Squealer wants to come with us," Gas said.

"Did you tell him where we're going?"

"Ixnay. You think I'm crazy?"

"He's got a quarter," Hershey said.

Pinky's Squealer showed Noah the quarter.

"All right," Noah said.

Old Annie, shaking her head sadly, watched the four boys start out across the fields. Noah led. Hershey, who came next, was Rabbi Druker's son; a scrawny boy with big brown eyes. His father had a small but devoted following. Hershey hung around the synagogue every evening and stopped old men on their way to prayers. "Give me a nickel and I'll give you a blessing." He didn't do too badly. "I'm holy as hell," he told Noah one evening.

Gas, trailing behind, was plump, fair-headed and freckled. The boys filed down the dirt road that led to the Nine Cottages, the sun beating against their brown bodies. They passed Kravitz's cottage, with its smelly outhouse, Becky Goldberg's place, and the shapeless shack that housed ten shapeless Cohens.

The tall grass at the foot of the mountain was stiff and yellow and made you itch. There were also mushy patches where the bullrushes grew, but they avoided those. The sheltering trees cooled the boys, but they had a long climb ahead of them. The soft plump ground they tramped on was padded with pine cones, needles, and dead leaves. Sunlight filtered deviously among the birch and maple and fir trees and the mountain had a dark damp smell to it. There was the occasional cawing of crows, they saw two woodpeckers and, once, a hummingbird. They reached the top of the mountain about one o'clock and sat down on an open patch of ground to eat their lunch. Gas chased around after grasshoppers, storing them in an old mayonnaise jar that had two holes punched in the top. After they had finished their sandwiches they started out again, this time down the other side of the mountain. The foliage thickened and in their eagerness to get along quickly, they scratched their legs and arms in the bush, stumbling into the occasional ditch concealed by leaves and bruising their ankles against jagged stones. They heard voices in the distance. Noah, who had been given the BB gun, pulled back the catch. Gas scooped up a rock, Hershey unstrapped his scout knife. "We'll be late for *shabus,*" Pinky's Squealer said. "Maybe we should go back?"

"Go ahead," Hershey said. "But watch out for snakes, eh?"

"I didn't say anything."

Voices, laughter too now, came splashing through the trees. The ground began to level off and, just ahead, they made out the beach. There were real canoes, a diving-board, and lots of crazy-coloured umbrellas and deck-chairs. The boys approached the beach cautiously, crouching in the bushes. Noah was amazed. The men were tall and slender and the women were awfully pretty, lying out in the sun there, just like that, not afraid of anything. There was no yelling or watermelon peels or women in bloomers. Everything was so clean. Beautiful almost.

Gas was the first to notice the soft drink stand. He turned to Pinky's Squealer. "You've got the quarter. Go get us Pepsis."

"Gas should go," Hershey said. "He's the least Jewish-looking of the gang. Look at his nose — Christ! They'll take him for a *goy* easy."

"You can have my quarter."

"Aw, go water your tea-kettle," Gas said. "Maybe I don't look as Jewish as you or Noah, but they can always tell by pulling down your pants . . . ."

They all giggled.

"It's not so funny," Hershey said. "That's how they found out about my uncle, who was killed in Russia."

"You're all chicken," Noah said. "I'm going. But I'm having my coke right out there on the beach. If you want anything to drink you'll have to come too."

A convertible Ford pulled away and that revealed the sign to them. Gas noticed it first. Suddenly, he pointed. "Hey, look!"

THIS BEACH
IS
RESTRICTED
TO GENTILES

That changed everything. Noah, his excitement mounting, said they would hang around until evening and then, when the beach was deserted, steal the sign.

"Yeah, and walk back in the dark, eh?" Pinky's Squealer said "'It's Friday, you know. Ain't *your* paw coming?"

Gas and Hershey looked puzzled. Both of them had been forbidden to play with Noah by their mothers. Pinky's Squealer made sense, but if Noah intended to stay they would look cowardly if they left him behind. Noah certainly wanted to stay. Having his father up for the weekend usually meant two days of quarreling.

"Aw, in a hundred years we'll all be dead," Gas said.

Pinky's Squealer waited, kicking the stump of a tree petulantly. "If you come with me, Hershey, you can have my quarter."

"Watch out for snakes," Hershey said.

Pinky's Squealer ran off.

The afternoon dragged on slowly, but at last the sun lowered and a strong breeze was starting up. Only a few stragglers remained on the beach.

"Is a Gentile a Catholic and a Protestant too?" Hershey asked.

"Yeah," Noah said.

"But they're different," Hershey said, "aren't they?"

"Different," Gas said. "You know the difference between Hitler and Mussolini?"

Noah decided that as it was getting late they would have to risk it, stragglers and all. The few couples who remained were intent on each other and wouldn't notice them if they were cunning. Noah said that he and Gas should stroll out on to the beach, approaching the sign from different directions, nonchalantly. It didn't look as if it was stuck very solidly into the sand. Hershey was to holler if he saw anybody coming for them. He had stones and the BB gun.

So the two boys sauntered innocently out on to the beach. Noah whistled. Gas pretended to be searching for something. The wind kicked up gusts of sand and the sun, sinking still lower, was a blaze in the opposite hills. Suddenly, frantically, the two boys were yanking at the sign. Gas shook with laughter, tears rolling down his cheeks. Noah cursed. They heard, piercing the stillness, a high-pitched shout. "Look out!"

Gas let go, and ran off. Flying for the woods.

"Hurry!"

Noah persisted. A man, waving a canoe paddle, was running toward him. Noah gave one last, frenzied tug, and the sign broke free. The man was about twenty feet away now, wielding his paddle viciously. His eyes were wild. "You little son of a bitch!"

Noah swerved, racing for the bushes. A shower of pebbles bounced off his back. The paddle swooshed through the air behind him. But he was fast. Once in the bushes he scampered off, zigzagging into the mountain. He ran and ran and ran. Finally, clutching the sign in his hands, he tumbled down on the pine needles, his heart hammering.

Noah couldn't find Gas anywhere, but Hershey loomed up from behind a rock. Darkness fell quickly and they soon realized they were lost. Lost, and without a flashlight. Possibly, they were moving in circles. For all they knew they might come out of the woods again at Lac Gandon.

Noah and Hershey had stopped climbing, they had reached a level bit of ground and then all at once they heard many voices. Light beams shot through the darkness. Hastily, the boys concealed the sign under a mess of decaying leaves and climbed up the nearest tree - their pockets filled with stones. The voices and probing lights came nearer.

''Hershey!''

''Noah!''

''Boys!''

''Hallo!''

The boys began to quake with laughter. Every able-bodied man in Prevost must have been out on the mountain that night, armed with pitchforks, rakes, clubs and baseball bats. Noah and Hershey had never thought they'd be grateful to Pinky's Squealer, but they were that Friday night. They slid down the tree and uncovered the sign and that was their night of glory in Prevost. Nothing was too good for them. Sunday morning Noah, Hershey, Mort Shub, and Gas planted the sign on their own beach. When the others came out to swim, they read:

THIS BEACH
IS
RESTRICTED
TO
~~GENTILES~~
LITVAKS

Sondra Gotlieb

The Wrongies

"The Wrongies"—an Excerpt from **True Confections,** Sondra Gotlieb's book of memoirs which describes growing up in North End Winnipeg during the '40's and '50's.

I certainly wasn't ashamed of my house.

It was on the best end of Machray Street, only a block from the Red River, near the big oak trees on the corner. Daddy said the only reason he didn't buy a house on the river was because he was afraid that my brother and I might roll down the steep bank and drown. My parents bought the house before I was born and I lived there until I was married.

Everyone on Machray planted snapdragons, salvias and sweet peas, bright annuals that flourished in the long days of Winnipeg's brief summer — except for Ida Bled who grew poppies for the seeds to make cookies and cakes. One day the Mounties knocked on Ida's door and asked to see her poppies because they thought she was growing *Papaver somniforum,* the opium flower. Ida panicked, tore her poppies out of the ground and planted snapdragons like the rest of her neighbors, although it turned out afterwards that her poppies were not the variety dope fiends liked.

Most of the people living near us were Jewish, small businessmen and their families, except for the Mercers who lived next door — he was a Methodist small businessman. In December the Mercers' house shone in the evening blackness for a good half mile because they had the only Christmas lights on the street.

Most of our Jewish neighbors were second generation Canadians who had moved away from their parents' small wooden bungalows on the other side of Main Street, which crossed Machray less than a mile from the Red River. The river end of Machray had bigger houses and more yard space for lilac bushes, bird baths, and lythrum.

Anyone who lived on the river side of Machray sent their children to Luxton school from grade one till nine. Consequently, half of Luxton's pupils were Jewish, but from varying social backgrounds. Machray was on the top of the social heap because we had a couple of lawyers and dentists on the street. Many of the pupils at Luxton were children of workers in the needle trade; few of them wished to follow their parents' footsteps.

Miss McCord once asked us what we wished to be when we grew up and every boy in my class answered lawyer, doctor or dentist. Some of the girls said home economist or teacher, but most of us believed that the best thing to be was "good wife and mother." A shock went through the class when a girl named Ruby, who sat in the back seat in the farthest row, answered "presser."

Miss McCord didn't understand.

"What's a presser?"

"It's what my mother and father do: iron clothes at the wholesale." Everyone in the class was embarrassed, partly because Ruby had such a low ambition, but mostly because her mother had to work.

The rest of the pupils came from middle and working-class Ukrainian families, and there were a few Anglo-Saxon kids whose parents had not yet moved to Fort Rouge, Crescentwood, of Fort Garry, anywhere away from the north end.

The teachers were mostly Scotch — names like McKay, McCord, McCloud, Duncan, and McKinley were as familiar to us, whose grandfathers or fathers came from eastern Europe, as to any child born between Dumfries and the Caledonian Canal.

The teachers dealt with the mouthy Jewish kids as best they could, realizing we hadn't been trained at home to keep quiet when another talked and to stand up when a lady walked in. There was little overt anti-Semitism — perhaps because we were in the majority.

Choir singing was the most important activity throughout the year. There was the girls' junior high choir, the boys' junior high choir, and the best mixed voice junior high choir. Each class was automatically formed into a choir as well, although less was expected from the sound. This meant there was no escape for the tone deaf who had to mouth their way through, "Step I with my Cromach to the Isles."

The Manitoba song book had one of the most complete selections of Scotch folk airs in all the educational systems of North America. Miss McCord, Miss Dunbar, Miss McKay and Miss McKinley enthusiastically led Wanda Kunka, Hymie Birnboim, Boris Bachynski and Shulamith Gorelick from the lowland Selkirk borders to Loch Maree in the highlands with "Sing Aye for the Bonnets of Bonnie Dundee."

Neither teachers nor pupils thought the song selection in any way incongruous.

Other than differences over the interpretation of the Gospels (and the desire to suppress the New Testament entirely on the part of militants like Kusy Gwertzman) our teacher-student relationship was satisfactory. Team spirit flourished during the home and school tea. The teachers asked the mothers to bring a "small square" for the event. On the day of the tea, the teachers would be overwhelmed by eastern Europe's culinary riches. Instead of shortbreads and matrimonial cake, the pupils would carry in eight-layered tortes filled with apricots, paper-thin strudels set with turkish delight, and a hundred different kinds of cookies made with strange ingredients: poppy seeds, buckwheat, honey, and prunes.

Unconsciously, the mothers' rule of thumb was: the worse their English, the more lavish their contribution. In this way they made up for social inadequacies during their talks with Misses Dunbar, McKinley, McIver and others. My mother felt no need for self-expression at the Luxton Home and School Tea, having been a teacher herself. Her contributions were aptly named nothings.

There were parts of the north end, past the Selkirk bridge toward the city hall, where mothers didn't bake for home and school teas, where people put newspapers on their windows instead of blinds, let alone curtains, and weeds grew. This was where many of the northend wrongies lived. The wrongies' parent's didn't speak English and were a symbol of the despised old country to their children.

The wrongies were mostly Jewish, except for a couple of straying Ukrainians. They liked to stand in front of the north end synagogue on Yom Kippur, when the pious fasted, and munch on pork spare ribs from a greasy brown bag. They considered their ploy successful if an apoplectic beadle rushed at them close enough so they could offer him a bit.

The boys found their pride and living space at certain cafes and snack bars along Main Street — the This is It and the Tophs.

I used to walk by Tophs with my eyes closed so the wrongies inside wouldn't catch me peeking at the sunbathing magazines displayed in the windows. None of the Carols or Normas ever went inside. Burt the Boozer, Chicken Brassiere and Kusy Gwertzman, who hung around playing cards, would be sure to make the atmosphere uncomfortable for girls from the river side of Machray Street.

Kusy was a kid with a mean streak who would sit on the streetcar with one leg tucked under so that the old ladies standing in front of him would think he was a child amputee. When he rose on his two good legs he'd smirk at their dirty looks. Kusy, Chicken and Boozer used to make money by enticing farmers into poker games at every fleabag hotel in Manitoba. No one from Mafeking or Mud Falls was safe when that trio hit town.

Chicken's mother was responsible for his first name. Her lungs had enlarged, trying to reach her son over the years. She would stick her neck out of the window from her upstairs apartment and bellow, *''Faigeleh, Faigeleh''* (little bird, little bird), an affectionate Yiddish diminutive used to lull infants to sleep.

Faigeleh was usually somewhere setting fires with his friends and didn't appreciate her old country manner of speech. The language of the street was English and none of the wrongies wanted it generally known that their parents spoke only Yiddish at home.

They even tried to encourage a little bilingualism. When Chicken's or Kusy's parents asked them, in Yiddish, where they had been for the last three days, they always replied, briefly and sullenly, in English. The most apt translation for *Faigeleh,* the wrongies thought, was Chicken.

The second part of Chicken's name was acquired in Latin class when Chicken awkwardly translated a passage from Latin into English, that read, ''And the Roman soldiers carried the flaming braziers high about their heads.'' Hence Chicken Brassiere.

Sometimes my brother Ronnie, a typical middle-class boy, ventured into Tophs. The wrongies once examined his watch, passed it from one to another and congratulated him. ''Best quality bar mitzvah type watch, boy. Leave it with us and we'll see that it gets properly cleaned.'' Ronny returned without the watch and my parents had nothing to say except, ''We told you not to go into Tophs.''

A.M. Klein

Beggars I Have Known

I get along very well with beggars. Perhaps it is because they feel that I shall soon be one of them.

Whenever I pass a panhandler on the street he buttonholes me. Even when I say, No I can't spare a dime, he never feels resentful. He knows I am telling the truth, even if I am wearing a new suit.

But when I have the change I give it to them. I am not one of those who go around making nasty remarks about beggars just because their mouths smell of beer. I know that when a fellow has only a nickel to his name he would rather, and it's much wiser, too, spend it on a glass of beer, than on a cup of dishwater. Coffee just washes your insides and keeps you awake, whereas beer fills you, tickles your guts and makes you drowsy. It's easier to sleep on hard benches that way, and besides, if your mouth smells of beer the flies don't fly into it when you're asleep with it open.

I remember once when I had a dime between myself and hunger, I thought of how to spend it. If I bought something to eat, I figured, I would be hungry again in no time and would have to walk the streets with an aching belly. So I went into a cheap movie and for four hours forgot all about my hunger, except now and again when I saw on the screen how the rich eat.

There is a man on our street, an old Jew, who lives in the Home for the Aged. Every day, except Saturday, you can see him walking around the block with his eyes glued to the sidewalk looking for cigarette butts. He keeps the butts in regular cigarette boxes which he picks up in the gutter. Whenever I see him nosing around for his butts, I always give him a brand-new cigarette; sometimes I don't notice him until he turns the corner, and then I run after him to give him his smoke. He always takes my cigarette and then blesses me. I should live to an old age: I should be rich: I should have pleasure from my children. I always feel good when I leave him, because he blesses with so much heart, caressing my shoulder at each blessing, as if he was loading them on my back.

I told him he could pick up a lot of butts outside the Arena on wrestling nights, because the fans go out to have a smoke between bouts and always at midnight there are hundreds of butts on the sidewalk. As a matter of fact, once when I was coming home from a show downtown at twelve o'clock, and walked up by way of Fletcher's Field, a beggar walked up with us and stopped at the Arena to pick up these butts. But the old Jew tells me he can't get out of the Home for the Aged after eight o'clock.

There is a beggar who rings our door-bell on Mondays. To tell the truth I never saw him ring it and I often wonder how he does it because the fingers of both his hands are all chopped off. My mother gives him a nickel— we're poor, too—and he grabs it off with his palms and with the stubs that are left of his fingers. When my brother, who is eating dinner, asks my mother who it was at the door, she always tells him, and begins to describe the buttons of flesh where the fingers should be, and my brother says, Can't you see I'm eating?

I know all the beggars of our city personally. Most of them are real beggars, but some of them are fakes. There are a couple of guys, for example, who patrol Peel and St. Catherine Street, who are nothing more than racketeers and who, if they are ever found out, will give begging a bad name. These fellows get themselves a pair of returned soldier buttons, and every time they nab a customer they flash the badge and say something about a country fit for heroes to live in. But Tommy Kinsella, on Place d'Armes Square, who is a real returned soldier, lost his badge and all he can show are two sawed-off legs. Everybody pities him, however, when he tries to get on a street car.

He's a funny case, too, this Tommy. He doesn't seem to mind his stumps so very much, but he's always complaining about getting T.B. because his nose is so near the ground. I suppose you get that way, from trouble.

Then take Steve Szopik. He is the fellow who hangs around our factory and runs messages. Occasionally he gets a sandwich and a Coca Cola. Now he's been trying to break into the beggar game for years. But he can't do it. He just can't get a license. No pull. Everything is politics.

On the other hand, a snob like Burke — the violinist in front of Christ Church Cathedral — has all kinds of pull, and gets a license, and one of the best spots in town. Stuck-up. That's not the word for it. He calls himself a mendicant.

It's the blind beggars who are really handicapped. When you're blind and a beggar you can't run after your clientele, it just passes you by. It doesn't even feel embarrassed. You're blind.

And they can throw into your box whatever they feel like throwing. You can't even know.

I just can't see old man Rosenbloom. He is blind and is led around by his little boy. He wears dark glasses and carries pencils in his hand. It's the idea of the pencils that I can't get. I imagine that if you are blind you are entitled to charity without giving away presents. Apart from the expense, it's foolish. What does he want, his patrons to write him a letter?

So, as I am saying, I get along swell with beggars. They remember that when I had money I was no piker. They tell me all their secrets: why the doorstep of some churches are more profitable than others; what restaurants throw you out, and which ones give you a hand; how to approach elderly ladies and how to tackle young slickers; where the bookmakers are, and what time the barbutte finishes, and the winners come out; how to feel the denomination of coins; what words to open up your plea with, and what phrases to leave out when the giver doesn't seem to pay any attention; when to talk clearly, and when to mumble; when to be bold and when to be humble; what districts have dogs in their porches; how to shake a coin-cup so that it should make the greatest amount of noise with the least danger of the coins falling out; and numberless other tricks of the trade.

As a matter of fact, they have often asked me to become one of them. They don't mind a little extra competition if it comes from a decent fellow, and they lead me to believe that I am such a fellow. They tell me, too, that it is a very happy profession, that you are out in the open all day, that you have no overhead expense, and that you can never be laid off because you are working for yourself. They've planned a union for beggars, but have found it impossible. It's a capitalistic society, they say. But even without a union, one can make a nice living. You can't strike in your trade, I said. People would be happy if you quit work. Would they, though? they said. A rich man can't live without a beggar. He needs him to protect his conscience. So they were trying to persuade me to join their ranks. My wife wouldn't stand for it, I said. She always talks about beggars in a sad voice, and gets herself weepy about armless sleeves and folded trouser legs and empty sockets and men with dumb, pitiable expressions.

That's nothing, they said. For us to be blind or crippled is only a school degree, like a doctor's or a lawyer's. That's the way we hang out our shingle. Our superiority over those who give us money is this: they still pity us, but we have stopped pitying ourselves.

Anyway, I said, I'll think about it.

I have been thinking about it. But I am afraid to broach the subject to my wife. I know that she will begin to cry. She is too proud. And I, too, am afraid that I can't afford to take this step — I have no ailments, I am not blind, I am not crippled, I am perfectly healthy. Only I am poor; and that's like being blind and crippled. Worse, because you feel helpless without any excuse. But I can't become a beggar; I can't learn to stop pitying myself.

Ed Kleiman

The Handicap

Our family has always lived with handicaps. Let me tell you what I mean. Not the lack of money and not the small house and not the North End that we grew up in — that hodge-podge district of slums, delicatessens, little musical groups, watch repair shops and local newspapers with limited circulations. Anybody can deal with those kinds of handicaps. In fact, some people wouldn't call those handicaps, but helps, aids, advantages. No! I'm talking about honest-to-goodness handicaps. My brother and sister and me — we've been struck violent blows by these handicaps.

Take my brother, for example. He was the first one to have a deal with the kind of handicap which our family, it seems, specializes in.

His handicap was a salami. I know! I know! You'll say who ever heard of a salami being a handicap. Well, if you really want to know, it's the worst kind — or almost the worst kind.

When my brother was twelve he insisted on going off to Scout Camp. Our family was outraged. So what was wrong with going along with the family to the beach? Or if it had to be camp, what about one of ours? Perhaps the B'nai B'rith, although it was a bit expensive; or if he was a fledgling Zionist, there was always the Habonim. The Mapam camp my father would have drawn the line at. They were too socialist, almost communist — ''Bolsheviks'', my father cursed — but, anyway, some arrangement, some compromise could have been arrived at. But by brother was adamant — it had to be a Boy Scout camp.

My father was even more outraged when my brother brought home the list of camp items he would need: a hatchet, a knife — all ''goyishe'' junk. The instruments of a barbarian. My father threw tantrums, argued into the night. ''You'll be the only Jew there,'' he thundered. But all to no avail.

My mother's strategy was more simple. She simply provided my brother with a salami. That was enough. That ''sufficed'', as they say. That salami was his handicap.

So how can a salami be a handicap? It's easy. Believe me.

The morning my brother left for camp he looked absolutely resplendent in his uniform: a green handkerchief knotted about his neck, a water canteen worn like a bandoleer around his back, and, at his side, the shiny hatchet my father hated. Poor father! He didn't know whether to curse or snicker. On the one hand, there was his oldest son — in a brown shirt, of all things; and on the other hand, there milling about in the railway station, among the hundreds of other uniformed children, were grown men — the counsellors — dressed in short pants.

When the time came for my brother to board the train, my father growled, by way of parting, ''You're leaving a Jew; I expect you to return a Jew.'' My brother Barry looked absolutely demolished. What assurances, after all, could he give? As far as my father was concerned, you must understand, Barry, with his brown shirt, knife, hatchet, canteen, was already something of an apostate.

My mother, her eyes filled with tears of anguish, gave her eldest son a long kiss that evoked cheers of derision the whole length of the train. And then as a final measure she dropped into the hands of my astonished brother — a salami. ''So you won't starve on all that goyishe food,'' she commented by way of explanation.

A less loyal son would have abandoned the salami in the washroom. But Barry — alas! — he was enough his mother's son at least to try heeding her wishes. And that was what destroyed his holiday. He stepped onto the coach a doomed child.

Almost two weeks later, my parents received a letter from the Scout Master asking them to drive out to the camp and retrieve their son. Some comment was made about an awkward and difficult situation having developed.

The day we drove out to the camp, the sun was shining like a golden crown in the heavens. The foliage on the trees was so green it seemed to sparkle like jade. It was Eden that day as we drove out into the country, despite my father continually uttering such remarks as, "I knew it. He was probably the only Jew there. They'd never stand for it. One of us among all of them. But what could one expect? A bunch of civilized people sleeping on the ground in dog tents. Pah!"

"Pup tents," I corrected.

"Now don't get smart with me, Mister," my father immediately responded. "You see with your brother what happens to smart guys who think they know more than their parents."

"Perhaps," sighed my mother, "I should have given him something else beside a salami. One salami for fourteen days. It wasn't enough. Perhaps a jar of chicken soup I should have put into his knapsack. And some pickles."

And I must confess, my brother didn't look too well when I saw him. There, in the campground, one could see tanned shouting boys playing baseball; others running along the sand beach to plunge into the crystal-clear waters; and still others chopping branches for a bonfire that night. And there in the midst of the laughter, the sunshine, the green paradise about us, stood my brother — a one-man ghetto. What I saw in his face were the ravaged remains of a small Eastern European town that's just barely survived a full-scale pogrom.

None of us ever did gain a fully coherent account of what happened during those twelve days my brother had been in camp. My father was content enough with the feeling that my brother had now learned his lesson. During the next few months, however, I was able to gain, from odd bits and pieces of information my brother let escape, the following impressions.

I have an image in my mind of Barry, during that first night in his pup tent, sneaking into the woods and suspending the salami from a high branch with a string. That night, it seems, he was observed by a counsellor, but his mysterious movements were put down to those of a young boy looking for the pit toilets, unable to find them, and then simply going into the bush instead.

But poor Barry had been seen, curiosity had been aroused, and all Barry's further nocturnal activities were ruthlessly scrutinized. Night after night Barry was observed as he made his furtive pilgrimage to the hidden shrine. And much as Barry gorged himself, no matter how much fury he displayed as he devoured the hated gift, the salami remained obstinate, shrinking slowly, taking its own sweet time.

In the meantime, speculation about Barry's comings and goings had become rampant. The rumours covered the whole spectrum of possibilities — and a number of impossibilities for good measure. At one extreme, there was talk of meetings with some Girl Guides from a nearby camp; there were suggestions of masturbation episodes; possible homosexual encounters among the boys; even vague hints of secret Jewish ceremonial rituals.

And while all these rumours swarmed back and forth and continued to grow in both intensity and number, my poor brother discovered that the secret of the hidden salami was not his alone anymore. It had been discovered by about ten million mosquitoes. At that point anyone else would have abandoned the whole project, thrown the salami into a garbage can, anything. But my poor brother was conscientious, you see. And so he wrapped the salami in a paper bag and buried it in the earth.

It was at about this time that he realized his nightly movements were being observed. Also, the salami had begun to acquire an unappetizing flavor and his attempt to devour it speedily had, on that account, met with some delay. Accordingly, several nights were allowed to pass before he could once more bring himself to sneak off into the bush. But when he came to where the salami should have been buried, he could find no trace of it. The mound in the earth was still there, but the salami seemed to have vanished. And while he was probing in the ground with his hunting knife — Oh, what lofty and adventurous images had excited his thoughts when he'd made the purchase! — at that moment, while he was puzzling over the disappearance of the salami, a dozen flashlights were suddenly turned upon him. Then, on all sides, were the counsellors of the camp.

He answered all their questions with a resolute silence. He might even have survived their interrogation, but what finally broke his spirit was the sight of the mound he'd been digging in. It was illuminated fully now by all the flashlights, and what he saw made his stomach leap and stretch and sink — all at the same time.

No wonder he'd been unable to find the salami. During the last few days, buried in the earth and wrapped in a paper bag, the salami had not fared too well. In fact, the salami — if the truth must be known — had, during his absence, been transformed into an anthill.

For the next few days Barry neither ate, slept, nor spoke. Slowly, steadily, he simply turned green. All questions and shows of concern were met with the same look of silent suffering. Finally, in exasperation, the Scout Master had written my parents.

For years Barry made other attempts at escaping. He joined the Y.M.H.A.; he joined the school debating society; he became editor of the school newspaper — all to no avail. Mother out-manoeuvred him on each occasion. Finally, after the Easter exams one year, without a word of warning to family or friends, he quit school and joined the army. It was the spring of 1943, there was a great need for volunteers, and a few months later Barry was safely wading ashore on the beaches of Sicily.

Of course, Mother was desperate. All through those months, she bombarded army training bases with little parcels of chopped liver, boxes of matzohs, jars of gefilte fish. But it was too late; Barry had made good his escape.

Having been forewarned by my brother's difficulties, I made my preparations carefully. When I made my dash for freedom, I didn't want the exit blocked by jars of borscht and loaves of pumpernickel. Accordingly, when summer came and I determined to register for a summer camp, I chose neither the Boy Scouts (''A bunch of goyim,'' I could hear my father thundering), nor an extreme Zionist group like the Mapam (''Revolutionaries,'' he would cry), nor the B'nai B'rith (''Spoiled, wealthy brats!''). No, I cunningly chose a Jewish camp called the Habonim. Its members were poor enough to be mildly socialist, wealthy enough to be anti-communist, and Jewish enough to insist that the boys not carry hunting knives or hatchets strapped to their waists.

So what can go wrong? I asked myself. An embarrassing kiss at the railroad station I dodged by warning my mother about smudging her powder and lipstick. When the food parcels started arriving at the camp, I promptly turned them over to the cook. ''My son,'' read one accompanying note, ''don't scrimp on yourself. If you're hungry, buy if you have to — whatever you need. Try not to feel too sad. We warned you, but now you know why experience is the best teacher. We'll see you Sunday.''

The first week left me feeling limp with joy. Freedom definitely did not taste of chicken soup and gefilte fish. It was swimming in sunlight, drinking sweet well water, breathing in the smell of grass and trees until it seemed that paved streets, houses, cities no longer existed.

And then on Sunday my parents arrived. ''Why aren't you eating?'' my mother immediately demanded. All protests that I had been were ignored in the loud rush of comments that followed: ''We paid them enough, more than enough; so why do they try to save? on food yet; but I — no I'm not surprised. Now you'll appreciate home — for a while anyway. But you'll forget. Still, it's a good experience for you, yes.

Photo 8: Zionist Youth Camp, Grimsby, Ont., 1946.

Now you'll appreciate . . . yes . . . . " And before I could realize what had happened, I was left with a cardboard box of food at my feet, a ten-dollar bill in my hand, and, no doubt, a puzzled look on my face, as my father's car lurched onto the highway and roared off into the distance.

Despite all maternal injunctions "not to be a fool" and share the food with my fellow campers, my first thoughts were of course to turn the whole box over to the cook. But lately the cook had begun to look annoyed as I paid my daily visits to contribute strudels, bagels, chocolate cake, herring. This last offering, I feared, would trigger an explosion. And so, that night, the whole works got dumped into Lake Winnipeg. I suffered terrible pangs of guilt. What if my act of betrayal were ever discovered? What if the next morning at swimming one of the campers said "Say, this water smells like chicken soup"? Yes, that's what I had done, turned all of Lake Winnipeg into a gigantic bowl of my mother's golden soup. What would the original Cree say to this latest cultural take-over? Lake Winnipeg - made Kosher overnight.

For two days I couldn't bring myself to enter the water. It looked too much like the golden broth I'd consumed, week in, week out, all my life.

But what really proved to be a stumbling block was that ten-dollar bill. Now that was a real stroke of genius — like giving my brother that salami.

The camp was vaguely socialist. Everyone knew that. What this meant in practice was that as soon as we had all arrived, everyone put his spending money — two, three, four dollars — into a common fund which was to be spent on marshmallow roasts, magazines, prizes for field day; in fact, anything that we could all agree to. One cabin even tried to get permission to spend its money for a dozen condoms, which were to have been inflated and suspended from the camp flagpole. The overwhelming majority of campers had been in favour of the project — the whole affair had the makings of a legend that would live for years — but at that point the camp briefly lost its socialist basis as the director turned dictator on us and vetoed the scheme.

But what was I to do with that ten-dollar bill? All spending money had been turned in a week before. To try contributing it now would immediately make me an object of suspicion. And it was such a large amount. Besides, I had already put several dollars into the camp fund. Also, people might suspect that I'd had the money all along and been hiding it. Why had I delayed? Hadn't I trusted them before? I would have mailed the money back home except that all our letters were being read by the camp director and his counsellors. There were no bones made about this. They did not want letters reaching our parents about near drownings, cases of poison ivy, bed-wetting and, above all, no letters about condoms being flown from the camp flagpole. All parents were to be left secure in the feeling that their children were enjoying a golden three weeks. Of course, exactly the reverse was true: most parents felt that it would do their spoiled little brats good to be ''out in the cold'' for a while.

In any case, the mails were denied me. So, in desperation, I slipped the ten-dollar bill into an envelope and buried it at the bottom of my suitcase, much as my brother had buried his salami in the woods. And — oh! — now that ten-dollar bill festered there. It poisoned my dreams and soured my days.

But, then, at the end of the week, my aunt and uncle arrived. They were staying at a beach a few miles down the road. They had brought along another cardboard box of food from my mother. Here I absolutely drew the line. That box of food was not — absolutely not — to be taken out of my uncle's car trunk. The ten-dollar bill was enough of a burden. And then I had a brainstorm, a stroke of genius, or so I thought.

I dashed into the cabin, pulled the suitcase from underneath the bunk bed, grabbed the envelope, and raced back outside. Would my aunt do me a favour? I innocently asked. Immediately she was suspicious and stared at the envelope as if it were a viper — which it was.

''So why such a fuss?'' she demanded. ''Why the big secret? Who ever heard of giving back spending money?''

But in the end she agreed, and it was with a joyous heart that I saw the envelope vanish into the depths of her voluminous summer straw purse.

I felt like an Indian snake charmer that's just managed to get a particularly ornery serpent back into its basket.

Of course mother was in a fury when she heard of my little defensive manoeuvre. All that last week I received one raging letter after another: Did I think our family was so wealthy that I could throw ten-dollar bills to the wind? Didn't I realize my aunt would never return that money and either I would have to ask for it myself or make it up out of my own allowance? Besides, why hadn't I hung on to that ten dollars? Our family's money wasn't good enough for me anymore, was that it?

A less hardy soul might have been demolished by the barrage of charges that kept arriving in the mail, but I had my own defence: the image of my brother — silent and broken —when we had come to collect him after his two weeks at Scout Camp. That image served as my shield.

But my greatest test, I knew, would occur that afternoon I got off the train back in Winnipeg. There must be no loss of nerve then, no retreating. I had, however, a secret weapon of my own prepared. Beneath my bunk bed I'd stored a cardboard box whose contents would safely see me through any barrage my parents could bring to bear. Let them bring on their bagels, latkes, pickles, chopped liver, herring — I was ready. If there was to be a confrontation when I stepped off the train, then I must come away from it with a clear victory, a triumph every bit as complete as my brother's escaping with the Canadian Army to the beaches of Sicily.

All that last week, as I went off on hikes, slipped off with others on secret midnight swims, sang folk songs around camp bonfires, I felt as if I'd been allowed to return to myself. The tyranny of my parents, I saw, was the tyranny of fear. They were terrified at what our relatives would say if my three weeks at camp were a complete success. (''Who can blame him? He has so little joy at home.'') My brother had been prevented from taking a paper route for the same reason. (''So now they even have to send an own son out to work. It must be very bad with them.'') These were fears impossible to overcome. My brother and I could never win any family argument of this kind.

So I made my plans accordingly. When I got off that train I wanted no assaults made upon my independence. It would be impossible to argue the question rationally with my parents. What was needed was some act, some gesture, which would place me forever beyond the reach of that tyrannical fear of theirs.

The train to Winnipeg was due to arrive at 3:30 Saturday afternoon. At 3:15 I entered the washroom with the cardboard box I'd kept under my bunk bed at camp. That box was my secret weapon. If it didn't work nothing would. I carefully timed my exit so that I came into the coach again just as the train was pulling into the station. The effect upon my fellow campers was galvanic. They froze into silence and wonder. Before anyone had a chance to recover, the train had jerked to a halt and I was marching smartly down the coach steps.

Further down the platform, I could see my parents and sister glancing anxiously from face to face. About me all sorts of touching scenes were being enacted. ''My son, what have they done to you?'' I heard one mother shriek at a fellow camper of mine whose blanched face, thirty seconds before, had been both tanned and relaxed.

''So now you know, smart aleck,'' I heard a father's voice drawl. ''Now you know what it's like to live out in the world.''

There were no doubt similar statements awaiting my return to the family fold. I could see that tears were waiting to flood from my parents' eyes as soon as they locked into recognition upon me. But when at last they did come to focus upon the figure bearing down upon them, their eyes widened in disbelief.

"Hi, Mom; hi, Dad," I called cheerily. They winced as if struck visible blows. Strangers turned their astonished gaze upon me. And to be quite honest about the matter, I suppose I did look quite a sight, standing there in my brother's old Boy Scout uniform, that absurd hat perched on my head, a hatchet at one side, hunting knife at the other. But the crowning touch, I suppose, was the salami which I twirled absentmindedly in front of me. "Hi," I shouted again.

"Fool!" my father thundered as soon as he was able to recover his voice.

But I wasn't ready to let the battle end so soon. "Hey Mom!" I shouted. "This was a great salami you sent me. Really great. Here, have some. Go ahead; it's just delicious." And without more ado I seized the hatchet from my side and began hacking off pieces of salami.

"Get into the car," my father hissed. "Quick. Before I kill you here and now."

But even for this kind of ultimatum I had made provision. I wasn't going to be taken off guard. By this point, of course, we were the focus of attention for more than just a few parents and their children.

"By the way," I asked innocently, "did Christine Dymkofski phone today? She said in a letter that right after mass tomorrow she'd be really keen on seeing a movie. *The Nun's Story,* I think it's called. Or maybe *I Was a Rabbi for the F.B.I.,* I forget which."

My father's slap across the head blotted out the sunlight, but it didn't matter. There I was with my brother, storming through the water, scrambling up the beaches of Sicily. The Germans would never stop us. I'd made it. At last.

Fredelle Bruser Maynard

"From Yon Far Country"

Excerpt from "**Raisins and Almonds**"

Into my heart an air that kills
From yon far country blows:
What are those blue remembered hills,
What spires, what farms are those?

They are not all happy highways where I went. What, then, drives me down them again, after all these years and another life? The effort, I suppose, to understand. Somewhere, in yon far country, lies the answer to the question that confronts me with increasing urgency. Who am I?

I begin with the simplest things. I was born a woman in a family where women were valued. Years later, encounters with the expectant father of popular mythology — craving a son to complete his manhood — astonished me. So too did the discovery that many girls felt themselves, by reason of sex alone, disappointing to their parents. I never doubted that mine preferred girls. In my mother, partiality was perhaps a reaction to the circumstances of her own childhood. She had grown up in a household where boys were kings and girls scullery maids. How I shuddered, as a child, at the tales of my grandmother, cruel as any legendary stepmother, making strawberry jam for her sons and allowing her daughters only a taste of the floating pink scum from the pot. More dreadful was the story of a crisis that occurred during the family's emigration to Canada. They had left Russia with their gold, literally, in their teeth, sacks of dried cherries for the journey, and five children. In London my grandmother became ill — too ill, she decided, to care for her sickly youngest girl, an infant in arms. "Anyway she will die," this extraordinary woman announced. "So we leave her here, in the railway station. It is easier then for us all." Lucy was not left behind; my mother, nine years old, strapped the baby to her back and carried her throughout the long ocean voyage. My mother never spoke of her own upbringing except with awe, the Jew's *derech-eretz,* and a muted regret for love never received. But the experience marked her, and when she acquired daughters of her own, she redressed the balance with a fierce protective joy. She made us queens— and my father paid homage. In him the feeling for women had always, I think, a strongly sexual element. He would have enthusiastically endorsed Robert Burns' view: "[God's] 'prentice han he tried on man And then he made the lasses, oh!" And indeed, now that I think of it, his delight in femaleness had just Burns' combination of energy and bawdy humor. He really liked girls, and, though a notably faithful husband, he never lost his connoisseur's eye. "She burns under her dress," he would say of a particularly lusty wench. Even when I was little, that remark told me something about my father, too. In a quite innocent and unselfconscious way, he treated us as sexual persons — future mothers, future brides. Being a woman, I knew, was a privilege. Women were *special.*

The fact that I was also a Jew reinforced this sense of uniqueness. Of course there were disadvantages. Many times, during my lonely childhood, I would have sold my birthright for a mess of pottage — but the chance never came. Every Jewish child has heard, in his heart's core, the cry Victor Hugo puts in the mouth of a tormented Moses: "*Laissez-moi m'endormir le sommeil de la terre!*" But when the common sleep of earth is denied, one learns to profit from the mixed blessing of eternal wakefulness. Being different anyway, the Jew must actively embrace and cultivate his difference; this theme ran through all my parents' injunctions. "It is not enough a Jew should be good," my father used to say. "He has to be *best.*" Not in everything, to be sure. Certain areas, like physical prowess, were unJewish; distinction here was meaningless, if not downright reprehensible. (My father told us once how, as a boy, he longed for a ball. He knew better than to ask Grandpa, but every day, when no one was watching, he would creep out to the stable, where the family horse was kept, and run his hand back and forth over the animal's back. In this way he acquired, gradually, a small springy coil of hair. At last — it took almost a year — the ball was the right size. He had given it just one good bounce when my grandfather appeared, outraged and incredulous. "Shame on you!" The old man snatched the ball and flung it into the pigpen. "You have no pride? That my son should make sport — *like a gentile!*")

In character, conduct, and intellectual pursuits, however, the Jew had an obligation to shine. For years I was driven, through school and then university, by a wild competitive urge — to get the highest marks, gather up all the prizes, and lay them at my parents' feet. It was a kind of madness. (Still, in dreams, I see myself called to take examinations for which I am not ready, and I wake sweating.) Blind, selfish, destructive . . . it was all these things. I took mathematics, which I hated, rather than the literature I loved, because math courses offered the best chance of a perfect score. I studied fifteen, eighteen hours a day, much of the time devoted to pure memorization. (One year I committed to memory the whole of *Silas Marner* so that I might embellish my exam paper with appropriate quotations.) At the height of the frenzy, I would not only have botanized on my grandmother's grave, I would have dug it up, if necessary, to ensure a scholastic triumph. And yet — such is the ambiguity of most gifts — the same forces which drove me to run faster plagued me with uneasy questions. *Why* was I running? And where? Bred in a tradition of respect for truth, because I was a Jew, I stopped at last to think.

Jewishness conferred upon me other gifts. Experiencing very young the effects of ignorant prejudice, I was made incapable of inflicting that particular savagery upon others. Aversion to violence, drunkenness, demagoguery — anything against reason — all this I acquired by osmosis. Also, in strange ways, I came to see my life as having significance beyond its obvious narrow limits. I was not just Freidele Bruser, the youngest child of a country merchant, but an actor in the cosmic drama that included Abraham and Isaac, David and Solomon and Daniel and Job. Scientists, scholars, philosophers, makers of music, my people had for centuries brooded on the burthen of the mystery and, sometimes, seen into the life of things. Einstein's conquest of space, Bergson's of time, and Freud's of the dark unconscious — these were my triumphs too.

Woman and Jew, I am also my parents' child. Inescapably. Had I been given a choice, I might have chosen different qualities to inherit.

(How I sighed, growing up, for my father's narrow hips and my mother's face! Later I reflected sadly on other gifts not given — but one must learn, in Maslow's phrase, to love one's fate.) Biologically, my father seems to have transmitted very little to me; it was my sister who inherited his physical grace and, perhaps, a certain incapacity for coping with the real world. I never felt *like* my father. I admired without desire to emulate, and yet his clear nobility provided a standard of value in my life. My mother's influence was overwhelming. I had only to look in the mirror to see that I too was a Slobinsky, the very name suggestive of the build. (It has taken me many years to value the rugged constitution which went along with a thickness of waist and ankle.) By blood or example, I acquired early my mother's need to be busy, to take charge. From her, too, came a need to achieve stability (or its illusion) in a world of change. Wherever we moved, she planted a garden. The most unpromising circumstances overnight became home. This wizardry she acheived, in part, symbolically. A Boston fern in a sunny window; bright embroidered pillows plumped on the sofa; a silver samovar; the lace bedspread laid over pink taffeta . . . . These assurances triumphed over dirt floors and outdoor toilets. Though my mother abandoned the elaborate domestic rituals of Jewish orthodoxy, a certain feeling for ritual remained — not worship the Lord in the beauty of holiness, but worship life in the beauty of order. There were no snacks eaten standing in our house. Even breakfast was a proper meal, with the table set and napkins rolled in silver rings beside glasses of freshly squeezed orange juice. Milk waited in a pitcher, jelly in crystal. While I never shared my sister's bright conviction that our family had secret reserves of wealth, I understood how she got the notion. Without money, we lived rich.

Part Three

Tradition and Faith

Photo 9: Hasidic youth studying Gemara, Montréal, 1960's.

Tradition and Faith

If the Canadian experience changed the ways in which many Jews practised their faith, the support offered by traditional beliefs acted also as a ballast, helping to stabilize the chaos of North American life. J.I. Segal's *Late Autumn in Montreal,* Eli Mandel's *Day of Atonement,* Irving Layton's *The Real Values* superimpose timeless verities on the New World's uncertainties; while, in contrast, other poems of Layton and Weintraub humorously chronicle the accommodations in their Judaism made by assimilating new Canadians. Murray Goldenberg's *Kol Nidrei* juxtaposes Canada's complacency in the Middle East's violence against the story of Isaac read during the High Holiday Services; the same Biblical tale becomes a moving resonance in Leonard Cohen's modern ballad. Such imaginative statements provide testimony to the fact that although challenged and changing, the faith of their fathers continues to be meaningful in the lives of modern Canadian Jews.

J. I. Segal

Late Autumn in Montreal

The worm goes back to the earth
the wind glitters and sharpens his sword;
where did all the colored leaves fly
to, anyway? The branches are all locked
in a vise of sleep; the skies aspire
to climb higher, their clear-blue
washes over the rooftops and stillness
assures us that all is well.
Our churchy city becomes even more pious
on Sundays, the golden crosses shine and gleam
while the big bells ring with loud
hallelujahs and the little bells answer
their low amens; the tidy peaceful streets
lie dreaming in broad daylight murmuring
endearments to me who am such a Yiddish Jew
that even in my footsteps they must hear
how the music of my Yiddish song sounds
through the rhythm of my Hebrew prayer.

Translated and adapted from the Yiddish
by Miriam Waddington

Matt Cohen

The Universal Miracle

***The Universal Miracle*—an Excerpt**
Harvey Zackman's mother died, leaving his father, Stanley, who had never been able to manage the family second-hand furniture store. The grandfather, Louis Zackman, took over. The "universal miracle" was an obsession of Louis Zackman,an invention intended to clean automobile oil so efficiently that it would never need changing.

When Louis Zackman died it was Harvey who had to call the funeral home. He looked it up in the business directory, trying to remember the place where Louis had once dragged him for the final rites of a friend. There was no large advertisement, but in the smallest possible type it was listed at the old address on Spadina Avenue. An old man with the kind of accent Louis only imitated for the purpose of doing business downtown, answered the telephone.

"My grandfather's dead."

"Get a doctor," said the man. "With some people you never know."

"He's dead."

"Get a doctor first. Then we'll come and dress him for you. Don't worry."

At the funeral home they left the coffin open. In it, Louis Zackman was dressed in his best black suit, a yarmulke, and the blue tie he always hated. Harvey bent over the coffin, forcing himself. In the three nights since Louis' death, Harvey had slept only a few hours. He had learned to pace the narrow halls of his town house, carrying the candle he had bought to console himself, a white mourner's wax candle in a glass; and he had begun, in the midst of his sleeplessness, to discover himself kneeling inappropriately on the white shag carpet of his library, trying to pray.

"If there's a God," Louis Zackman used to say, "there's some things he should attend to."

But in these three nights Harvey did not know the feeling of God's eye on his soul. All he felt was one generation closer to the grave. "Soon it will be me," he thought. Again he was aware of his own skin, the imperfections he had at first ignored but now saw as signposts to his own death.

"It's natural to be afraid," Sarah Chernik told him. "To be afraid of your own fear is the worst."

"That sounds familiar."

"You can't afford to be clever now, Harvey."

This spoken in the darkness of Harvey's bedroom, exactly one mile from the Princess Margaret Hospital for Cancer. And when he bent over his grandfather's coffin, looking at the freshly pinked cheeks, Harvey suddenly saw Dorothy on the edge of his vision; she had interrupted her weeping to inspect him curiously, as if his own mixed anger and shame were equally painted on his face.

As the service started, old drunks at the back of the chapel chanted and muttered in company. These derelicts, unknown of course to the family, were a compulsory part of the funeral, and in accordance with the mortician's instructions Harvey had tried to pay for their good graces, handing out a whole pocketful of two-dollar bills.

He was so tired that even the harsh music of the prayers was soothing. He had been forced to study Hebrew, learned to read and write the characters so he could follow in the book, but he didn't actually understand more than a few words. So finally he found it most restful just to close his eyes and listen to the hired cantor, a hoarse-voiced man who poured out his messages to God in a quick river of half-articulated phrases countered by false trills and moans, drawn-out high notes far beyond his reach. With his hands in his pockets, shoulders hunched and bent, tears beginning to collect, Harvey rocked back and forth on his bench, trying to remember his grandfather.

And then the rabbi, sleek with a complacently round face and shiny black suit, began to deliver the penultimate tribute. "We who knew him," he began. But of course he hadn't. Harvey, with his father's help, had needed to supply the rabbi with the details of Louis

Zackman's life so this elegy could be constructed, and as the rabbi spoke, the mutterings of the drunks grew louder and began to escalate into outright laughter. Looking back, Harvey could see them: indeterminately old men in shabby suits with paper-wrapped bottles in their hands, leaning against the back railing and sitting in the last row, gossiping and joking as if even the last Judgment would only be another free movie. And in some strange way Harvey felt comforted by their presence, even while other members of the family were trying to shut them up, because the rented rabbi and cantor could never have known or cared about Louis Zackman, but these old drunks, in palmier days, might actually have shopped at Zackman's store, bought cheap furniture on credit and paid three times its worth in interest, and at least now they were getting something back from Louis Zackman, one last laugh.

The era after Bella died and the store became Zackman's Furniture was when Harvey entered high school. By the time Louis Zackman had returned to the pursuit of The Universal Miracle, Harvey had started to learn about science, which Louis always extolled, the wonderful perfect way in which the whole universe was made up of billiard balls, each set assembled in a tiny replica of the solar system, tricky billiard balls which could themselves break apart into an infinity of fragments and in doing so, according to Albert Einstein and others, possibly blow up the whole world.

During bomb drill, while kneeling under his desk with his hands crossed over the back of his neck to protect his medulla oblongata, Harvey would think about the marvels of science and especially Louis and the crazy filter he had attached to his new automobile.

In the midst of the depression, when he first worked on the project, Zackman had lacked test vehicles. Now, with the riches he had forcibly inherited from Bella's safe, he had purchased a long black Oldsmobile with silver trim.

"He was a wise and moderate man," said the rabbi. "A man who knew where his own universe ended and God's began." Nothing could have been further from the truth about Louis Zackman: his universe never ended, not for other people or for God. After blowing three engines out of the Oldsmobile, he began to connect his filters in series, trying two and three designs at once, so whereas at first it would take him two months to ruin a motor, eventually he could do it in a week.

After school, Harvey would have to clean and dust the furniture, wash windows, procure coffee for Louis Zackman and tea for his father; and there was no place in the store from which he couldn't see out front to where the black Oldsmobile stood. It was in fact, as he pointed out to his friends, nothing less then his mother's hearse, bought with her death money, and every time more cash from the store was poured into it, Harvey was further rankled. Until one day when Louis Zackman poked his long finger into Harvey's chest, Harvey poked back and began to scream.

''Science knows nothing of anger,'' Louis finally said.

''Oh, take your damn —'' And that was all. His throat was raw, he didn't know what to say, he stomped out of the front door and up the side stairs to the apartment above the store; there he went into his own old room and helplessly knelt in the position of atomic attack.

* * *

At the graveyard, everyone waited around in the cold until the coffin finally arrived. With a great clanking of chains, tipping and threatening to spill open, it was lowered into the grave; and as it went down, and after it was resting, the drunken professional mourners rained stones upon it. Which thunked mutedly into the cheap composition board of the coffin, making only the occasionally satisfying clang at the hinges and trim.

Over this absurd and disturbing noise the rabbi began to read the final prayers, but as clods of earth and larger rocks succeeded the pebbles, the words got confused. Without knowing it, Harvey had started crying; he was holding onto Dorothy while her skinny arm dug through his wool coat, holding onto her and crying for the first time since his mother died. Then, cutting across and above his own voice, he heard a high quavering wail: it was his father. Stanley, standing on Dorothy's other side, had thrown his hat into the grave and was rocking back and forth, his high voice keening across the empty cemetery. Soon others joined in; the combined chorus grew so loud that the rabbi was silenced. Harvey looked at him, the treeless grounds, the apartment buildings that stood in the gray sky looking like particularly large monuments, and then he closed his eyes and began to cry again, letting himself be filled and carried by the sound, until finally the city disappeared, his self-consciousness disappeared, and he began to grow in his soul the image of the grandfather he had once known: Louis Zackman — wing-headed, stocky and muscular, The Universal Miracle printed to his genes.

When he opened his eyes, others were opening theirs, too, looking around, embarrassed.

"That was the way it used to be," Dorothy said. "At home; I remember now."

At his own home, Sarah Chernik was waiting for him and the kitchen was filled with the steam of cooking. Wearing a turban around her head, olive skin perspiring in the heat, cheeks flushed as his own had been, she turned to him as he walked in the door.

"What are you doing here?"

"I felt like cooking. How was the funeral?"

"Terrible."

"You look nice."

He was wearing a black striped suit he had bought only a month before, and with it a white silk shirt. But only now, as he poured himself a drink, did he realize that for Louis Zackman's funeral had he dressed himself up in his best clothes, everything from his Spanish patent leather boots to the Cardin tie for which he had paid twenty-five dollars.

"That was the way it used to be," Dorothy had said, and with a weird but contented smile on her face had sat proudly between Stanley and Harvey as they drove back to the suburban split-level house Louis Zackman had bought with the profits of Bella's early demise. The whole family came too; a funeral not followed by drinks and food could not be imagined, and while the distant uncles and cousins drank their straight scotch and brandy and ate stale cookies and buns provided by the funeral home, Harvey sat on the corner sofa with his father.

"With a Zackman, all things end at the stomach," Louis used to say. In fact, even his cancer had ended there, after progressing downward from his chest, the exploded particles and mutant cells following inside him the voyage his planetary crust had taken years before. And as Harvey stood in his kitchen, watching this woman trying to console him with food, he couldn't force out of his mind the image of Stanley, now endowed with a new aggressive confidence, voraciously attacking the food and spreading crumbs about himself like manna.

Stanley, with Louis' death, had prospered. Stanley, who after the sale of the store came back into his parents' house, a room with its own bathroom in the basement, now seemed to have doubled in size. When he stood up to greet newcomers at the door, his back straightened, his voice lowered. After the drive home, he had uncharacteristically leapt out of the car and held the door open for Dorothy. Now it could almost be believed he would move upstairs.

All through Sarah Chernik's dinner, Harvey worked at his scotch. Afterward they danced; her hand pressed warmly into his back, he let himself be led through the house, stumbling, laughing, secretly crying, he moved from room to room with her, trying to feel the warmth coming into his own deadened body, trying to let her exorcise the ghost.

But it was only late that night, with Sarah gone home and the house dark and silent, that Harvey finally began to get drunk. With each sip, he felt new radioactive particles invent themselves and explode beneath his skin. ''Science can do anything,'' his grandfather had said. Smiling beneficently at Harvey, he drove him every day from the downtown store to the bright suburban bungalow, the works of the black Oldsmobile purring with its magical filters. And even on the very last day of his scientific career, when a piston flew up and through the shining black hood, pierced the gleaming clean wraparound windshield, and came sharply to rest in the seat between Louis Zackman and his skeptical wife, Dorothy, even on that day Zackman's grandson was put to bed with a book about the wonderful world of the microscope.

Holding his scotch in one hand and his wax-filled mourner's glass in the other, Harvey stumbled up and down the narrow stairs of his town house, going from one shag-carpeted room to the next, until he finally ended up in the library. There he went down on his knees, but though he tried to remember the words of the funeral prayers they escaped him; all he seemed to know was the blessing for bread. As he repeated that over and over to himself, the sound of the words melted into the earth and rocks homing into the coffin; and the sight of his own praying dissolved into old men's faces, drunk and delighted to be paid in two-dollar bills to stand and kibbitz during a funeral, old men's faces laughing at these crazy Jews so lost from themselves they needed professionals to stone a cheap coffin down to the grave.

Miriam Waddington

Traffic Lights at Passover

HERE, by some sorcery, lies the avenue
With its boulevard and elms,
Its gracious width of street and stone decor;
A gear flick away, a moment ago
We were on Côte des Neiges with Montreal
Engraved in antique colors on a map below.
The cars like pastel lozenges
Spilled between the bus-bright circuses
And aimed to transcend space
With every moment between nine and five.

If only we could transcend as easily
This dryness which no sense can irrigate
Or travel to, and cross our mountainous griefs
To the legendary valley, there to rest
If not in elms, then firm upon the wings
Of the forgotten angel, death.
Oh seldom-thought-of-angel, memory as rare
As Hebrew melodies and rituals once a year
Which speak their melancholy chanting
Through unfamiliar seasonable prayer:

We ate the bitter herbs, but did we pass
Through cleaving oceans? My spirit lay
As dark as Egypt in a solitary kiss,
And the wine held my trembling breath
Upon its surface like a skin;
Grandfather's beaker shone ironically,
And the open door was left
Untranslated for Elijah's coming.

There are no surprises; the light changes,
We shift and fly across the city's desert
To the burgeoning arteries where buildings sway
Above each new oasis; *hayom yom shaini.*
We gulp the gas fumes of the air
And exiled, live another year.
We send our Hebrew God this alien prayer:
Lead us from Egypt and our misplaced faith
To the white paschal lamb and the mayflower
  wreath
And find for us a single leavened hour.

Miriam Waddington

Unquiet World

Prophet dream us a palm of light
and make it bloom in our hands
until Friday's festival
spreads its peace like wings
over the unquiet world.
Fold us smooth as shining hair
of a pious wife in slumbers sweet
then wake us fresh with sabbath bread
From enchanted sleep and look
with us past the templed ruins;
deep as the cratered earth
plumb our purpose and hallowed be
the heady wine of our hope.

Phyllis Gotlieb

Kaddish

The men who say the
prayers for the dead surge
forward, fall back *Yis*
gadal their harsh voices ring
break and replicate *v'yiskadash*
pure throbbing against
stone under the stamping
feet, vibration
bursts into the boundless
arena of a Lord

sanctified and magnified

Eli Mandel

Day of Atonement: Standing

My Lord, how stands it with me now
Who, standing here before you
(who, fierce as you are, are also just),
Cannot bow down. You order this.
Why, therefore, I must break
If bend I will not, yet bend I must.

But I address myself to you thus,
Covered and alert, and will not bare
My self. Then I must bear you,
Heavy as you are.
                                        This is the time
The bare tree bends in the fierce wind
And stripped, my God, springs to the sky.

A. M. Klein

And in That Drowning Instant

And in that drowning instant as
the water heightened over me
it suddenly did come to pass
my preterite eternity
the image of myself intent
on several freedoms

                                        fading to
myself in yellowed basel-print
vanishing

                        into ghetto Jew
a face among the faces of
the rapt disciples hearkening
the raptures of the Baalshem Tov
explaining Torah

                                    vanishing
amidst the water's flickering green
to show me in old Amsterdam
which topples

                                into a new scene
Cordova where an Abraham
faces inquisitors

the face
is suddenly beneath the arch
whose Latin script the waves erase
and flashes now the backward march
of many

I among them

to
Jerusalem-gate and Temple-door!

For the third time my body rises
and finds the good, the lasting shore!

A. M. Klein

Portraits of a Minyan (Excerpts)

LANDLORD

He is a learned man, adept
 At softening the rigid.
Purblind, he scans the *rashi* script,
 His very nose is digit.

He justifies his point of view
 With verses pedagogic;
His thumb is double-jointed through
 Stressing a doubtful logic.

He quotes the Commentaries, yea,
 To *Tau* from *Aleph*, —
But none the less, his tenants pay,
 Or meet the bailiff.

PINTELE YID

Agnostic, he would never tire
 To cauterize the orthodox;
But he is here, by paradox,
 To say the *Kaddish* for his sire.

REB ABRAHAM

Reb Abraham, the jolly,
Avowed the gloomy face
Unpardonable folly,
Unworthy of his race.
When God is served in revel
By all his joyous Jews,
(He says) the surly devil
Stands gloomy at the news.

Reb Abraham loved Torah,
If followed by a feast:
A *milah*-banquet, or a
Schnapps to drink, at least.

On Sabbath-nights, declaring
God's praises, who did cram
The onion and the herring?
Fat-cheeked Reb Abraham.

On Ninth of *Ab*, who aided
The youngsters in their game
Of throwing burrs, as they did,
In wailing beards? The same.

For in a single breath to hiss
The ten outrageous names of those
Who on the Persian gallows rose —
Oh, this was pleasure, joyance this!

SWEET SINGER

O what would David say,
Young David in the fields,
Singing in Bethlehem,
Were he to hear this day
Old Mendel slowly hum
His sweetest songs,
Old Mendel, who being poor,
Cannot through charity
Atone his wrongs,
And being ignorant,
Cannot in learned wise
win Paradise,
Old Mendel who begs Heaven as his alms
By iterating and re-iterating psalms?

JUNK-DEALER

All week his figure mottles
  The city lanes,
Hawking his rags and bottles
  In quaint refrains.

But on the High, the Holy
  Days, he is lord;
And being lord, earth wholly,
  Gladly is abhorred.

While litanies are clamoured,
  His loud voice brags
A Hebrew most ungrammared.
  He sells God rags.

HIS WAS AN OPEN HEART

His was an open heart, a lavish hand,
His table ever set for any guest:
A rabbi passing from a foreign land,
A holy man, a beggar, all found rest
Beneath his roof; even a Gentile saw
A welcome at the door, a face that smiled.
The chillest heart beneath his warmth would thaw.
And for these deeds, God blessed him that he saw
The cradle never emptied of its child.

AND THE MAN MOSES WAS MEEK

This little Jew
Homunculus
Found four ells too
Capacious.

He never spoke,
Save in his prayer;
He bore his yoke
As it were air.

He knew not sin.
He even blessed
The spider in
His corner-nest.

The meek may trust
That in his tomb
He will turn dust
To save some room.

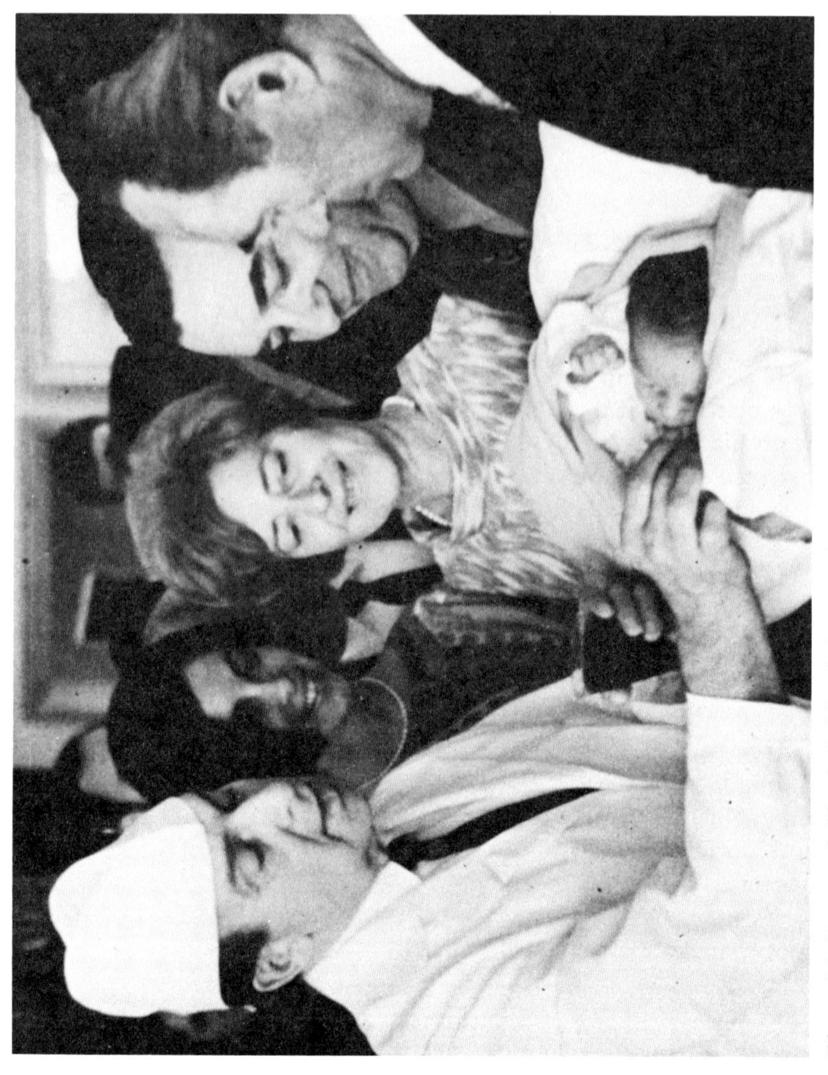

Photo 10: Reverend Charloff ("Mohel"), performing circumcision ceremony, 1972.

Phyllis Gotlieb

A Ceremonial

With bloodwine left from the Passover
the morning's quorum waits for the
ritual doctor. Imagine a train of bearded
patriarchs, dirty and holy
transparent in his shadow? he only
lays out a clean cloth and boils a knife,
serious and intent for the fivethousandth time.

Last Friday old men in beards and skullcaps drank
beer and ate peppered chickpeas here, singing:
Hi, di, diddle diddle di,
hi diddle, di diddle,
di, di, di!

Today's song is the
whimper of the weekold boy in the
arms of his godfather leaving
his mother empty and conceived at last,
still weak and ill on the bed, two grandmothers
beside her locking glares in the blinddrawn room.

The knife rises, the men
bite their lips and know the sensitive
and the outraged howl
rings down all the halls of Solomon and his temples.

The doctor dips his finger in the wine
and rubs the lips of the little Jew and he sleeps
— then (a father of five daughters) raises his
hat, and leaves them to
murmurs and silences, except one
grandmother, who sniffs: heh, all
the little pieces, he couldn't get a boy!

J. I. Segal

A Song about My Son

I have shelves of old books
where I dig for gold,
the tales I tell my son.

When I have no time —
the weekdays take away my time
and turn it to dust and sand
and need —

My beautiful son holds off.
He lets me be.
All he asks of me is a book from the shelves.

I grant him that. He stands on a stool,
turning pages
and searching,
very thoughtful, very deep.

He lights on something,
something moving,
but a look at me and he catches himself
and the word he was about to say.

He returns to turning pages,
and buries his head in one book after another.
My wonderful, zealous,
understanding seven-year old.

I get up out of my corner. I go to him
and look straight into his eyes.
Where are you now, Reb Nachum?
Wandering in world after world?

And I start to chant the tale
of the temple. How it was built,
The copper lions, the deer,
the sacred bread

and the seven-branched Menorah.
The white wicks burn bright
and the high priest stands at the threshold
in deep blue and purple robes.

And the chant lifts as if of itself
like a golden crown.
Then open wide ye gates
God in his glory has come.

I lift up my head to walls and corners
in the quiet after sunset.
I see a golden snake coiled
on the pillars of the temple.

Translated from the Yiddish
by Seymour Levitan

William Weintraub

Sport in the Old Testament

This selection was Chapter 18 of **Why Rock the Boat?,** William Weintraub's humorous novel of modern Jewish life.

They arrived at the synagogue just as Rabbi Sheldon Cohen finished shining his riding boots. The handsome, beardless cleric had been a three- letter man at Rabbinical College and his zeal for sport had never died. He was getting a bit old now for water polo and jiujitsu, but he still played his daily eighteen at the golf club and wielded an eager broom at the curling club. And he had just been elected Master of Fox Hounds of the Disraeli Hunt, Montreal's first Jewish pack. It was currently being organized and would be restricted to those of good character and extreme wealth.

Still wearing his new scarlet hunting coat, the Rabbi crossed the broadloomed floor of his study to greet his two visitors.

"Shalom, shalom, peace be with you," he said. "Please sit down. What can I do for you?"

"Well, Reverend," said Erskine, "it's about the speech you'll be giving tomorrow." He took his copy of the text from his briefcase.

"Oh?" said the Rabbi. He had been worrying about this.

Harry watched carefully, aware that he was about to see public relations in action.

"I'm just wondering, Reverend," said Erskine, "whether you've picked the right topic."

"Well," said the Rabbi, "I chose a Talmudic subject because of the conference's intellectual nature. Let me have a look at it again, will you?" He took some typewritten pages from his desk and leafed through them. Damn it, he shouldn't have bought this thing from Rabbi Epstein without reading it all the way through. But then again, the old man had assured him that it was extremely intellectual.

"To be quite frank, Reverend," said Erskine, "I wonder whether the reporters covering this speech will be able to understand it. And what's the point of a speech if it doesn't hit the papers?"

"Hmmm . . . . the Talmud is very complicated, Mr. Erskine."

"For instance," said Erskine, "this section where you tell about a theological argument those two old men had in Lithuania in 1654. That runs to about ten pages, doesn't it?"

"Yes . . . hmmmm . . . " The Rabbi sat down at his desk and looked distastefully at the script, badly typed and phrased in Epstein's sketchy English. To think he had paid the old chiseler ten dollars for this wretched thing.

"Have you ever heard of Rabbi Epstein, Mr. Erskine?" he said. "The great Talmudic scholar."

"Can't say that I have."

"A fascinating man. He has a very colorful little congregation over in the Jewish part of town. I've incorporated a few of his ideas." With disgust, the Rabbi looked down at the old man's cabalistic fulminations; Erskine was right, this thing was totally incomprehensible. He must have been out of his mind even to buy it, let alone deliver it to a big convention. What could he have been thinking of? This fox hunt was taking up too much time.

"Actually," said Erskine, "I was rather hoping you'd give us your 'Sport in the Old Testament'. I've heard it several times, Reverend, and personally I never tire of it."

The Rabbi got to his feet and thoughtfully examined the riding breeches that lay folded on a chair.

"Upon reflection, Mr. Erskine," he said, "I shall be pleased to address the BUMTA convention on 'Sport in the Old Testament'. In our troubled times, I feel — excuse me —" His telephone was ringing and he picked it up and engaged in a long argument with someone at the other end regarding how often foxhounds should be fed.

"So many details," the Rabbi sighed, hanging up the phone. "Today's clergyman is so beset by detail that he has no time left for policy matters. I sometimes envy the medieval rabbinate, in their quaint black caftans and their funny old hats. No telephones, no broadcasting, no committees. Yes, in the ghetto a man could sit down and concentrate on the big picture."

"Well, then, Reverend," said Erskine, "I wonder if you could let us have a text of your speech."

"But I don't use a text. I know that speech fairly well, you know."

"In that case," said Erskine, "I wonder if you could deliver it now."

"Now?"

"Yes, right here. Young Barnes will take notes and write some releases. We'll hand them out to the press in the morning."

"I suppose I could do that," said the Rabbi.

"Fine," said Erskine. He rose to go. "Here's two dollars, Barnes," he said. "When you're finished, grab a cab down to the hotel."

Erskine left and Harry took out his notebook. "Whenever you're ready, Your Reverence," he said.

The Rabbi paced up and down, flirting his riding crop self-consciously. "It's strange," he said, "giving a speech to only one person."

"Just pretend I'm a large crowd, Your Reverence."

"Very well then." The Rabbi took up his stance behind his desk and cleared his throat. "Mr. Chairman," he said, "Ladies and Gentlemen, Friends. As we forgather here today in the spirit of interfaith, I am reminded of — excuse me —" The telephone was ringing again and Harry waited, pencil poised.

"Don't argue with me, Solly," the Rabbi was saying into the phone. "There's a wholesale and a retail price for everything and horses are no exception. We are definitely not buying our horses on the retail level. Now you just go back to the dealer and make that quite clear to him."

The Rabbi hung up and continued his speech. As his pencil flew over the paper, Harry realized what a fine professional Larry Erskine must be in the field of public relations. In just a few minutes he had completely changed the course of events, and for the better. The Rabbi was happier with his new speech, the conference would probably also be happier, and the public would most certainly be happier.

"And so, friends," the Rabbi was saying, "we must face up to the very sad possibility that our beloved Montreal Canadiens may fail this

Photo 11: Ryerson School Basketball Team, Toronto, 1915.

year to win the Stanley Cup, emblematic of hockey supremacy in this broad land of ours. And in the heaviness of our hearts we will wonder if it is righteous to place the blame squarely on a coach who has very seldom shown even the slightest familiarity with his business. If we turn to the curious old pages of the Book of Deuteronomy . . . .''

No wonder this speech was popular, Harry thought. The Rabbi was being highly partisan about the biggest of all sports controversies. Spoken in a tavern, these words would cause fisticuffs.

''And in conclusion, dear friends, let us remember those old prophets who many many years ago walked the sun-baked hills of Judea, let us remember that those prophets were pondering the very problems we ponder today, at this important BUMTA conference: how to build a healthier, happier community; how to achieve peace of mind and sound mental health; how to formulate a meaningful program for teen-agers; how to choose between the many worthy causes that make such demands on our time; how to keep the Arabs out of Israel.

''And as they pondered these problems, those colorful men of yore, they realized one thing: that man does not live by bread alone. No, our daily toil must be complemented by meaningful use of leisure. And what builds better bodies, for a better future in this broad land of ours, than sports?

''And so it was that those bearded old prophets questioned themselves, in their heart of hearts. 'Why do we play?' they asked. 'Do we play to win? For the glory? For the spoils? . . . . No,' they said. 'No, we play for the sake of the game. Play up, play up, and play the game!' And they wrote it on their parchments, in their squiggly old Hebrew letters.

''So today, as then, let us be good sports, ladies and gentlemen. For remember — a good sport is a good Canadian. Thank you. Shalom. Peace be with you.''

''If I may say so, Your Reverence,'' said Harry, ''that was very good.''

''Thank you, thank you. By the way, do you think this fits me?'' The Rabbi took off his skullcap and tried on a hunting cap with an extravagantly long peak.

''A perfect fit, sir.''

Leonard Cohen

Out of the Land of Heaven

for Marc Chagall

Out of the land of heaven
Down comes the warm Sabbath sun
Into the spice-box of earth.
The Queen will make every Jew her lover.
      In a white silk coat
Our rabbi dances up the street,
Wearing our lawns like a green prayer-shawl,
Brandishing houses like silver flags.
      Behind him dance his pupils,
Dancing not so high
And chanting the rabbi's prayer,
But not so sweet.
      And who waits for him
On a throne at the end of the street
But the Sabbath Queen.
      Down go his hands
Into the spice-box of earth,
And there he finds the fragrant sun
For a wedding ring,
And draws her wedding finger through.
      Now back down the street they go,
Dancing higher than the silver flags.
His pupils somewhere have found wives too,
And all are chanting the rabbi's song
And leaping high in the perfumed air.
      Who calls him Rabbi?
Cart-horse and dogs call him Rabbi,
And he tells them:
The Queen makes every Jew her lover.

And gathering on their green lawns
The people call him Rabbi,
And fill their mouths with good bread
and his happy song.

Eli Mandel

Psalm 24

What did you expect?
You, who drove me to mad alphabets
and taught me all the wrong words.

Isn't it enough that I've failed?

It's your scripture. You read it.

Irving Layton

Synagogue in West Palm Beach

Too elegant, too white, too spacious.

I halt, embarrassed, on the wide boulevard
down which Caesar's legions might march
or a duke's retinue with swords and halberds.
It should be dark and smoky
like God's word,
foreboding and rueful as the eyes of my father,
twisted like crushed limbs.
What, will the Almighty
descend these broad steps in sneakers,
wearing a Panama hat?
Will his voice be a soft breeze
stirring the palmleaves above his house?
Will a limousine stop for him
while his man runs to take the tablets
from his hands?
Will he smile to me in greeting,
displaying perfect manners and teeth?

I miss the smell of onions and piety
and of ancient gaberdines
that shone like boyhood rinks at twilight.
The black-bearded fanatics
whose long bony fingers
hobbled after me like arthritic Hebrew letters
to nightmare my sleep.
The ecstatic cries only torment could reproduce.
Where are the prayers that resounded like curses?
The yellow-black stumps in the beseeching mouths?

Who are those sleek impostors with coiffured heads
and upright backs?

Irving Layton

The Real Values

Rabbi, why do you move heaven and earth
to blow breath
into this lifeless body,
drowned under the surfeit
of Chinese food and pizzapie?

The good life destroyed him:
distilleries, supermarkets.
Long ago he packed away his soul
in the clothing industry.

Examine the hideous, putrefying face,
the fishy eyes
and gross mouth, open
as though to swallow
another cooked lentil.

Isaiah, hop to it, Moses —
bring on the condiments, the plum sauce —

Your noble gas
about Torah, Halachah
affords a passing tingle
to worshippers breathless with emulation,
especially to wives and daughters
musing on fabled hairdos.

Save your breath, rabbi.
No, save your money.

And learn from your bloated flock
bored by whisky and wifeswapping,
the burnt offerings on Sunday,
how to invest sensibly
in real estate values.

So that you can speak the truth
as I do.

Leonard Cohen

Story of Isaac

The door it opened slowly
    My father he came in
    I was nine years old
And he stood so tall above me
    blue eyes they were shining
    and his voice was very cold.
Said, "I've had a vision
    And you know I'm strong and holy
    I must do what I've been told."
So he started up the mountain
    I was running he was walking
    And his ax was made of gold.

The trees they got much smaller
    The lake a lady's mirror
    We stopped to drink some wine
Then he threw the bottle over
    Broke a minute later
    And he put his hand on mine.
Thought I saw an eagle
    But it might have been a vulture,
    I never could decide.
Then my father built an altar
    He looked once behind his shoulder
    He knew I would not hide.

You who build the altars now
    To sacrifice these children
    You must not do it any more.
A scheme is not a vision
    And you never have been tempted
    By a demon or a god.
You who stand above them now
    Your hatchets blunt and bloody,
    You were not there before.
When I lay upon a mountain
    And my father's hand was trembling
    With the beauty of the word.

And if you call me brother now
    Forgive me if I inquire
    Just according to whose plan?
When it all comes down to dust
    I will kill you if I must
    I will help you if I can
When it all comes down to dust
    I will help you if I must
    I will kill you if I can.
And mercy on our uniform
Man of peace or man of war
    The peacock spreads his fan.

Photo 12: Blowing of the Shofar for High Holiday Services.

Photo 13: Reading from the Torah at Beth Jacob Synagogue, Winnipeg, 1930's.

Murray Goldenberg

Kol Nidrei

So I find myself once more
Standing in the synagogue
Beside an aging father (is he really sixty?)
Surrounded by men who pray and
Gossip and speculate on the next football
game and the cantor's wages

The building is familiar as an old sneaker
Here I spent seven noisy years
Snugly growing up to be a Jewish mensch
Learning about Hebrew and Algebra and boredom
And all the contradictions

Yesterday half a world away
A sunbaked square in Tel Aviv
Trembled to the chants of
Four hundred thousand
''Am k'shai oref'' — a stiffnecked bunch
Who roared ''Enough . . . Dayenu!''

No placards wave here on the quiet prairie
The Arab bombs the guns of the Falange
Do not intrude
Winnipeg is too distant for the
Desperate young men of Paris and Beirut
The only fireworks come from the Rabbi
Eloquently judging those who
Criticise in public

The long day's prayers continue
Children run and chatter in the outer hall
Old men ascend before the scrolls
To sing the ancient praise
I fumble in the prayerbook
Lost and bored as always
My sister says I have no principles
Perhaps there's truth in that
I tell my friends it's just an easy way
To please the folks

And yet the cry of "all our vows"
Strikes with surprising force
And in the shofar's blast
I hear the hard and high command
To stay the slaughterer's knife
And when I join the rising, gyring chant
Something in me finds

its home

Part Four

Holocaust and Israel

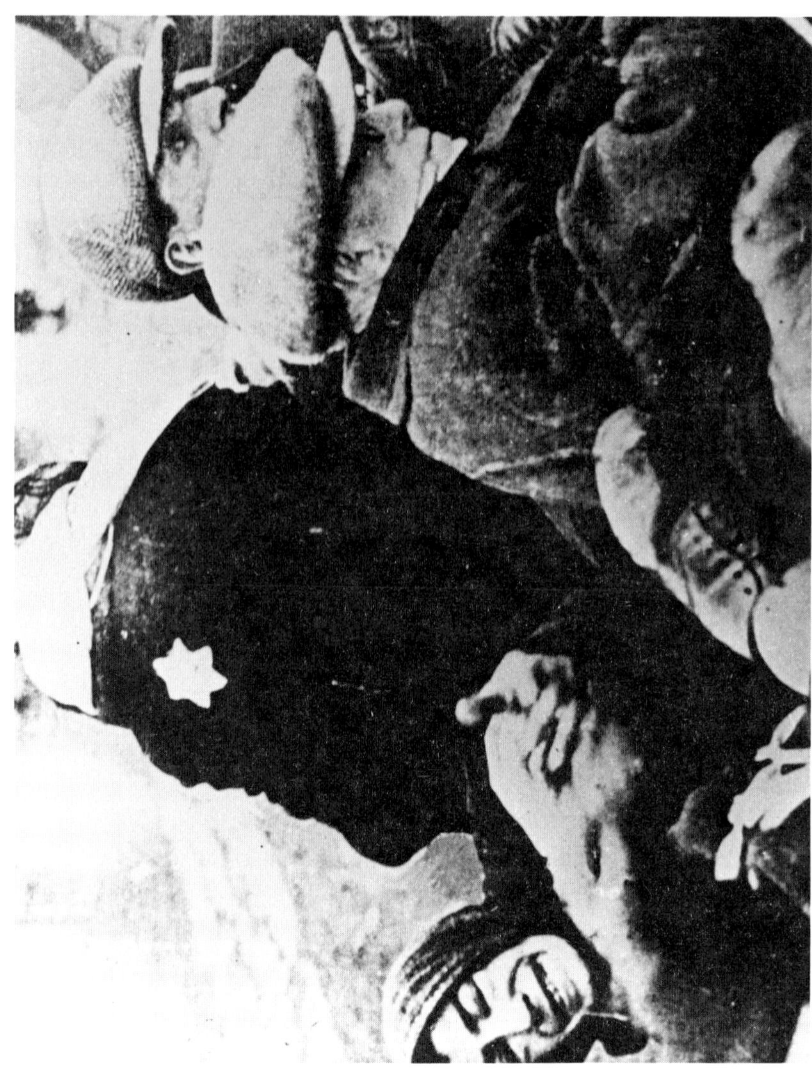

Photo 14: Jewish Holocaust victims during evacuation of a ghetto, c. 1943.

Holocaust and Israel

Central to the literature of *all* contemporary Jewish artists are images of two significant realities of twentieth century Jewish experience: the unspeakable horror of the European holocaust and the triumph of the emergence and continued vitality of the State of Israel. Included in this section are works by Layton, Klein, Segal and Cohen which attempt, despite the inadequacy of any language in the face of such atrocity, to convey the brutality, inhumanity and tragedy of history's blackest time. The need to confront this overwhelming evil and deal with it creatively is at once an act of memorial, of catharsis and of transcendence.

The State of Israel, rising from the ashes of the Holocaust, is imaginatively linked to the psychology and fate of all Jews by several of the authors represented here. Heralding the metamorphosis of a 'new Jew', Layton advises his sons symbolically to be 'gunners in the Israeli Air Force', while Cooperman vows: ''If we die it will be as the lion dies . . .'' The pride, the concern, and the natural duality experienced by the Canadian Jew in relation to the new state is effectively captured in Richler's satiric tale *This Year at the Arabian Nights Hotel.*

Rachel Korn

My Mother Often Wept

A birch tree may be growing on the mound
heaped by a murderer's hands
in thick woods near the town of Greyding,
and only a bird goes there to honour the dead

where my mother lies in an unknown grave,
a German bullet in her heart.
And I go, go, go there only in dreams,
my eyes shut, my mouth dumb.

I remember that my mother often wept,
and I, I imagined
Abraham's son, bound for the sacrifice, looking to her
from the yellow pages of her prayerbook
while she lived Sarah's fate

and we tumbled, laughed, and played,
despite our father's early death —
Had he lived, our good father,
he would never, never
have taken us to Mount Moriah to be sacrificed.

And yet my mother wept so often —
Did she know
that heaven had prepared
to open wide its gates
and take her sons
in billowing clouds of smoke?

And I was left behind, her only daughter,
like a thorn in dry ground,
and I am the voice of my mother's tears,
I am the sound
of her weeping.

Translated from the Yiddish
by Seymour Levitan

J. I. Segal

Aunt Dvorah

Our only aunt called Dvorah
Has gone and left us too,
And on her grave is carved a small Menorah
And on each side a slender stalk of wheat.

That is how the stonecutter Reb Nachem
Worked it out, and in between, her name;
We stand and gaze into religious silence
As from our lips there falls a last amen.

No member of her family survived her,
Her comely daughters, Esther and Hadassah,
Were lost in the great burning
Beyond the ghetto walls, in some side street.

And when they brought them home to her,
Their bodies raped and spoiled, well do I recall
How Dvorah clamped her mouth in iron silence
And sat, held in its bitter vise for days.

Widening her sorrow by their narrow graves
Our auntie used to sit, and in the evenings take
Her children's clothes and thoughtfully caress
Their measure; then shivering and bleak

She'd close the trunk and draw over her face
A darkness deeper than cavernous wastes
Of empty cupboards and more desolate
Than all those hangers peeled and bare.

Translated and adapted from the Yiddish
by Miriam Waddington

Seymour Mayne

Zalman

The name was curiously given
Both families agreed the firstborn's
would be chosen from the mother's side.
Her father's name? No, he may still be alive —
May '44 — if the Nazis hadn't killed him yet.
Who knew of his end then?
                                        But the mother's mother,
Zlateh — she who had married twice
and amassed money and means —
a boy named after a woman? Was it a forbidden thing?
And the name rooted from the Marranos
and hidden observance: Zalman;
Suleiman — did they know of the Turkish origins?
Not drawn from the Pentateuch,
no, a name of the orient, the eastern Diaspora
and linked in the beginning, the first consonant,
with a grandmother whose only lasting image:
the block of stone carved with Hebrew
in Bialystok's cemetery and her youngest son,
the uncle, standing there in the photo
just weeks before Poland fell —
the rest of her brood caught in a burning synagogue
before they could buy passage to New Jersey or Montreal.
She was dead then, her ears stopped
with that terrible silence marking its way
from the din of outrage — the flames licked the night
and the polish and german murderers
prepared for a Saturday night off, the air incensed
with smoke of scrolls and flesh.
Enough, we begin again, the father said, name him.
She will live.
                          — On their lips and in my face.

J. I. Segal

Scenario

The enemy returns
home to his German village,
and the white blossom on the tree
waves to him, bends to him,
smiles to him, ''Welcome!''

His dog jumps up to meet him
and trembles with recognition,
and all around him lie his fields
as fresh and frank as summer.

In the doorway of his house
waits the housewife, pale and dear.
Lost in the joyous pulse of dream
she stands rooted and still as a bird.

He runs toward her
and she falls into his arms;
all is husband and wife between them.
together they enter their warm house.

But I, whom the German enemy destroyed
in seed and root, in branch and bud,
whose last living child he has killed,
and whose native city he has bent
from its ancient Polish pride —
I am the one who in my rags,
my ribbons, and my pure bright hate,
remain outside, and like a beaten cur
I must watch and see
How these German trees still celebrate
the summer's whiteness, and German fields
submit their earth to the sharpened plow,
while in the barn German horses

Bear German colts, silky and fair,
which German lads will mount and ride
possessing July and the burning sun
between fertile forests of wheat and rye.

And Jewish children? Sealed within winds
and their quenched ashes and desolate crumbs;
and only the emptiness of street
will remember and miss them, and only
the echoing cobblestones will weep.

I know they will not ever be transformed
to innocence, they will never be
angels astride on palominos
in a blossoming heaven; they will never be such
as tumble through fields and gamboling, shout,
''Welcome!'' around the feet of God.

Translated and adapted from the Yiddish
by Miriam Waddington

A. M. Klein

The Second Scroll

"The Second Scroll"—an Excerpt
The novel excerpted here covers the times between the Russian pogroms of 1917 and the year after the founding of the Jewish State in 1948. It is the history of Jewish suffering in European exile, in exodus and in settling the Promised Land. Melech Davidson is the wandering uncle of the narrator. A religious scholar, Melech abandons his faith after the Russian persecutions, blaming God for permitting them. He joins the Communist Party but renounces it when the Soviets deliver eastern European Jewry to the Nazis. At this point he has survived the massacre of Kamenets and writes to his sister's family in Montreal.

"I pray your forgiveness for not having written to you all these years; nor will I enter now into explanations for my silence. It is too late for explanations." (Did Uncle Melech know?) "It is surely not because I haven't thought of you, it is because — let us say that it is because, having taken upon myself the yoke of exile, I deemed it also my duty that I should sunder myself from kith and kin. As if that were ever possible . . . . In the light of all that has happened, I know now that I was in error, in grievous error. Forgive.

"Today I write as one who having fled from out a burning building runs up and down the street to seek, to find, to embrace the kinsmen who were with him in that conflagration and were saved. And we were all in that burning world, even you who were separated from it by tbe Atlantic — that futile bucket.

"I bless the Heavenly One for my rescue. It is wonderful to be alive again; to know that the trouble, the astonishment, the hissing is over; to eat, not husks or calories, but food; to have a name; and be of this world. Even now I do not know how it happened or by what merit it was I who was chosen, out of the thousands who perished, to escape all of the strange deaths that swallowed up a generation. At times I feel — so bewildered and burdened is my gratitude — that the numbered dead run through my veins their plasma, that I must live their unexpired six million circuits, and that my body must be the bed of each of their nightmares. Then, sensing their death wish bubbling the channels of my blood, then do I grow bitter at my false felicity — the spared one! — and would almost add to theirs my own wish for the centigrade furnace and the cyanide flood. Those, too, are the occasions when I believe myself a man suspect, when I quail before the eyes of my rescuers wondering *Why? Why did this one escape? What treaty did he strike with the murderers? Whose was the blood that was his ransom?* I try to answer these questions, but my very innocence stutters, and I end up exculpating myself into a kind of guilt.

"I try — I look about me at the Jews of this camp, the net of our accounting, and try to compose backwards from these human indices the book of our chronicles. I hear from the neighboring tent the voices of the castrati and evoke the images of the white-robed monsters who deprived them of race. I scan the tattooed arms — the man before me bears the number 12165 —and wonder whether it is in gematria that there lies the secret of their engravure. I see them all about me, the men who cheated the chimney, those who by some divine antitoxin were preserved from the thirty-two fictitious diseases. Through the kindergartens of the orphans I proceed, and talk to children, and observe. I observe how it is that so many of them wear little lockets that break open, like cloven hearts, to reveal the picture of father or mother or brother lost, old-fashioned, poorly taken snapshots of the formal stance or the gay moment — they are everywhere — and I conceive the multitudinous portrait-gallery of our people: it hangs pendent from the throats of little children. Our small cenotaphs. And here in the secretariat of the camp I keep counting over and over again the puny alphabetical files to which we have been reduced. Yet from all of these studies and encounters I am not able to make me a chart of what actually happened; it is impossible. When the Lord turned against the captivity, I was like one that dreamed.

"All I can follow in clear sequence — and even here at the critical connectives it is only the hand of God that can explain — is what happened to me. It was late '39, and when the enemy swarmed over Poland, I found myself in Kamenets, still abashed by the treachery of the pact that the Soviets had made with the sons of Belial. In the midst of our anguish we were regaled with a dialectic which proved that fascism was but a matter of taste. The taste was bitter unto death. Almost I made my own the counsel of Rabbi Simon ben Yochai concerning those best of serpents who, too, ought to have their smooth skulls crushed. With a stroke of the pen, a dart of the tongue, they had handed over to perdition, those two-faced masters of thesis and antithesis, three and a half million souls. My ideology had been a saying of grace before poison.

"How it came to pass that during the more than four years that I had to remain in Kamenets I was not denounced as the Communist I no longer was — it would have been an ironical but just visitation — I shall not ever know. Perhaps it was because everybody was busy devising means for himself to remain obscure, unnoticed by the death's-heads who terrorized our streets, that no one thought of me; perhaps it was the loyalty of the valley of the shadow. There had been, indeed, occasions when the men with the eyes of ice had gone searching for their various categories of *Zigeuner* and *Bibelforscher* — I, in fact, could fall under both classifications — but the fact that I was now caftaned, bearded, and befringed apparently rendered me harmless. Is it not written that in the place where the repentant one stands, not even the complete saint may stand?

"These were years obsessed by a premonition of doom continually postponed. We were ghetto-ized, with none coming or going without special permission. We were catalogued: blue cards, yellow cards, red cards — our oppressors changed them at their whim so that even starvation in its various penultimate hues was uncertain. With the six-pointed Star of David we were inoculated against the world. We lived from prayer to prayer.

"Then one day — I remember it well, it was the Sabbath of the Bar Mitzvah of Rabbi Zelig's youngest son and came at the end of a long, shuddering week — the town was suddenly surrounded at all its exits. The commanding officer of Kamenets had been missing for over a fortnight, our oppressors had accused the Jews of having kidnapped or murdered him, and the ultimatum issued to the Town Council to produce him, if alive, within the week, had expired. In the public square the placards offering a reward for the discovering of the Commandant's body still glowered their gothic menace. In the meantime searches, which were but an excuse for brutality and pillage, were carried on in all houses.

"The Commandant was not found.

"It began in Rabbi Zelig's home, where a number of his relatives and some worthies of the community had gathered to congratulate the young boy who this day was being confirmed into the congregation of Israel. The boy, standing in front of Rabbi Zelig's Ark of the Covenant — public worship had been forbidden — was making his speech of self-dedication when there burst into the house a turmoil of heavy-booted soldiers. They were under the command of a young lieutenant who, it soon appeared, prided himself on being a specialist in Semitic affairs . . . . How shall I tell you, how shall I bring myself to write down, the abominations which took place that day! The Scroll of the Law was polluted: between its rods upon the parchment an infant was set and then tossed in the air — the specialist shouted: *'Hagba'* — was allowed to fall to the ground, its skull cracked crying: 'Father!' Our women were made to strip and circle the room — *hakofos,* explained the specialist — while the soldiery indulged in their obscene jests; and our men were each in turn called up to the improvised pulpit — *aliyoth,* said the authority — to receive their beard-pluckings and blows. Some — I among them — were allowed to go unscathed. It was these arbitrary exemptions, together with the guns which threatened immediate death, that induced and compelled the performance of the unspeakable ritual.

"The sport over, we were ordered out of the house, and outside observed that similar rituals were taking place in the other habitations of our ghetto. In the street there stood a truck with spades and mattocks; these were distributed to all the men. The specialist then addressed us. Information had come to the authorities, he said, that the body of the Commandant had been buried outside the town, near the abandoned mill. We were to dig that ground until we came upon it.

"Oh, that we had used our spades in a last battle for an honorable death!

"We dug that whole Sabbath afternoon. The suspected place, a considerable area, had been marked out, and after about three hours of digging — every stone we struck sent terror through our hearts — we stood in the midst of a great pit, deep and wide.

"The Commandant's body had not been found.

"It was as, at the order of the specialist, we climbed out of the pit that we realized that the revenge of our tormentors had not been staved off; for the whole horizon before us was dark with smoke, streamered here and there with tongues of flame. Fire had been set to the town. A great weeping arose among the women, crying: 'Our children! Our children!'

"We cursed in our hearts the man, whoever he was, who had laid hands upon the Commandant and made all of us the hostage of his luxury.

"Some rushed forward to go back into the burning town. It was as one of these was shot down that there screamed up the road which led to the mill a high-powered car, sounding its horn loudly. As it sped toward the field of the pit and skidded to a stop, there stood up in it, giving the outstretched salute, a tall, bemedaled, arrogant figure. The Commandant! He was alive! We had been saved!

"'Praise be to the lord!' cried Rabbi Zelig. 'He sleeps not, neither does He drowse, the Custodian of Israel!'

"Among the women ululations now alternated with crazy uncontrolled laughter.

"'Silence!' The specialist was deeply conscious of his role. 'Do you not think that you Jews owe some celebration, some festivity, to the Commandant for his miraculous appearance?'

"The Commandant beamed.

"'In front of the pit! Line up! Quick!'

"The order was obeyed.

"'Now where are your musicians?'

"There stepped forward from the line our wedding company of four fiddlers, two flute-players, and the drummer.

"'Give them' — the specialist turned to the soldiers in the truck — 'give them their instruments.'

"And there they were, in the truck, the fiddles, the flutes, and the drum. All in readiness. The whole thing — disappearance and sudden miraculous appearance — all of it had been a prearranged plan. Terror gripped us. A wind passed over my face, as if a door of the world to come had been left ajar.

"'And where is Itzka, your town idiot? He must lead the orchestra!'

"Itzka was pushed forward and a baton placed in his hand.

"'Now, a *freilichs*!'

"Led with fantastic gestures by the flattered Itzka, the musicians trembled over their tune, at first hesitatingly, as if seeking and probing out their theme. Soon they reached the high ecstatic and repetitive notes, the expression of the bride's and bridegroom's ineffable union, the notes beyond which it was impossible to reach, so strange, so otherworldly — "'Fire!'

"The specialist's voice had barked; barked, too, the guns. The volley reached its marks: screams, *shma-Yisroels,* upflung arms, and great toppling into the pit.

"The Commandant beamed. The plan had worked according to schedule. The cunning Jews had been outwitted.

"The shooting continued for some time. Myself, I had been pushed at the first volley by a falling body onto one of the upper ledges of the pit, where I lay motionless. Two others fell upon me; their blood trickled on my skin. Now and again I heard the running agony of some who, holding their wounds, tried to flee; they were pursued and beaten to death. *One bullet to a man!* Rabbi Zelig's youngest son, the *bar mitzvah,* having been incompletely shot, crawled out of the grave. He was grabbed by one of the soldiers and flung back. *You are supposed to be dead, little Jew! Stay that way!* Soon the number of bodies heaped upon him stifled his cries.

"And all this time the musicians continued with the *freilichs,* which now and then trailed off into whinings, breaks, and falsettos. It was during one of these hesitations that the final volley was heard. The music was silenced; a last fiddle scraped.

"Darkness had fallen, and as I lay beneath my burden, my wrist under my mouth providing space for breathing, I could hear the soldiers pushing the pile of earth that had been dug up during the day back into the pit. The soldiers were exhausted, and contented themselves with simply a general covering layer of earth.

"The grave groaned.

"A soldier slapped with the back of his spade upon the place that had groaned. 'We'll finish it tomorrow,' he said, 'the Jews are bedded for the night.'

"As their footsteps died away, I heard one of them shouting, as if he had turned back: 'You may go now, Itzka. Kamenets is yours.'

"It was the middle of the night when I rose from the grave. All was now silence; the groans had ceased; the earth trembled no more. I rose up and, a shadow of the shadows of the night, I made my way toward the neighboring forest.

"There will be, I hope, other occasions when I may write you of the times that went over me, of the kindness of the wild beasts of the wood who did *not* seek my life, of the ruses and deceptions I used to disguise myself, and of that good peasant family over whose house there presided the image of the man of Galilee, who hid me and fed me and preserved me. Of them, and of how they kept alive in me the human mind so that I did not collapse to walk on all fours, I shall at another time attest. Now I hasten toward my future.

"When the end came, when the highways of Europe were at last cleared of the cogged armored monsters, I came out of my concealment and joined in camp after camp the remnants of our people. And now I am at Bari; I am promised that soon I shall be able to board ship for Haifa.

"Already there come to this harbor the rescuing ships of the Israeli navy. I stand here on the shore and watch them as they take on their passengers. Clarion names they bear, these ships: *Negba* — to the south! *Kedma* — to the east! *Atzmaouth* — independence! I stand on the shore here watching them, it is my one engrossing vision. Before me there extend the waters of the Mediterranean — blue; and its foam — white: an Israeli flag. Above me there stretches the Mediterranean sky — blue; and its clouds — white: an Israeli banner. And between flag and banner and banner and flag there proceed these the pauperized rich argosies of our future. Oh, let the nations of the world keep their mighty armadas, their hosts of dreadnoughts, their potent fleets sweeping the waters of the deep! Theirs be the leviathans of steel and plate; the proud galleons, the sweated galleys — theirs! Ours, these overhauled corvettes, these leaking tubs, these discarded bottoms all of steerage compact — no flotilla in the world can rival them, no navy compare! For they carry a cargo unknown to the annals of the sea — a cargo of re-membered bones — and to the last landfall they make their way — a Navy of Redemption!

"I long to board one of these ships. But I must wait my turn. In the meantime I pause over my hope, I revolve it — as ben Bag-Bag was wont to do to the texts of Holy Writ — about and about. I weigh it, savor it, seek in all aspects to realize and absorb. I make an introspective game out of it, a sacred play, as if with palm leaf shaken to the four winds, as if with citron held and palmed and blessed.

"A game; I say it to myself in language Biblic:

> *And it came to pass that the word was*
> *spoken unto Melech ben David, saying:*
> *Get thee out of thy country, and from thy*
> *kindred, and from thy father's house. And*
> *go thee forth to thy kinsmen and thy kins-*
> *men's country, to the house of thy father's*
> *father, which in these latter days has been*
> *builded and set up again. And I will shew*
> *thee a land . . .*

"Or I read to myself a Mishna:

On the day of the redemption and at the
time of the rebuilding of Erez Israel,
what shall be the benediction to be uttered?
The benediction of shehichianu. Rab says:
The benediction prescribed to be said on
the appearing of a monarch, or wise man.
Others say: The benediction of theTish-
bite.

"And I make Talmudic commentary:

The benediction of the Tishbite — what is
it? It is a benediction not yet composed,
the Tishbite Elijah will compose it. Said
the learned men of Babylon: Israel not yet
reconstructed — how then is one to know
the form prescribed for such occasion. Let
the time come, and the heart talk.

"Or I let my soul gambol among the cumuli of Cabbala:

When the years were ripened, and the
pears fulfilled, then was there fashioned
Aught from Naught. Out of the furnace
there issued smoke, out of the smoke a
people descended. The desert swirled, the
capitals hissed: Sambation raged, but
Sambation was crossed . . . ."

Photo 15: Jewish refugees arriving in Canada from Europe, c. 1947.

Photo 16: German Jewish refugee presents Torah to Canadian Jewish Congress, c. 1949.

Irving Layton

Das Wahre Ich

She tells me she was a Nazi; her father also.
Her brother lies buried under the defeat
        and rubble of Stalingrad.
She tells me this, her mortal enemy, a Jew.

We are twenty years removed from war.
She urges on me candied biscuits and tea,
and her face is touched by a brief happiness
when I praise her for them and for the mobiles
        she has herself fashioned
in the comfortless burdensome evenings.

Her face is sad and thin as those mobiles
moving round and round in the small wind
my voice makes when I thank her
and she bows her frail proud head into her hands.

The terrible stillness holds us both
and stops our breath
while I wonder, a thrill stabbing into my mind:
"At this moment, does she see my crumpled form
        against the wall,
blood on my still compassionate eyes and mouth?"

Mordecai Richler

The Holocaust and After (Excerpt)

The Germans are still an abomination to me. I do not mourn for Cologne, albeit decimated for no useful military purpose. I rejoice in the crash of each German Starfighter. No public event in recent years has thrilled me more than the hunting down of Adolph Eichmann. I am not touched by the Berlin Wall.

That much made clear, let me add that for some time now I've been reading published memoirs about life in the Warsaw ghetto, the *Paradies-ghetto* of Terezin in Czechoslovakia, Treblinka, and the Janowska camp near Lvov, Poland. After all these years, the record is still terrifying, enraging, and impossible to digest more than a small chunk at a time.[1] Take *Scroll of Agony,*[2] The Warsaw Diary of Chaim A. Kaplan, for instance. Here German soldiers roaming the streets looking for Jews to whip and torture, rounding up girls for obscene sport, and smashing babies' skulls against lamp posts, is soon made to seem like the good old days, the high-spirited prankish days, a phony war once the more

[1] Approximately six million Jews were systematically murdered by Germans during World War II.

[2] London, Hamish Hamilton, Ltd. 1965.

scientific "final solution" is set in motion in 1942; and the *Judenrat,* the sometimes notorious Jewish "self-government" answerable to the Nazis, is compelled, to begin with, to deliver 6,000 Jews a day for re-settlement in the East.

Adam Czerniakow, President of the Warsaw *Judenrat,* committed suicide by poison rather than sign the expulsion order. Unfortunately, another quickly rose to take his place. "The expulsion is reaching its peak," Kaplan wrote (optimistically, as it turned out) on July 29, 1942. "It increases from day to day. The Nazis are satisfied with the work of the Jewish police . . . . This criminal force is the child of the criminal *Judenrat.* Like mother, like daughter. With their misdeeds they besmirch the name of Polish Jewry . . . . " Others, especially those heroic men and women who were later to rise in hopeless but magnificent rebellion, brought undying honour to the same people.

The intrepid and diligent Kaplan was not a natural writer; he was clumsy, without a reporter's ear for dialogue or a gift for the telling detail, but all this somehow enhances his diary. Where art might have been inadequate, even suspect, the diary of a bewildered, appalled man utterly convinces. The Warsaw ghetto, it seems, was always rife with wishful rumours. Mussolini has been murdered. Hitler has had a heart attack. Roosevelt is intervening for the sake of the Jews. Another rumour spoke of extermination camps, mass murder, gas chambers, but it was not generally believed.

Terezin was something else, a transit ghetto for the Jews of Moravia and Bohemia. More statistics. Of the more than 125,000 Jews who were squeezed into this garrison town with sufficient accommodation for 7,000, some 33,000 died from malnutrition and disease before they could even be transported to the extermination camps. "While the Jews in Terezin," Goebbels said, "are sitting in the café,drinking coffee, eating cakes, and dancing, our soldiers have to bear all the burdens of a terrible war, its miseries and deprivations, to defend the motherland."

Before the gas chambers were installed it was commonplace for the Jews in the Janowska camp, near Lvov, to be lined up and shot, to tumble into a mass grave they had dug for themselves. Then, once the tide of war had turned, the S.S. felt it prudent to dig up the graves and burn the evidence. Leon Wells, who was compelled to dig with one of the death brigades, writes, in *The Janowska Road,*[3] that one had to be very careful sinking a hook into one of the corpses, already in an advanced

[3]London, Jonathan Cape Ltd. 1966.

Photo 17: First religious service for Canadian Jewish servicemen in Germany, March, 1945.

state of decay, because it might break in two. The corpses were stacked in pyramids of 2,000 and then burned. Stubborn bones were put through a pulverising machine. Then another squad, humorously called *die Goldsuchern von Alaska* by the Germans, sifted the ashes for gold.

I could go on and on, the catalogue of atrocities is endless and after all this time still unbelievable, but in retrospect there are other questions. There is, for instance, the question of the Good Germans. By 1966, only twenty years after the holocaust, we had already witnessed the astonishing emergence of the Good German. Those dashing generals, soon to come to your local Odeon screen, who plotted against Hitler in 1944, or were so besotted with culture as to spare Paris. And let's not forget the sporting *luftwaffe* pilots of the Battle of Britain, who always behave decently, and the chivalrous submarine captains who surfaced after each clean kill to search the sea for survivors. These men, portrayed on the screen by such as Marlon Brando, Kurt Jurgens, and Peter O'Toole, all have one remarkable quality in common: they were anti-Nazis. In fact, seen from today's disinterested vantage-point, such were the number and charm of anti-Nazis in the German armed forces that one wonders how Hitler came to power in the first place — survived — fought —and damn near won. All the same, I must agree that these fictional Germans *are* credible, while the many real ones who surely knew about the concentration camps and the few who made them work are not.

Even looking at the actual photographs of the Warsaw ghetto in *Struggle Death Memory,* I find it difficult to credit. Big assured German soldiers, each one holding a rifle ready, leading a group of starved ragged school children to a railway car that will carry them to the death chambers. The children did not know where they were going. They sang songs.

Other photographs show German soldiers grinning as they torment bearded Jews. There are pictures of incredibly emaciated Jews, lying dead and frozen on the pavement. It is all so foreign. How much easier, drawing on our own sheltered experience, to identify with Eichmann's stalwart son telling the press, "I'll stand by my father" than with these gruesome photographs of swollen-bellied, wildeyed Jews. And while we're at it, why didn't they resist?

What is surprising is that so many did resist. By the time the Jews were transported to the extermination camps they were so broken in spirit and body, so obviously deserted and despised by the world outside (their international socialist brothers, the Pope, England, America) that death must have seemed a deliverance. Earlier, going back to the days before the war, it should be remembered that many of the most astute of German and Polish Jews clearly saw what was coming and left for Palestine, England or America, so that by the time the war and ghettoes had come, the Jews had already been shorn of many of their natural leaders. Other leaders, too many, as has already been noted by Chaim Kaplan and Hannah Arendt, behaved dishonourably. Still, there was resistance, but how pathetically easy it was to stop, and how amazed and encouraged the Nazis were that so few world leaders outside cared what they did with "their" Jews.

If a Jew in the Warsaw ghetto was bold enough to strike back or even shoot down a German soldier, an early incident Kaplan notes in his diary, then the next morning one hundred innocents including women and children, were rounded up, tortured, and shot. If a Jew managed to escape from a concentration camp, as two men did from Janowska, then the families they left behind and many more were murdered as a reprisal. But once it became clear that death was to be everybody's lot, there was resistance in Warsaw and elsewhere.

How very, very difficult it was too. The Jews, unlike say French or Italian partisans, could not fall back on a friendly populace. On the contrary. Minimal help was forthcoming by the way of guns and ammunition from the Polish underground to the heroes of the Warsaw ghetto, and those others who escaped to form partisan bands in the forests had not only the Germans to contend with. Anti-Semitic Polish partisans hunted them down on one side and Ukrainian fascist partisans on the other.

Let no one ask why there wasn't more resistance. Let them ask instead, as Chaim Kaplan did in *Scroll of Agony,* on April 12, 1940, "Is there any revenge in the world for the spilling of innocent blood? I doubt it. The abominations committed before our eyes cry out from the earth: 'Avenge me!' But there is no jealous avenger. Why has a 'day of vengeance and retribution' not yet come for the murderers? Do not answer me with idle talk — I won't listen to you. Give me a logical reply!"

Kaplan did not survive. He is presumed to have been exterminated in early 1943. Leon Wells, who did survive, writes that after the war the need for vengeance slowly died within him. "How can one live despising the world?"

Eli Weisel, another survivor of the holocaust, the enormously talented autbor of *Night,* returned to Germany seventeen years after the holocaust and found, to his regret, that he was unable to sustain his hatred for the Germans. He wrote in *Commentary,* "Yet today, even having been deserted by my hate during that fleeting visit to Germany, I cry out with all my heart against forgetting, against silence. Every Jew, somewhere in his being, should set apart a zone of hate — healthy, virile hate — for what the German personifies and for what persists in the

German. To do otherwise would be a betrayal of the dead."

Speaking for myself, I am a believer in obligatory voyages, Gehenna being as necessary as the heavenly spheres, and so I've been to Germany as well as Jerusalem.

On my first day in Munich, in 1955, I went to meet a friend at the American Army Service Club, formerly Hitler's *Haus der Kunst.* Drifting into the lobby, I was confronted by a life-size cardboard hillbilly which held a poster announcing that Friday would be "Grand Ole Op'ry Night." Over the information desk, there was another announcement that I used in my novel, *St. Urbain's Horseman.* This one set out Saturday's diversions. Visiting GIs were assured that promptly at 1400 hours a bus would leave for nearby Dachau: **"BRING YOUR CAMERAS! VISIT THE CASTLE AND THE CREMATORIUM."**

I was in Germany again in 1963, this time to write a piece about the Royal Canadian Air Force base on the outskirts of Baden-Baden. Young, distinctly small-town Canadian school-teachers attached to the air base breathlessly assured me the Germans were "a simply fantastic people." So modern, so clean, "We have a lot to learn from them," a science teacher told me. "From their leisurely way of life."

The next evening I went to the Social Center, mixing with teenagers at a dance. "What have you seen in Europe?" I asked them.

"Venice."

"A bullfight in Barcelona."

"Dachau."

Dachau. The boy was only fourteen. His parents, he said, had taken him to Dachau when he was twelve. To my astonishment, most of the other children had been there too.

"Do you know what Dachau is?" I asked. "They used to punish people there."

"Naw. Like it was extermination."

"No, no. They just hung guys there. They never used the gas chambers."

"Who told you that?" I asked.

"The Germans."

I asked if they had found Dachau a chilling place.

"It's not used any more, but."

"Yeah, it was only during the war. They used to torture guys there."

"Why?"

"Um, there were too many prisoners so they had to kill some off."

"Jews were against Hitler so they had to exterminate them."

"What else?" I asked.

"It was," a boy said, "an unusual place to visit."

Kenneth Sherman

Alien

My student (aged 21)
has never heard of Auschwitz
His eyes are vacuous
like one of those aliens on *Star Trek.*

He's seen every single show,
can tell me Spock's first name,
the thousand and one ways
Capt. Kirk faced death.

Yet he has never heard
the names Goebbels, Rudolf Hess —
and Hitler now
some hard luck hero.

On his arm a tattooed knife
has got it in for a heart.
He dreams beer river
and the ultimate overhead drive.

Perhaps minds like his
are controlled from some
far away hostile planet.

Bleep, bleep. Bleep, bleep.

Someone
something
speaking through him
of a future dark and brutal.

Leonard Cohen

All There is to Know about Adolph Eichmann

EYES: .... Medium
HAIR: .... Medium
WEIGHT: .... Medium
HEIGHT: .... Medium
DISTINGUISHING FEATURES: .... None
NUMBER OF FINGERS: .... Ten
NUMBER OF TOES: .... Ten
INTELLIGENCE: .... Medium

What did you expect?

Talons?

Oversize incisors?

Green saliva?

Madness?

Leonard Cohen

Hitler

Now let him go to sleep with history,
the real skeleton stinking of gasoline,
the mutt and jeff henchmen beside him:
let them sleep among our precious poppies.

Cadres of SS waken in our minds
where they began before we ransomed them
to that actual empty realm we people
with the shadows that disturb our inward peace.

For a while we resist the silver-black cars
rolling in slow parade through the brain.
We stuff the microphones with old chaotic flowers
from a bed which rapidly exhausts itself.

Never mind. They turn up as poppies
beside the tombs and libraries of the real world.
The leader's vast design, the tilt of his chin
seem excessively familiar to minds at peace.

Stanley Cooperman

Masada (Poems 1,4,5)

1. TERMS OF AGREEMENT
The function of a Jew
is to die.
That is his function;
or to survive wrapped in psalms,
violins,
rags
    money . . .
an object for your (discreet)
sympathy,
astonishment that still
he breathes, and walks,
refusing to settle
on the garbage dump of History
which
    kindly
you define, being ready
to forgive his existence.

The function of a Jew
is to splatter chicken-fat
on the smooth tables
the kitchens
the ovens
of your love:
the hunchback you entertain

who squats
                comic
on piles of his own dead,
wailing
under the moth-eaten canopy
of his beard: you give him more
than he deserves.

The function of a Jew
is to dance
like a soft-shoe beggar
with a bible stuck in his mouth, greasy coins
between his fingers:
not for him the earth, not
for him
unborrowed sky . . .
the function of a Jew is
to be
     allowed.

4. THE TOURIST

After tea at the YMCA,
after smiles
Idaho
conversation, when even the bacon
was blond,
we walked toward Jerusalem:
I held my camera
like a bullet-proof vest,
our guide
twirled his dry moustache
and glittered at his pilgrims.

It was 24 hours
after I had signed a paper
that I had no ''Jewish blood'' . . .
the man at the Embassy
said
he had no control,
the eagle behind his desk
had no control,
and I dipped my pen in gall
being good, being agreeable, being
what was necessary
to be
a pilgrim
to the holy city of Jerusalem.

When we arrived at a wall
where goats
fed on their own excrement,
our guide paused, wiped his sleeve
and smiled:
''a Jew place'' he said
pointing to the inscriptions,
tatters of cloth,
30 centuries of tears
eaten into rock;
''they came to cry'' he said
wrinkling, and we
the pilgrims
smiled back, nodding,
hanging out of our teeth,
comforted, familiar:
the lady from Idaho complained
of the smell.

Later
we climbed the Mount of Olives
pious; the road was holy,
sweat beaded our skin like rosaries,
and all around us
stones lay on the yellow earth,
burial urns
with their names painted out,
red paint smeared over their verses:
from Minsk and Alexandria,
Cracow, Berlin:
old men had come to be buried . . . .
I watched them
scream under the earth,
their beards
opened like empty hands, their eyes
filled with mud,
with thorns:
our guide watched me
and I
watched my face.

5. HOMECOMING

The function of a Jew
is to die.
that is his function;
that
    was
his function: we have come home,
and if we die
it will be without your permission,
and without your love:
we have tasted your love
and it burned us . . .
it flows through the world
like a sewer of used blood.

Listen: our hands are no longer empty,
and our dreams
are of olive groves,
oranges
planted on the edge of despair;
if we die
it will be here,
if we die
it will be as the lion dies
protecting his young.

Mordecai Richler

This Year at the Arabian Nights Hotel

Jake was sitting in a projection room at Pinewood, idly probing his scalp for bumps and nascent tumours, then placing a hand over his heart to listen for palpitations. He was waiting for the others to arrive so they could run through the second reel together, when Sid whacked the door open to say he had just heard, on his car radio, that the fighting had started. An Israeli spokesman had declared that, in response to an Egyptian attack, Israeli armour had gone into action. A fierce tank battle was in progress in Sinai.

Soon there were ten of them in the projection room, chain-smoking and drinking coffee round the transistor radio. This time, Jake thought, the bloody Egyptians would suck Israeli armour deeper and deeper into Sinai, then Jordan would throw everything into an assault on the Sharon Plain, cutting Israel in two where it was only twelve miles wide. Jake would have to volunteer. He would be obliged to fight.

— Golly, Dad, where'd you get those hooks?

— Had a little disagreement with a land mine, son. The mine won. But look at it this way: I won't have to worry about dirty fingernails any more.

Cairo claimed forty-four planes shot down. There was dancing in the streets. The headline in the first edition of the *Evening Standard* proclaimed that Germany was to send Israel 20,000 gas masks. ''About twenty-five years too late,'' Jake hollered at the others, crushing the *Standard* into a ball.

As a high school boy in Montreal, during the forties, Jake had joined Habonim, the Labour-Zionist youth movement. On Friday nights he listened to impassioned speeches about soil redemption and saw movies glorifying life on the kibbutz, girls dancing round orange trees, their breasts jiggling. Early Sunday mornings he was out ringing doorbells for the Jewish National Fund, righteously demanding quarters, dimes, and nickels to help reclaim the desert in Eretz Yisroal. In the summertime he went to a camp in a mosquito-ridden Laurentian valley, heard more speakers, studied Hebrew, and, in the absence of Arabs, watched out for fishy-looking French Canadians. But Jake did not actually get to Israel until the spring of 1963. On arrival, he remembered, it was balmy, marvellously bright and blue; and what with London's wet gummy skies only six hours behind him, he began to feel elated. Jake stopped the first taxi he saw. ''How much do you want to take me to Tel Aviv?'' he asked.

''Are we getting married? Do we need a rabbi? We'll settle the fare when we get there. So, how do you like it in Israel?''

''There's only one thing that worries me. Will it be all right to tip you? Another Jew.''

''Next to Japan,'' the driver said, wheeling onto the highway, ''we have the highest accident rate in the world.''

Jake whistled, impressed.

''And that,'' the driver added, ''is without benefit of drunken drivers.''

Checking in at the Garden Hotel, in Ramat Aviv, Jake, his mood altogether frivolous, toyed with the notion of announcing himself as Mr. O'Brien, just to see what sort of room, if any, they would offer a goy; but he let it go. He stopped by a poolside table for a gin-and-tonic. Lots of foot-weary, middle-aged tourists were sunning themselves.

''Have you heard their English yet, Sadie?''

''What?''

''So help me, they speak better than us. They speak like the British.''

Among the tourists was Mr. Cooper. Shooing flies away with a rolled newspaper, pondering his toes as he curled and uncurled them, the portly, bronzed Mr. Cooper, his eyes shaded by a peak cap, basked in a deck chair, his manner proprietorial. "And where are you from?" he asked Jake.

"London," Jake said, hastily adding that he was in fact a Canadian.

"Ah ha. And how long are you here for?"

"A week. Ten days maybe."

"Longer you couldn't stay? This is Israel. Don't be a cheapskate." Jake laughed.

"And tell me, Mr. Hersh, you came over on one of our planes, you were impressed?"

"They're Boeing 707's, you know. A Gentile product."

"And what about the pilots? Eh? This country it's a miracle. I been here seven years ago and what we done since it's remarkable. I'm not a millionaire, Mr. Hersh, and I'm not poor. I'm in sporting goods. I sell guns, sleeping bags, tents. You'd never catch me spending a night in a sleeping bag. Goys are crazy. I should complain. So, Mr. Hersh, what line of business are you in?"

"The junk business," Jake said, and he retired to his bungalow to consider the script Leopold had given him in London. One cursory glance was sufficient to depress him. Jake poured himself a brandy and rehearsed his Academy Award non-acceptance speech once more. "As long," it began, "as there are no Negro directors in our industry and a Protestant can rise no higher than a grip, I must, in all honesty . . ."

Traditionally, producers were the butt of most film jokes, but Jake had found Leopold surprisingly engaging. The most uncomplicated of con men. "On her deathbed," Leopold had said, contemplating the ceiling with wet eyes, "my mother, may she rest in peace, made me promise that one day I would make a picture in Israel."

"Did she specify a sexy thriller?" Jake asked.

"I need your fresh, exciting talent. You're the only man who can direct this picture for me."

He was also the fifth choice, Jake knew, and could not afford to be choosy.

Early the next morning a bellboy rapped on Jake's bungalow door: a Colonel Elan was waiting on the terrace for him. Elan, who was Leopold's Israeli partner, the moneyman, was to drive Jake to Jerusalem. Elan was squat and sinewy, his solemn face hardened by the wind. He was casually dressed. "Shalom," he said.

"Shalom."

Mr. Cooper passed arm-in-arm with his wife. Mrs. Cooper wore a floppy straw hat, winged sunglasses, and flower-print pedal pushers. "So, Mr. Hersh, have you decided to settle here yet?"

"What about you?"

"Me, I'm too old to dance the hora. So I come here and spend. It's the children's money. Do I want to be the richest man in the cemetery? The less I leave, the less the children will have to fight over, God bless them."

Elan smiled and shook his head, his grey eyes scornful. No sooner had Jake climbed into his Ford station-wagon than Elan said, "I wonder what that man's name was before it was Cooper."

"And what," Jake asked indignantly, "was yours before it was Elan?"

"You'll find that we're a new kind of Jew here. We have restored Jewish pride."

"By taking German reparation money?"

"It's easy to criticize."

"I'm an old-fashioned Jew. I criticize."

The other side of Ramle, the car began the slow winding rise and fall, rise and fall, through the bony, densely cultivated mountains. Arab villages jutted natural and ravaged as rock out of the hills. The gutted shells of armoured trucks lay overturned round bends in the narrow steepening road. Here a dried wreath hung on a charred chassis; elsewhere mounds of stone marked where a driver, trapped in the cab of his burning truck, had died an excruciating death. These ruins, spilled along the roadside, were a memorial to those who had died running the blockade into Jerusalem during the first Arab-Israeli War, at a time when the Arab Legion had held the vital heights of Bab el Wad and Kastel, an ancient Roman encampment and crusaders' castle which dominate the closest approaches to the city. "Look here, Elan," Jake said suddenly, "have you read the script yet?"

"Yes."

"It's cheap, sentimental stuff. Sex on the kibbutz. Murder. Why don't you tell Leopold to go get stuffed?"

"Because we need the foreign currency."

In the afternoon Jake assembled with some two hundred others for the tour through Mea Shearim, the fiercely orthodox old quarter. The group, predominantly American, was composed of gaudily made-up matrons and their cigar-biting husbands, harnessed with cameras, light metres, filters and binoculars. "Look who's here," Mr. Cooper said, nudging his wife.

Jake waved. It was a stifling afternoon. A spritely boy hurried through the narrow, squalid streets, blowing a horn to announce the coming of the sabbath. Poor men with glazed eyes watched as the chattering tourists shuffled past, others slammed their doors as they wound towards them. Once Mrs. Cooper poked the guide with her dimpled elbow and pointed out a forlorn, olive-skinned little girl skipping rope on a square. ''Is *that one* Jewish?'' she asked.

''Oh, yes,'' the guide said. ''She's from Persia.''

''Shabbat shalom,'' Mr. Cooper sang out; and he pressed a five-dollar bill into the child's hand.

Later Mr. Cooper stopped, pushed open the door to a sinking corner house, and beckoned to his wife. ''Look, Sylvia, it's not so bad inside.''

As they twisted up yet another cramped alley, Mr. Cooper turned to Jake and said, ''Take a deep breath. Stinky, isn't it? But this is holy ground, you know. I'll bet you couldn't buy a lot here for any price.''

''Possibly,'' Jake said, irritated, ''you should not push open doors to peer into strangers' homes —''

''What are you talking *strangers?* We're all Jews in Israel. The soldiers are Jewish. The trees are Jewish. Even the flowers have the wrong accent. Shouldn't I feel at home here?''

Mr. Cooper was not only determined to feel at ease in Zion, he appointed himself goodwill ambassador by the poolside of the Garden Hotel, dealing severely with the least grumble.

''Tell me, Cooper, is it right I have donated so much to build this country . . . it costs a man thousands to come here . . . is it right they should charge me extra I want a cup of tea in the afternoon, I'm parched?''

''Is it right? They should squeeze every penny out of you, what they're doing here, it's a miracle. Isn't that so, Mr. Hersh?''

''Absolutely.''

''We Jews don't have to die to go to heaven. We're already here. What do you say, Mr. Hersh, you're an educated man?''

''You took the words out of my mouth.''

On Tuesday Jake drove to Ako with Elan, to look at possible locations. Old sacks had been stretched across the narrow stinking streets of the Arab marketplace, offering shade to venders and buyers alike. Donkeys, chickens, and goats wandered somnolently through the maze of stalls. The wares the venders had on display were pathetic. Rusty keys for ancient locks, faded cotton dresses, and split boots reclaimed from junk piles. Barefoot boys scampered through the muck. Flies were everywhere. ''They don't have to live like that,'' Elan said. ''A lot of them own property. They bury their money in jars.''

''I've even heard,'' Jake said, ''they have a secret plan for world domination. It's all outlined in something called the Protocols of the Elders of Islam.''

''Actually,'' Elan said solemnly, ''there is no such thing as an ''Arab''. What, for instance, has an Arab in Cairo in common with a Bedouin from Iraq?''

''What,'' Jake asked, ''have I got in common with a Yemenite Jew?''

''Jerusalem. All the Arabs have in common is the fact that they're Moslem. We must teach them that it's not such a bad thing to be an Arab in Israel.''

''Possibly,'' Jake said, ''the trouble is they have loyalties outside their own country. Like my friend Mr. Cooper.''

The next morning Jake drove to Beersheba with Elan to look at the Arabian Nights Hotel, then still under construction. About a half hour out of Tel Aviv, the station-wagon wheeled into a lush cultivated belt. ''When I used to fly over this area in forty-eight,'' Elan said, ''it was almost impossible to navigate. It was all desert. Look how green it is now.''

It was, Jake agreed, truly impressive. Then, quite suddenly, they were streaking across desert. ''We are seventy miles wide here.'' Elan said. ''One day this will be our bread basket.''

Finally, the station-wagon rocked to a stop on the outskirts of Beersheba. Squinting against windblown sand, Jake saw an enormous roadhouse rising abruptly out of the desert. The proprietor, a Mr. Hod, hurried towards them. ''I'm putting up the finest hotel in Israel,'' he said. ''We're going to have a golf course, hot springs — the works. Soon we'll have the biggest neon sign in the country: THE ARABIAN NIGHTS HOTEL. I'm even organizing a society to be called Sons of the Arabian Nights.''

''Dreamy,'' Jake said.

A chauffeured limousine pulled in down the road. ''More stockholders,'' Hod said, somewhat exasperated. But he was ready with a smile as the middle-aged couple alighted from the car.

''Say,'' Mr. Cooper said, ''you've got quite a baby here.''

''Have you ever seen anything like it anywhere in Israel? On the execution and investment side this is the most modern hotel in the country. The best.''

Mr. Cooper beamed. ''Quite a country, eh, Mr. Hersh?''

"In more ways than one."

"You know how they say "Next Year in Jerusalem", Mr. Hod? Well, we'll be saying "Next Year at the Arabian Nights Hotel," won't we, Sylvia?" Sidestepping wet cement, Hod led them inside an unfinished suite. Mrs. Cooper stopped, her brow wrinkled, before some nudes a worker had drawn in pencil on the framework of the bathroom door. "I suppose," she said, "this *does* come off —"

"Sure, sure," Hod said, with a wink for Elan. He led the Coopers over planks and puddles to the second wing of the hotel. "We were not going to build this wing for another two years, then the demand for reservations was so high —"

"You hear, Lou?"

"— that we decided to build big before another hotel opened across the road,"

Hod led the Coopers to the unfinished Sheik's Suite. "Ooh," Mrs. Cooper said, holding a hand to her cheek.

"You know what it says there," Mr. Cooper said, pointing at the archway. "It says reserved for Lou and Sylvia Cooper."

"Want to make reservations, speak to Mrs. Ginsburg."

"Oh, good," Mrs. Cooper said. "Em, what will stockholders have to pay when you open up?"

"Stockholders will be allowed to sign for a month's credit. Like to see our kitchens?"

"We want to see everything. But . . . Em. what will stockholders have to pay?"

"Never mind, Sylvia. Who cares? This is Israel, not Miami."

"In the United States, you know," Mrs. Cooper persisted, "if you bring a guest and you're a stockholder, well, once a month the guest is free . . ."

Hod scratched his head. Elan raised his eyebrows as if to say, these people, these people.

"It's very smart, you know. It makes for goodwill."

"The waitresses will wear veils," Hod said, as they emerged from the hotel again. "I'm going to have a doorman with a long sword standing here."

"That's for me," Mr. Cooper said. "I'll take the job."

Hod didn't even smile. Jake, trailing behind, turned on Elan. "Hod might show a little more kindness, don't you think? Mr. Cooper and his kind happen to pour a lot of money into this country.

"It's ill-begotten."

"I don't see anybody turning it down."

"It's blood money. We risk our lives here. They're paying off their guilt for not settling here."

Hod was escorting the Coopers firmly to their limousine. Mr. Cooper looked back longingly at the garden table lavishly set for a buffet lunch. "Wait," Jake called after them. "Won't you join us for lunch? I'm sure Mr. Elan would be delighted."

It was a mistake. A stupid mistake. Hod grudgingly offered everybody drinks.

"Only H_2O for me," Mrs. Cooper pleaded with a weak laugh.

"Is it kosher?" Mr. Cooper asked, grinning.

"Don't worry," Hod said impatiently. " It's kosher, it's kosher."

"He was only joking," Jake said, accepting a large whisky.

Elan, Jake saw, was smiling icily. He was watching Mrs. Cooper wipe her knife and fork on the edge of the tablecloth.

"Let me drink to the Israelis at our table," Mr. Cooper said, standing up. "As I said to Mr. Hersh here when we first met, this country it's a miracle. I been here seven years ago and what we done since, it's remarkable. *L'chaym.*"

"*L'chaym.*"

We, Jake thought, utterly miserable, did he have to say *we?* And he hastily poured himself another large whisky.

As things turned out, Jake wasn't the only compulsive drinker. Come coffee time, Hod was knocking back large snifters of brandy. "One day," he said, "I met a Spaniard in Beersheba. A rich man. He told me that in Madrid he was an anti-Semite."

"So what else is new?" Mr. Cooper said.

"He said he didn't believe these Jews could ever build a country, so he thought he'd go and see for himself. "Well, I've seen the country," he said, "and it's marvellous!"

"Second the motion."

" 'It wouldn't surprise me,' he said, 'if you people had the atom bomb in five years and took over the Middle East in ten. But you're not Jews; you're different. The Jews in Spain would only fight for their families and their businesses. You're different here,' he said."

"A new kind of Jew," Jake said, looking directly at Elan.

"Stinking Jews," Hod exploded, "that's us. *But we happen to like our smell here.*"

"Well, next time you run into your rich Spanish friend you tell him that the Jews in Canada have not only fought for their country — some of them even fought for Spain."

Elan rose gravely from the table. "Come with me one moment, Hersh. And you too, Mr. Cooper." He led them to his station-wagon, where he flicked open the glove compartment, revealing a service revolver. "I always carry this with me, because the *fedayin* used to be very active on this road. I tell you this, Hersh, because it seems your lousy

Jewish heart bleeds for the poor Arabs. Well, the feeling is not reciprocated. The Arabs hate us. They sit by the radios in their villages and listen to venomous broadcasts from Cairo. They are waiting to slit our throats. But we do not cringe here, we are not the type. If war comes again we will fight hard and they must know it. Either we live in Israel or we drown in the sea."

"God forbid," Mr. Cooper said feelingly.

But Elan was not to be placated. "And you, Mr. Cooper, do you eat kosher in America?"

"Not always."

"But when you come to the holy land, you expect us to be good little boys, you want us to keep kosher for you. You come here to delight in Jewish cops and Jewish soldiers, well then you pay for it, you can pay through the nose for it."

"That's a hell of an attitude," Jake began, "that's —"

"Oh, you're fastidious, aren't you, Hersh? You wonder why we have vulgar hotels like this and would finance cheap exploitation films. It's because we need the currency. And that's why we also take German reparation money. So if you mean that we have compromised our lousy Jewish souls here, then you're right. This state lies and cheats and deals, just like any other. If we didn't, we couldn't survive. There are only two possibilities for the Jew," Elan said. "Assimilate. Or settle here."

On the long drive back to Tel Aviv, Jake feigned sleep, anxious to avoid a further exchange with Elan. Finally, Elan dropped him outside the Garden Hotel. "See you tomorrow," Jake said lamely.

Elan said nothing. He nodded curtly, but he did not turn up the next morning. Late in the afternoon there was a cable from Leopold: PICTURE POSTPONED STOP EXPLAIN LONDON STOP RETURN IMMEDIATELY.

Mr. Cooper was taking his afternoon tea by the pool-side.

"So, Mr. Hersh, I can see that you've been drinking again."

"We're surrounded by anti-Semites here, Mr. Cooper."

"It's the whisky talking, Mr. Hersh, not you."

"Maybe. But we're surrounded by anti-Semites all the same. Ever read Koestler?"

"Who?"

Darkness at Noon. When Rubashov is in prison, as they march him up and down the yard for afternoon exercise, the crazed man behind him, another old bolshevik, repeats over and over again, 'This could never happen in a socialist country.' Rubashov hasn't the heart to tell him they're actually in Russia."

"Very interesting. But this . . . Koestler; he's a communist?"

"He used to sell lemonade right here in Tel Aviv."

"Mr. Hersh, I'm an older man, a grandfather. You live in London, is that correct?"

"Yes."

"I been to London. Over there, everything's happened. There's only the past. Here it's a new country. Here we got to give them a chance. We got to wait and see."

As long as the six-day war lasted, well-meaning acquaintances bought Jake drinks in the pub at Pinewood Studios.

"You've got to hand it to the Israelis," a grip said.

"Bloody good show," somebody else said, slapping him on the back.

"That Dayan is quite the lad, isn't he?"

Yes. The truth was Jake felt immensely relieved by the Israeli victory, even somewhat jubilant. He was also astonished. Elan, he thought, would not be the least bit astonished. Jubilant, yes; astonished, no.

Before Jake had finished editing the second reel, the six-day war was over. A blintzkrieg, *Time* called it. Israelis swam in the Suez Canal and camped on the banks of the Jordan. Jerusalem was theirs. Jerusalem, Jake thought, surprised to discover himself deeply thrilled. Somebody passed Jake the issue of *Life* magazine with the lead picture story on the Israeli war. And there, among the group of officers conferring with Dayan at the Wailing Wall, stood Elan, Colonel Elan, looking uncommonly handsome and capable.

Jake had never seen Elan again after the day at Beersheba. Neither had he ever run into the Coopers elsewhere. Elan, Jake assumed, had fought bravely, leading his men, not following after. And Mr. Cooper wherever he was today had, Jake felt sure, given generously to support the Israeli war effort. So had all the Coopers everywhere. A man came round to collect from Jake too. And much to his own embarrassment, Jake hesitated. Dayan, melodramatic eyepatch and all, was a hero. Our hero, Jake thought, with a certain pride. And yet — and yet — put this arrogant general, this Dayan, in an American uniform, call him MacArthur, call him Westmoreland, and Jake would have despised him. Jake wrote out a cheque, but unhappily. Being the old kind of Jew, a Diaspora Jew, he was bound to feel guilty either way.

Photo 18: Yiddish play at Queen's Theatre, Winnipeg, 1918.

Part Five

In Search of Identity

Photo 19: Jewish firemen, Victoria, B.C., c. 1870.

In Search of Identity

The collection closes, appropriately, with the quest for selfhood. Living in a milieu in which the search for Canadian identity is itself precarious and cliché-tainted, Canadian Jewish writers are doubly beleaguered. "To be a Canadian and a Jew is to leave the ghetto twice", Mordecai Richler has commented. Growing up Canadian and Jewish has meant coming to terms with both ethnic and national ambiguities, with episodes of anti-Semitism, and with unprecedented possibilities. Joe Sherman's *Commentary on the Jewish Problem* confronts the fact of cultural stereotypes, while the excerpts from Leonard Cohen's *Favorite Game* reflect the relationship of an upper-middle class teenager to the values of Anglophone and Francophone Montreal, both of which he will ultimately reject. An assimilated academic is forced to examine his roots in Henry Kreisel's thoughtful *Chassidic Song,* and J.I. Segal, musing on the same past, concludes that "like a talisman of homecoming . . . it longs to gather all us Jews from our spaceless boundaries of loss". Alternatively, Tom Wayman's *Jews* voices a pious prayer that after all the wanderings in search of a home, Jews will join with all nations and religions and become part of an indivisible family of mankind.

Secular and religious, unique and communal, reminiscent and anticipatory, the Canadian Jewish experience is vibrant, multiple and never static. The patterns of this kaleidoscope have been effectively captured by several generations of imaginative writers whose impulses have been to preserve and appreciate the nature of that experience. We, the readers, are the fortunate recipients of their visions.

Leonard Cohen

The Genius

For you
I will be a ghetto jew
and dance
and put white stockings
on my twisted limbs
and poison wells
across the town

For you
I will be an apostate jew
and tell the Spanish priest
of the blood vow
in the Talmud
and where the bones
of the child are hid

For you
I will be a banker jew
and bring to ruin
a proud old hunting king
and end his line

For you
I will be a Broadway jew
and cry in theatres
for my mother
and sell bargain goods
beneath the counter

For you
I will be a doctor jew
and search
in all the garbage cans
for foreskins
to sew back again

For you
I will be a Dachau jew
and lie down in lime
with twisted limbs
and bloated pain
no mind can understand

Irving Layton

Post Crematoria

Gray-haired, soft-spoken, and her blue eye bright,
No, she's not your graceless anti-semite;
For while decrying them does she not use
That nice word *Israelites* instead of *Jews?*

Irving Layton

For My Two Sons, Max and David

The wandering Jew: the suffering Jew

The despoiled Jew: the beaten Jew

The Jew to burn: the Jew to gas

The Jew to humiliate

The cultured Jew: the sensitized exile
    gentiles with literary ambitions aspire to be

The alienated Jew cultivating his alienation
    like a rare flower: no gentile garden is complete
    without one of these bleeding hibisci

The Jew who sends Christian and Moslem theologians
    back to their seminaries and mosques for new arguments
    on the nature of the Divine Mercy

The Jew, old and sagacious, whom all speak well of:
    when not lusting for his passionate, dark-eyed daughters

The Jew whose helplessness stirs the heart and conscience
    of the Christian like the beggars outside his churches

The Jew who can be justifiably murdered because he is rich

The Jew who can be justifiably murdered because he is poor

The Jew whose plight engenders profound self-searchings
in certain philosophical gentlemen who cherish him
to the degree he inspires their shattering aperçus
into the quality of modern civilization, their noble
and eloquent thoughts on scapegoatism and unmerited agony

The Jew who agitates the educated gentile, making him pace
back and forth in his spacious well-aired library

The Jew who fills the authentic Christian with loathing for himself
and his fellow-Christians

The Jew no one can live with: he has seen too many conquerors
come and vanish, the destruction of too many empires

The Jew in whose eyes can be read the doom of nations
even when he averts them in compassion and disgust

The Jew every Christian hates, having shattered his self-esteem
and planted the seeds of doubt in his soul

The Jew everyone seeks to destroy, having instilled self-division
in the heathen

Be none of these, my sons
My sons, be none of these
Be gunners in the Israeli Air Force

Joseph Sherman

Commentary on the Jewish Problem

On the first night of the Going Out Of Business Sale
 a loud longtime customer
 hip-waded into the melee
 dragging for bargains

Spotting me
 she moved her large arms
 in an encompassing circle
 and asked waggishly
 "What's old Abie up to now
 with all this   Hasn't
 he got enough money   ?"

So I turned
 and told her slowly
 that my great-uncle Abraham
 was dead
 didn't she know?

Her mouth opened fish-like
 just for a moment
 yet I knew she would find
 polite escape

but for that same moment
 I stood
 wishing for this patroness
 to show her teeth

wanting her to slough "that wouldn't stop old Abie"

Joseph Sherman

The Only Game in Town

As we were choosing up sides
the only other Jewish boy
in Bridgewater
winked me aside
and told me what he was

Later
when I shot him
it was with more pleasure
and less guilt
than I would have thought possible

Leonard Cohen

The Favourite Game

The Favourite Game—Excerpts
Lawrence Breavman, the central character, is strongly drawn from Leonard Cohen's own adolescence in Montreal's Westmount. Breavman, brilliant, privileged and deeply alienated, breaks away from one relationship after another as he searches for his own vision of life. The selections are taken from the early part of the novel.

Palais D'or

Suspended from the centre of the ceiling a revolving mirrored sphere cast a rage of pockmarks from wall to wall of the huge Palais D'or on lower Stanley Street.

Each wall looked like an enormous decayed Swiss cheese on the march.

On the raised platform a band of shiny-haired musicians sat behind heavy red and white music stands and blew the standard arrangements.

There's but one place for me
Near you.
It's like heaven to be
Near you

echoed coldly over the sparse dancers. Breavman and Krantz had got there too early. There was not much hope for magic.

"Wrong dance-hall, Breavman."

By ten o'clock the floor was jammed with sharply dressed couples, and, seen from the upstairs balcony, their swaying and jolting seemed to be nourished directly by the pulsing music, and they muffled it like shock absorbers. The bass and piano and steady brush-drum passed almost silently into their bodies where it was preserved as motion.

Only the tilt-backed trumpeter, arching away from the mike and pointing his horn at the revolving mirrored sphere, could put a lingering sharp cry in the smoky air, coiling like a rope of rescue above the bobbing figures. It disappeared as the chorus renewed itself.

"Right dance hall, Krantz."

They scorned many public demonstrations in those prowling days but they didn't scorn the Palais D'Or. It was too big. There was nothing superficial about a thousand people deeply engaged in the courting ritual, the swinging fragments of reflected light sweeping across their immobile eye-closed faces, amber, green, violet. They couldn't help being impressed, fascinated by the channelled violence and the voluntary organization.

Why are they dancing to the music, Breavman wondered from the balcony, submitting to its dictation?

At the beginning of a tune they arranged themselves on the floor, obeyed the tempo, fast or slow, and when the tune was done they disintegrated into disorder again, like a battalion scattered by a land mine.

"What makes them listen, Krantz? Why don't they rip the platform to pieces?"

"Let's go down and get some women."

"Soon."

"What are you staring at?"

"I'm planning a catastrophe."

They watched the dancers silently and they heard their parents talking.

The dancers were Catholics, French-Canadian, anti-Semitic, anti-Anglais, belligerent. They told the priest everything, they were scared by the Church, they knelt in wax-smelling musty shrines hung with abandoned dirty crutches and braces. Everyone of them worked for a Jewish manufacturer whom he hated and waited for revenge. They had bad teeth because they lived on Pepsi-Cola and Mae West chocolate cakes. The girls were either maids or factory help. Their dresses were too bright and you could see bra straps through the flimsy material. Frizzy hair and cheap perfume. They screwed like jack rabbits and at confession the priest forgave them. They were the mob. Give them a chance and they'd burn down the synagogue. Pepsies. Frogs. Fransoyzen.

Breavman and Krantz knew their parents were bigots so they attempted to reverse all their opinions. They did not quite succeed. They wanted to participate in the vitality but they felt there was something vaguely unclean in their fun, the pawing of girls, the guffaws, the goosing.

The girls might be beautiful but they all had false teeth.

"Krantz, I believe we're the only two Jews in the place."

"No, I saw some BTOs on the make a couple of minutes ago."

"Well, we're the only Westmount Jews around."

"Bernie's here."

"O.K. Krantz, I'm the only Jew from Wellgreen Avenue. Do something with that."

"O.K. Breavman, you're the only Jew from Wellgreen Avenue at the Palais D'Or."

"Distinctions are important."

"Let's get some women."

At one of the doors in the main hall there was a knot of young people. They argued jovially in French, pushing one another, slapping back-sides, squirting Coke bottles.

The hunters approached the group and instantly modified its hilarity. The French boys stepped back slightly and Krantz and Breavman invited the girls they'd chosen. They spoke in French, fooling no one. The girls exchanged glances with each other and members of the party. One of the French boys magnanimously put his arm around the shoulder of the girl Breavman had asked and swept her to him, clapping Breavman on the back at the same time.

They danced stiffly. Her mouth was full of fillings. He knew he'd be able to smell her all night.

"Do you come here often, Yvette?"

"You know, once in a while, for fun."

"Me too. *Moi aussi.*"

He told her he was in high school, that he didn't work.

"You are Italian?"

"No."

"English?"

"I'm Jewish."

He didn't tell her he was the only one from Wellgreen Avenue.

"My brothers work for Jew people."

"Oh."

"They are good to work for."

The dance was unsatisfying. She was not attractive, but her racial mystery challenged investigation. He returned her to her friends. Krantz had finished his dance, too.

"What was she like, Krantz?"

"Don't know. She couldn't speak English."

They hung around for a little while longer, drinking Orange Crush, leaning on the balcony rail to comment on the swaying mob below. The air was dense with smoke now. The band played either frantic jitterbug or slow fox trot, nothing between. After each dance the crowd hovered impatiently for the next one to begin.

It was late now. The wallflowers and the stag-line expected no miracles any more. They were lined along three walls watching the packed charged dancers with indifferent fixed stares. Some of the girls were collecting their coats and going home.

"Their new blouses were useless, Krantz."

Seen from above, the movement on the floor had taken on a frantic quality. Soon the trumpeter would aim his horn into the smoke and give the last of Hoagy Carmichael and it would be all over. Every throb of the band had to be hoarded now against the end of the evening and the silence. Soak it through pressed cheeks and closed eyes in the dreamy tunes. In the boogie-woogie gather the nourishment like manna and knead it between the bodies drawing away and towards each other.

"Let's get one more dance in, Breavman?"

"Same girls?"

"Might as well."

Breavman leaned over the rail one more second and wished he were delivering a hysterical speech to the thick mob below . . . . and you must listen, friends, strangers, I am binding the generations one to another, o, little people of numberless streets, bark, bark, hoot, blood, your long stairways are curling around my heart like a vine . . .

They went downstairs and found the girls with the same group. It was a mistake, they knew instantly. Yvette stepped forward as if to tell Breavman something but one of the boys pulled her back.

"You like the girls, eh?" he said, the swaggerer of the party. His smile was triumphant rather than friendly.

"Sure we like them. Anything wrong with that?"

"Where you live, you?"

Breavman and Krantz knew what they wanted to hear. Westmount is a collection of large stone houses and lush trees arranged on the top of the mountain especially to humiliate the underprivileged.

"Westmount," they said with one voice.

"You have not the girls at Westmount, you?"

They had no chance to answer him. In the very last second before they fell backwards over the kneeling accomplices stationed behind them they detected a signalling of eyes. The ring-leader and a buddy stepped forward and shoved them. Breavman lost his balance and as he fell the stoolie behind him raised himself up to turn the fall into a flip. Breavman landed hard in a belly-flop, a couple of girls that he had crashed into squealing above him. He looked up to see Krantz on his feet, his left fist in someone's face and his right cocked back ready to fly. He was about to get up when a fat boy decided he shouldn't and dived at him.

"Reste la, maudit juif!"

Breavman struggled under the blankets of flesh, not trying to defeat the fat boy but merely to get out from under him so he could do battle from a more honourable upright position. He managed to squeeze away. Where was Krantz?

There must have been twenty people fighting. Here and there he could see girls on their tiptoes as though in fear of mice, while boys wrestled on the floor between them.

He wheeled around, expecting an attack. The fat boy was smothering someone else. He threw his fist at a stranger. He was a drop in the wave of history, anonymous, exhilarated, free.

"O, little friends, hoot, blooey, dark fighters, shazam, bloop!" he shouted in his happiness.

Racing down the stairs were three bouncers of the management's and what they feared most began to happen. The fighting spread to the dance floor. The band was blowing a loud dreamy tune but a disorganized noise could already be heard in opposition to the music.

Breavman waved his fist at everyone, hitting very few. The bouncers were in his immediate area, breaking up individual fights. At the far side of the hall the couples still danced closely and peacefully, but on Breavman's side their rhythm was disintegrating into flailing arms, blind punches, lunges, and female squeals.

The bouncers pursued the disruption like compulsive housekeepers after an enormous spreading stain, jerking fighters apart by their collars and sweeping them aside as they followed the struggle deeper into the dance floor.

A man rushed onto the bandstand and shouted something to the bandleader, who looked around and shrugged his shoulders. The bright light went on and the curious coloured walls disappeared. The music stopped.

Everyone woke up. A noise like a wail of national mourning rose up and at the same time fighting swept over the hall like released entropic molecules. To see the mass of dancers change to mass of fighters was like watching a huge highly organized animal succumb to muscular convulsions.

Krantz grabbed Breavman.

''Mr. Breavman?''

''Krantzstone, I presume.''

They headed for the front exit, which was already jammed with refugees. No one cared about his coat.

''Don't say it Breavman.''

''O.K. I won't say it, Krantz.''

They got out just as the police arrived, about twenty of them in cars and the Black Maria. They entered with miraculous ease.

The boys waited in the front seat of the Lincoln. Krantz's jacket was missing a lapel. The Palais D'Or began to empty of its victims.

''Pity the guys in there, Breavman — and don't say it,'' he added quickly when he saw Breavman put on his mystical face.

''I won't say it, Krantz, I won't even whisper that I planned the whole thing from the balcony and executed it by the simple means of mass-hypnosis.''

''You had to say it, eh?''

''We were mocked, Krantz. We seized the pillars and brought down the temple of the Philistines.''

Krantz shifted into second with exaggerated weariness.

''Go on, Breavman. You have to say it.''

Leonard Cohen

The Favourite Game

The Favourite Game—Excerpts

The Park

At night the park was his domain.

He covered all the playing fields and hills like a paranoiac squire hunting for poachers. The flower-beds, the terraces of grass had an aspect of formality they did not have by daylight. The trees were taller and older. The high-fenced tennis court looked like a cage for huge wingless creatures which had somehow got away. The ponds were calm and deadly black. Lamps floated in them like multiple moons.

Walking past the Chalet he remembered the masculine smell of hockey equipment and underwear, the thud of skates on wooden planks.

The empty baseball diamond was blurred with spectacular sliding ghosts. He could hear the absence of cheers. With no bikes leaning against them the chestnut tree and wire backstop seemed strangely isolated.

How many leaves have to scrape together to record the rustle of the wind? He tried to distinguish the sound of acacia from the sound of maple.

Just beyond the green rose the large stone houses of Westmount Avenue. In them the baseball players were growing their bodies with sleep, resting their voices. He imagined that he could see them dimly through the walls of the upper storeys, or rather the sheets they were wrapped in, floating row upon row over the street, like a colony of cocoons in a moonlit tree. The young men of his age, Christian and blond, dreaming of Jewish sex and bank careers.

The park nourished all the sleepers in the surrounding houses. It was the green heart. It gave the children dangerous bushes and heroic landscapes so they could imagine bravery. It gave the nurses and maids winding walks so they could imagine beauty. It gave the young merchant-princes leaf-hid necking benches, views of factories so they could imagine power. It gave the retired brokers vignettes of Scottish lanes where loving couples walked, so they could lean on their canes and imagine poetry. It was the best part of everyone's life. Nobody comes into a park for mean purposes except perhaps a sex maniac and who is to say that he isn't thinking of eternal roses as he unzips before the skipping-rope Beatrice?

He visited the Japanese pond to ensure the safety of the goldfish. He climbed through the prickly bushes and over the wall to inspect the miniature waterfall. Lisa was not there. He somersaulted down the hill to see if it was still steep enough. Wouldn't it be funny if Lisa of all people should be waiting at the bottom? He sifted a handful in the sandbox to guard against polio. He did a test run on the slide, surprised that it squeezed him. He looked gravely from the lookout to guarantee the view.

"My city, my river, my bridges, shit on you, no I didn't mean it."

The bases had to be run, the upper ponds examined for sail-boat wrecks or abandoned babies or raped white nurses. Touch the tree trunks to encourage them.

He had his duty to the community, to the nation.

At any moment a girl is going to step out of one of the flower-beds. She will look as though she has just been swimming and she'll know all about my dedication.

He lay under the lilacs. The flowers were almost gone, they looked like molecular diagrams. Sky was immense. Cover me with black fire. Uncles, why do you look so confident when you pray? Is it because you know the words? When the curtains of the Holy Ark are drawn apart and gold-crowned Torah scrolls revealed, and all the men of the altar wear white clothes, why don't your eyes let go of the ritual, why don't you succumb to raving epilepsy? Why are your confessions so easy?

He hated the men floating in sleep in the big stone houses. Because their lives were ordered and their rooms tidy. Because they got up every morning and did their public work. Because they weren't going to dynamite their factories and have naked parties in the fire.

There were lights on the St. Lawrence the size of stars, and an impatient stillness in the air. Trees as fragile as the legs of listening deer. At any minute the sun would come crashing out of the roofs like a clenched fist, driving out determined workers and one-way cars to jam the streets. He hoped he wouldn't have to see the herds of traffic on Westmount Avenue. Turning night into day.

"Hello there."

A stout man of thirty in an Air Force uniform stood above him. He had been the centre of attention in the park a few days before. Several nurses complained that he had been too enthusiastic in the fondling of their male children. A policeman had escorted him to the street and invited him to move along.

"I thought you weren't allowed in here."

"Nobody's around. I just felt like talking."

His uniform was sharply pressed. Really, he was too clean for that time of the morning or night or whatever it was. Breavman isolated the smell of shaving lotion from the lilac-laden air. He stood up.

"Talk. You have my permission. I'm going home."

"I just thought . . ."

Breavman looked back over his shoulder and shouted, "Talk! Why aren't you talking? It's all yours — the park's empty!"

There were gardeners in faded clothes on his street. They called to one another as they swept, all Italian names. Breavman studied their brooms made out of wire-bound branches. It must be nice to use something that real.

Henry Kreisel

Chassidic Song

Huge, full-bearded, the figure stood in the passage-way that separates the first-class from the tourist compartment. His eyes surveyed the compartment carefully, as if to see who was in the plane and how many seats were not yet taken. Arnold Weiss, sitting by a window in the back, felt the eyes upon him. For a moment he was mesmerized. The dark eyes held him. Then they swept past him.

The figure moved slowly into the compartment, a strange, totemic apparition. Incongruous, thought Arnold Weiss. A Chassid on a plane, flying from Montreal to New York. Why strange? And if a nun wearing a black habit and wimple or a priest in a long cassock had come down the aisle, would I have been astonished? Then why now? The long, black garbardine caftan swished softly as he walked.

Behind him now other black-caftaned, black-hatted figures appeared, moved forward. Arnold Weiss counted them. One, two . . . five . . . ten. The first, the tallest, stopped, checked the seat number on his boarding pass, took a step or two, and then sat down beside Arnold Weiss. The others followed, took their seats. All around him now Chassidim sat. Surrounded, thought Arnold Weiss, on all sides. He shifted in his seat. He smiled.

The Chassid beside him took off his broad, round, black hat. Underneath he wore a black skull cap, a *yarmulke.* He adjusted it, then reached deep into the pocket of his caftan and brought out a small, dog-eared Hebrew book and began to read. He stretched one of his legs sideways into the aisle, and Arnold Weiss noticed his high, black boots. All around him the Chassidim talked, some in Yiddish, some in English. The Chassid beside him remained silent, reading his book. Now and then his lips moved, as if he were praying. The seat could barely contain his huge frame.

Quietly, smiling, a stewardess walked through the aisle, looking to see if all the seatbelts were fastened. She stopped. Smiled. Said gently, "Please fasten your seatbelt."

Arnold Weiss instinctively reached for the belt, then remembered that he had fastened it some time ago. Her quiet command was addressed to the Chassid, who put his book on his lap and began to struggle with the two ends of the belt. He had to extend the belt to its full length, and even then barely managed to snap the buckle shut. Impossible, thought Arnold Weiss, that the belt could restrain a frame that was like the trunk of a tree if anything should happen that would really test the strength of the belt.

The plane began to taxi out to the runway. Arnold Weiss felt the man beside him tense up, and the tension communicated itself to him. The engines roared, the plane gathered speed on the ground. The Chassid gripped his book, but his eyes looked to the side, out of the window. The upper part of his body swayed slightly, back and forth. His lips moved.

Now they were airborne. His body relaxed. The tension went out of his face. He looked at Arnold Weiss and smiled. Arnold Weiss returned the smile. Then looked away, out of the window, saw the landscape arrange itself into geometric patterns, the St. Lawrence river cutting through the squares, winding its way east.

"Are you going to a *Farbrengen?*" His head turned away, towards the window, Arnold Weiss heard himself speak, the words shaping themselves almost involuntarily, as if it was someone else's voice that was speaking.

The Chassid looked up from his book. Half-startled, half-puzzled, he cried out, "How did you know that word?"

Arnold Weiss turned towards him. "That word?" he repeated.

"A *Farbrengen.*"

"A *Farbrengen*. A *Farbrengen*." Arnold Weiss repeated the word softly, as if he were trying to fathom its strange sound. "I don't know. I don't know how it came into my mind."

"Such a word. So unusual. And you don't know how it came!" There was an undertone of mockery in the voice of the Chassid. "Do you even know what it means, that word. A *Farbrengen*."

Arnold Weiss hesitated. "Isn't it," he ventured at last, "isn't it a — a kind of gathering where Chassidim come together, to eat and to drink, to talk and to listen. And to sing."

"But who told you the word?"

"I don't know any more. I can't remember any more. I haven't heard the word in — God knows how long. Thirty, thirty-five years."

"So. You heard the word. A long time ago. But you heard it. And where did you hear it?"

"I don't know exactly," said Arnold Weiss. "But it must have been in my grandfather's house."

"In Canada?"

"No. No. In Poland. In my grandfather's house. When I was a child."

"You are from Poland?"

"My grandfather lived in Poland. But my mother and father lived in England. My father had gone to England right after the first world war, and then went back to Poland to marry my mother, and brought her to England. I was born there. But from time to time we used to go to Poland to visit my grandparents. And in my grandfather's house I heard about a *Farbrengen*."

"So. And your grandfather. Was he a Chassid?"

Arnold Weiss thought for a while. "I don't know," he said then.

"I don't really know. I wasn't aware. We went there in the summer two or three times before he died. In 1932 or 1933. That's when he died."

"So he was spared," said the Chassid.

"Spared? Spared what?"

The dark eyes turned on Arnold Weiss. "You have to ask?" the Chassid said then, with a hint of a reproach in his voice. "Spared what, you ask . . . The war. The Hitlerites. The holocaust."

Arnold Weiss nodded his head. "Yes," he said, his voice suddenly hoarse, his mouth feeling dry. "Yes. He was spared. If you put it that way."

"He must have been a Chassid," the other speculated. "Your grandfather. Or else why would he have talked about a *Farbrengen*?"

"Yes, I suppose," said Arnold Weiss. "He was probably close to the Chassidic movement." For a moment he was sunk in reverie. "He had a long beard," he continued softly. "I used to sit on his knee, and I stroked the beard. I remember that. But I don't think I ever saw him wear a caftan. He didn't wear the — the uniform. The Chassidic uniform." He smiled. But if he expected a smile in return, he was disappointed.

"If he talked about a *Farbrengen,*"the Chassid reasoned, as if be were explicating a passage in the Talmud, "then he must have gone to a *Farbrengen* when you heard him talk about it. Or he must have been planning to go to one.... Where did he live? Your grandfather. In what town?"

"In Stanislavov."

"Was there a Rebbe in Stanislavov?"

"I don't know."

"I think there must have been," the other asserted. "He must have gone to a *Farbrengen* there. Your grandfather. To be with the Rebbe. To hear the wisdom of the Rebbe. To drink from the fountain. To sing. . . . What was his name?"

"My grandfather's?"

"Yes."

"Moses. Moses Drimmer."

"And yours?"

"Arnold Weiss."

"Do you keep the commandments?"

Impertinence. What right did he have to ask such a question? Out of the blue. Overbearing, he seemed to tower over him, assuming a kind of moral superiority. Arnold Weiss felt pressed against the window. He did not wish to enter into an argument. "What is your name?" he asked, ignoring the question.

"Josef Shemtov," said the Chassid. "I came from Hungary. But after the war. I survived . . . . But I asked you a question. Do you keep the commandments?"

"What is it to you?" Arnold Weiss demanded. His voice rose slightly, though he tried to keep it under control, to keep it calm.

"I think a grandson of Moses Drimmer should keep the commandments," said Shemtov. He spoke as if he had known the other's grandfather and so had a right to question him and to issue moral commands.

"Who says that a man must do what his father did, let alone that a grandson should follow the grandfather?"

''But you sat on his knee and you stroked his beard. So you should honour his memory and keep the commandments.''

''What of my father's memory? Perhaps he didn't keep the commandments, and I follow him.''

Shemtov would not be deterred. ''All the worse,'' he said. ''And even more necessary that you should return to the faith of your grandfather.''

Arnold Weiss laughed. He couldn't take him seriously.

But Josef Shemtov persisted. ''Don't laugh. Don't laugh. Moses Drimmer hasn't forgotten.''

''Where is this leading?'' asked Arnold Weiss, now clearly irritated. ''Why did you start all this?''

''What do you mean — I?'' exclaimed Shemtov. ''Did I start this? What did I start? Did I talk to you first or did you talk to me first? Did I tell you where I was going? Or did you ask me? Who mentioned the *Farbrengen?* Did I or did you?'' He was silent for a moment, lost in thought. Then he said very quietly, ''But even did you? Or perhaps it was Moses Drimmer speaking through you. Not the father. The grandfather.'' He paused, triumphant. The dark eyes challenged Arnold Weiss.

Bemused, but mesmerized almost, Arnold Weiss groped for words, but before he could find what he wanted to say, Shemtov continued.

''The *Rebonoh shel Olem* — the Almighty — blessed be the name — works in very mysterious ways. How could we know that Moses Drimmer — blessed be his memory — who used to sit at the feet of a holy Rebbe and listened to the wisdom of the holy words, and who sang and danced at a *Farbrengen,* would be with us here in a plane and speak through you, his grandson?''

''You are mad,'' said Arnold Weiss.

''Mad? Who spoke to you? Who whispered to you that word? A *Farbrengen.* When did you ever speak the word before? When did you remember before? His questions were now challenges. ''When?'' he demanded.

''You can make a lot out of a little word,'' said Arnold Weiss, trying to sound very casual, but suddenly feeling eery, as if his grandfather were really here, on this plane, flying from Montreal to New York. He looked about him, turned his head, to see the other Chassidim filling all the seats around him.

''It is not an ordinary word,'' said Shemtov. ''It is a very special word. And you knew it. How long is it since you spoke the word?''

Arnold Weiss cleared his throat. "So far as I know," he said then, "I have not spoken the word in thirty, thirty-five years. Come to think of it, I don't know if I have ever spoken the word. I heard it, but I don't think I ever used it. But then — why should I have? I had no reason to."

"But you did. When I saw you, I didn't know you. I had no intention to speak to you. When you said the word, I was completely astonished. I didn't even think you were Jewish. You don't even look like a Jew."

"Because my hair is short and I don't have sidelocks . . . *peyes-* . . . and I don't wear your uniform?" He thought he had turned the tables on Shemtov. The taunt in his voice proclaimed his sense of satisfaction.

Shemtov shook his head. His hand reached up and touched the *yarmulke* on his head. "A soul is bare," he said. "But so long as we live here we have to wrap up the body. And what a man wears has to speak also. A man is weak. He has to remind himself who he is and what he is. Sometimes the burden is heavy. How easy it would be to sink away into the crowd, to become like all the others. No one would see. No one would notice. But no! No no! We cannot do that. We have to show our faith."

"There are many varieties of faith," said Arnold Weiss.

"Are you faithful?"

"In my fashion."

"When you married — did you marry out of the faith? Did you marry a *shikse?*

Arnold Weiss felt the blood rush into his face. "What — what is this?" he stammered. "What right have you to ask me these questions? Are you my conscience? Who appointed you?"

Without a moment's hesitation, Josef Shemtov, said, "Moses Drimmer appointed me. The grandfather. I sit for him."

"Tomorrow," Arnold Weiss said, "I'm going to meet my wife in New York. She's coming from Vancouver. I was away for a week — in Montreal. You might say . . .," he stopped and smiled, "that I was at a kind of *Farbrengen.* I was at a conference that was concerned with the work of James Joyce . . . . Have you ever heard of him?

Shemtov shrugged his shoulders, non-committal. "But I asked *you* a question."

"He was an Irish writer," said Arnold Weiss. "He was born a Catholic, but one of the great characters he created was a Jew. Leopold Bloom. At this conference I gave a paper that was concerned with Leopold Bloom's Jewishness."

''And your wife?'' Josef Shemtov insisted.

''She is Jewish, too,'' said Arnold Weiss.

*''Gott sei Dank,''*said Josef Shemtov, with a great sign of relief.

In the front of the compartment the stewardess had begun to serve a lunch of cold sandwiches. Smiling, she made her way along the aisle, handing out trays. The Chassidim declined. Josef Shemtov looked at Arnold Weiss, waiting to see what he would do. For a moment it seemed as if he would decline also, but then he reached out with a sudden motion and accepted the proffered tray. It contained two sandwiches, one cheese and one ham, and a piece of chocolate cake.

Arnold Weiss sensed the disapproving eyes of Josef Shemtov upon him, but could not bring himself to face him. He began to eat the cheese sandwich, slowly, deliberately. When at last he glanced sideways he saw that Shemtov had opened his book and was reading. Or was he praying?

Suddenly, he closed the book, but continued to hold it with both his hands. He began to speak very softly. '' I was not yet thirteen years old when the Hitlerites stormed through the town where we lived. In a few months I was going to be *Bar-Mitzvah* and I was already learning and preparing. I came from a *balebatische* family, a respectable family. We were orthodox, of course, but we were not a chassidic family. My father was a modern man. There were Chassidim in the town, but we had nothing to do with them. My father thought they were fanatics. I went to the *Gymnasium* in the town, and in the afternoon I went to Hebrew school. I didn't go to the *Yeshivah,* where the chassidic boys went. I knew some of them because I used to meet them, and sometimes we played together, but I thought the way my father did. I couldn't imagine myself dressed the way they were dressed.'' A thin smile creased the corners of his mouth. ''The way I am dressed now . . . . But once the fire started to burn, it didn't make any difference how we were dressed. We trembled and we huddled together. When I came back, the house was empty. I didn't know what had happened. A cold hand pressed my heart. I ran to a neighbour's house. It also was empty. Then I saw a beggar in the street and he told me that soldiers had come and driven them all away. So I left alone. I hid myself. I begged. I wasn't going to let myself be caught. I slept in forests. I huddled in dark corners.

''Then I was taken in by a *goyische* family. They gave me food and they let me sleep in their house. They had mercy on me, they had *Rachmones*. For this I bless them. So it pleased God to save my life. But I had to pay a price. I had to deny myself. My family. My religion. I went to church with that family. I heard the mass. I made the sign of the cross. I was blessed by the priest."

Beads of perspiration formed on his forehead, and he pulled out a handkerchief that had been tucked into his sleeve and wiped them away. Arnold Weiss had stopped eating. The ham sandwich lay untouched on the tray.

"So I survived," Shemtov went on. "The only one in my family. Why? What reason did the *Rebonoh shel Olem* — blessed be the name — what reason did He have that I should survive? And in such a manner. Only in my heart of hearts I kept the faith, and I prayed that one day it should shine out. When the end of the war came, I was not yet sixteen. I ran away from that town, from that family. I didn't know where I was running. Finally I landed up in a camp. I was caught in a net, like a fish. With hundreds, with thousands of others. They were like me and they were not like me. Now I was free to practice my own religion. To pray in the holy language. Only now everything was bitter. The *Rebonoh shel Olem* deserted me. Of all my family, He had saved only me, and now He deserted me . . . . In the camp when I came there was already a *shul.* Three times a day they prayed there. All day long some sat and learned there. At first I went with a glad heart. After I had denied who I was for so long, I could pray again to my own God in the holy language. Only now my heart was a desert. I couldn't sing. I had no joy when I said the prayers . . . ." He reached for his handkerchief again and wiped the perspiration from his brow. "Why should this happen? Was it a punishment? Was it a test? I didn't know, and I became very bitter and very angry. The *Rebonoh shel Olem* — blessed be the name — had cast me out. He had saved me. And then He had cast me out. Why? How could this be? It was a great, great riddle. But it was a riddle I couldn't solve. So — if He had cast me away, I would cast him away. For ten years, the Presence withdrew itself from me, and I withdrew myself from the Presence. For ten years."

He stopped. It seemed as if he were waiting for Arnold Weiss to say something, but Weiss, stunned by the intensity of Shemtov's words, remained silent.

Shemtov continued. "Then I was scooped up again. Like a stone in a great shovel. With other young people I was sent to Canada. To start a new life. I went to Winnipeg. And there I lived with a nice Jewish family. They treated me like a son. They gave me love. They were wonderful people. Only what did they believe?"

"But they gave you love," Arnold Weiss protested.

''Yes,'' said Josef Shemtov, ''yes, they gave me love. But it wasn't enough. There was still in me a desert, an emptiness. And they couldn't fill it. Deep in my heart of hearts there was a darkness. They sent me to school. I studied. I became an accountant. Then I left Winnipeg and I went to Montreal . . . One day there, on Friday evening, in the winter, I saw a Chassid. I have never before seen Chassidim in Canada. Not in Winnipeg, and not in Montreal before that moment. He walked in the opposite direction from me. And then suddenly something in me told me — commanded me — that I should turn around and follow him. He went to his *shul* and I went with him. And there that evening, when the Chassidim welcomed the bride of the Sabbath, there was so much joy that I couldn't believe it was possible. I couldn't believe that it was true. God had taken away every reason for singing, and still they sang. . . . Then suddenly, the Presence entered into me, like a stream. I cried out. I sang. I sang, too. I had no reason to sing, and yet I sang.''

A male voice announced, first in English, than in French, that the plane would be landing in New York shortly, and asked all passengers to fasten their seatbelts.

Josef Shemtov fell silent. He fumbled with his belt, fastened it, and opened his book. Arnold Weiss wanted to ask him some questions, but Shemtov's whole bearing now discouraged any further conservation.

Smoothly the plane touched down. Shemtov looked up from his book. *''Boruch Hashem,''* he murmured.

The plane came to a halt. People began to move out into the aisle. Josef Shemtov put on his broad black hat. Slowly they moved towards the front of the plane, Josef Shemtov just ahead of Arnold Weiss. As they were about to leave the plane, Shemtov turned round and held out his hand. Arnold Weiss took it.

''Seit gesund,'' Shemtov said. ''Remember your grandfather. He knew that the tongue is the pen of the heart, but melody is the pen of the soul.'' He nodded his head slowly. ''He sang. Your grandfather. Oh, yes. He sang, too.''

Elliott Bronstein

The Ritual Hour

It was only filial duty that brought me back to the Temple. I hadn't been inside for years, and felt uncomfortable the whole time. As soon as the benediction was over, I put my hands in my pockets and started to leave. Then we saw each other. Beside the President of the Temple stood Benjamin Lazar. Nodding to himself, he glided over to me. Instead of shaking my hand, Benjamin Lazar cupped it between both of his and pressed it like a waffle iron.

"I saw your father just a month ago," he said. "Did he ever tell you we had a coffee together downtown?"

"Yes."

"I gave him a message for you. Did he give it to you?"

"I don't remember."

"I told him to say, 'You should come out to our ritual hour one Sunday morning.' Just to see what it's all about. You might like it."

" . . . . . " I mumbled, not making sense.

"I really enjoyed talking to your father. He was a fine man. He was a religious man."

"Do you think so?"

"Oh yes. He was very happy to see how I'd come around. Like so many others of that generation—my parents too—who'd let the faith slide. He felt tremendous guilt. He was glad to see one of his son's old crowd take up the traditions."

"Guilty? My father? He wasn't even a member of the Temple. We—my family—had to buy a membership so we could bring him in here. In fact, I've never known anyone who thought about it less than he did. He thought about it . . . less than I do."

"He never lost his belief," Benjamin Lazar said. "No one does."

I brought my shoulders up. "My father—you met him once for coffee—you're entitled to your own opinion." I was anxious to get out of there. "It was good to see you again," I said.

"Do you have a car? No? Then let me give you a lift home."

"I'm not going home. I'm going downtown, to the Employment Bureau."

"Then I'll drive you downtown!" he said.

Once inside the car he said,

"So, and what are you doing now? Not too much of anything, eh? Still not tired of it yet? I admire your patience! Do you still see Morris? I hear he's very successful now. You see, I don't begrudge his success. I'm very happy for him."

We stopped alongside a small park, where he rolled down his window.

"I know you must think I'm crazy," he said. "You can't believe I'm sincere!"

"I don't doubt your sincerity," I interrupted.

"Because you're still trying to protect your parents! We all do that. They were the first to drop the ball, you know. We were raised outside it, outside the faith; naturally we ignore it too."

"It's getting late, unfortunately; I wanted to spend the morning looking for a job."

"I won't keep you! For your father's sake. Why did you come otherwise? Stay a few minutes more."

He closed his eyes and pulled at his beard. He resembled a young man listening to classical music. I began to compose a colorful account of the incident for Morris and the others, none of whom had seen him since his acceptance of the faith. As an anecdote it was bound to amuse them — but there was something very disturbing at the heart of his story. With the strain of recent events, I sometimes had felt the firm grasp of mind upon the facts of life begin to slip, like tires spinning on ice, slipping. The deepest treads can't get a grip. It was hard to be sure of anything.

"You never expected this to happen to me," he said. "You think of it as a surrender. You probably believe I've betrayed you." (It was true.) "So harsh! When the fact is I feel just the same - only better of course. I haven't changed so much that any of the old gang should fail to recognize me. My ears are just as prominent. My voice still cracks when I get excited. Even with my beliefs, I swear I'm the same person!"

Anxious to be conciliatory, I said, "Although you must've understood our surprise when we heard . . . "

"Of course! I haven't lost my sense of humor. I knew what comments you'd all make, after all the drugs. I wish I had the words to describe it to you. Those drugs—I don't touch them anymore, by the way—made these beliefs possible. It's like . . . leaving home, being driven to the airport, and they tell you, "We have to say goodbye to you here, we can't go past this point." He smiled nervously and said, perhaps needlessly, "I am very happy now."

"You remember," he asked me, "that I was the one who first persuaded you to experiment with drugs?"

"I'll never forget it," I answered. "You gave some to all of us. Where you got it from I never knew. How you learned about it—where you first found the courage to try it—because in the beginning you were on your own, there was no one (I imagine) to say, 'Trust me', which you told each of us and which we repeated whenever we gave it to others, whom you never met, but whose lives you also changed—" I shook my head. I felt glad to be talking to him, even though it was an inconvenience. I desperately needed to find a job.

He said:

"But don't you see the Temple is the same? The rituals aren't just random actions. There *were* people thousands of years ago, just like us, who witnessed the original revelation which so convinced them that they made their sons repeat it, and their sons repeat it, and their sons repeat it, till it came down to us: why would they lie to us? Did I lie to you? Did you promise the others something you couldn't give? If I say that the sensation of prayer is *exactly* the same we used to have—and I swear it is—" he whispered as if it was a secret everyone is the world leaned forward to hear: "I thought of you as it ripped through me, and tried to reach you through your father - why won't you trust me now?"

Joseph Sherman

Notes toward a Jewish Poem

At one point during the summer of 1965, I stood waiting for a bus at the corner of an intersection in Côte St. Luc. I wore green pants and a white nylon windbreaker featuring a university crest. A Québecois arrived at the same stop — French-Canadian beneath his crisp pants, plaid jacket, and sculpted fedora: ''Has the number five bus been here yet?'' ''Not since I've been here.'' I told him. Pause. ''Are you a Jew?'' I heard him ask. Pause. I said yes.

The number five bus arrived soon after, and we went off to our own important places. I have told the story of this encounter several times, each time transforming my listeners into a concerned audience. Obviously the man harboured a deep resentment and insatiable curiosity about Jews. Obviously. He probably made a practice of telling himself and friends that he could pick a Jew out of a crowd or thin air, if there was a neighbourhood of *Juif* in proximity. Probably.

I should feel a victim but I don't — at least not of the man with the question. I feel amused. Still. Sometimes I wonder if I ought to feel guilt — not for being a Jew, but for being obvious.

It was a good question. The ''interrogator'' did not realize it, but a smidgen of thought occupied the silence of that pause before I gave my answer. From the standpoint of consistent observance and devotion, I might have qualified my reply at the very least, but my masters had taught me well. They told me that I was a Jew, and I believed them. I even felt Jewish — a strange feeling at times. I have worn this feeling with its variations forever. It cannot be discarded, I was told. And I believed them.

I mentioned my masters. They came and sporadically continue to come in all weights and sizes. In the early 1950's, when I was trudging up the slope of Mount Pleasant Street after school to the Cheder lessons at the synagogue, I might hear unsubtle asides about Jews. These were not regular, but I remember the occasions and the language. During one of the universal cycles of Nazi revivalism, ignoramuses painted inverted swastikas on synagogue walls. I recall having a troupe of gentile kids, my own age and younger, fly by me crying. "Jew! Jew!" I even looked behind me to see who else might deserve this. These, the flying *goyim,* were some of my masters. I took a lot for granted in those days — I still do. But if I ever doubted my inheritance, my own bequest, here I was reminded of it by scruffy little *goyim* who seemed fascinated by the way "Jew" came shooting off the collective tongue. They weren't doing so bad at picking up "the torch." Anyway, they did more for establishing my racial identity, so-called, than my own Jewish instructors. I might conceivably suspect my own people, but never outsiders. If they thought that I was what they called me, I must have been.

I was born a Jew. I was born of a Jewish mother and a Jewish father, with a heritage and history made to order. My family and I will not let me forget it. "What if I had been orphaned and raised a Moslem by a Moslem family?" I seem to recall shouting once at my mother. "God forbid!" she replied to her child in mock horror. "You would still be a Jew, only you wouldn't know it."

In my small birthplace of Bridgewater, Nova Scotia, devoid of blacks, and nearly devoid of Jews, even my doctor somehow managed to be a Jew. So I was pulled from a Jewish belly by firm Jewish hands, sixty-nine miles from the nearest synagogue, and the doctor married to a gentile. I cannot help but feel that there must have been a conspiracy shared at the moment of my birth — by the doctor and my truly suffering mother — that the poor *shiksa* nurses could never have shared. "Aha!" the doctor would say as I slithered up and spluttered out of the waters. My mother would groan sympathetically. That would be enough.

There are times when I use the term "Jew" as if it were interchangeable with the term "human being." I was born a human being. I was born of a human being mother and a human being father — and there it stops. For it is my heritage and the history of a people who claim me as one of their own that cause me to use labels, and more important to be the label I use — for I am a Jew, not because I was told, but because I accepted it. "Jew" has been used so often as an expletive, that it's hard to decide what you would like to be called, but I really have little choice.

Many people fail to understand racial nationalism. Often, it is beyond comprehension. I am too introspective as a "thinking Jew," much too close to it to be anything but a subjective person straining for a better vantage point. I know that I have my own prejudices, and I am daring with my ethnic chip. I know because I am told, one way or another.

As a human being I have absorbed sensations all my life. Some of what has been taught me might legitimately result in an opinion, or an outlook, that is biased and offensive to others. I am supposed to sort it all out, as a living individual without recourse to name or conditioned belief, because there is no excuse for blindness here. I take the responsibility. I can extract the best from my learned traditions, or I can draw on that that should be discarded because of the harm it does. It is too easy to warp, to fall back on one's mortality and consequent limitations as a defense. I write about some Jews at some times, because I think I recognize them. I claim no more. I may be wrong in what I say, in my manner of saying it, in my too frequent failure to judge myself accordingly. In the end, I have, despite a reputed ruling to the contrary, at least one other "god" before me and that is myself.

I wish my children to know what paints and different sorts of building blocks have gone into their creation. I will tell them this, and while they are still young I will probably make them wear a sort of epidermal identity. They will be able to play it like an instrument. Finally, they will decide for themselves what they are and if they cannot lay claim to being individuals first, it will not be because they have not been taught. But then, they have every right of rejection and adoption. I know it.

The supermarket was crowded with shopping carts morally requiring licenses and registration. As I reached across a parked food buggy I heard its operator ask of me. "Are you a Jew?" Without any noticeable hesitation I unscrewed the cap of my freshly acquired jar of Mrs. White's Kosher Dills, offered my aisle companion one, and answered, "I am a person." I believe I smiled as I said this. And he laughed, and said, "That's funny, so am I!" And we were both laughing, and it must have been contagious because a lot of other people found themselves laughing with us. I was inwardly pleased, and not a little proud that I, for once, had been able to respond so quickly, and truthfully, and well. Actually, this incident has not happened yet. I just thought of it. But I can wait.

Avrum Malus

I Am a Modern Jew

I do not put on *tefilin*
I run each day

I put on my running shoes
heavy sweatsocks
and limp or fly
or do something between limping and flying
around the track

around and around the track I go
a modern Jew
on running shoes
limping and flying

Tom Wayman

Jews

A weird family to come from
like most families. And if you trace it back
you have to stop at the great-grandparents:
the most distant lives anyone remembers.
Behind them, only a few names
can be recalled.

Herschel, born in 1897
my father's mother's brother
remembers *his* father
Louis Altschuler, born 1859
in Russia, lived in Mglin
also known as Amlin.
Louis trained as a rabbi
but decided it was the rich
who ruled the synagogues.
So he gave it up and in 1899
emigrated to Bracebridge
Ontario, where he worked as a pedlar
carrying all the objects he sold door-to-door
farmhouse-to-farmhouse, laid out and
wrapped in one huge square of cloth
gathered at the four corners and hoisted
onto his back. By 1904
he had saved enough to bring over
his wife and five children, including Herschel

so he quit peddling as unsuitable
for a family man and worked
at a number of jobs
and moved to Barrie, and then in 1913
to Toronto, by this time with a sixth child.

Herschel remembers the other Jew in Bracebridge:
a man who made a living
by selling the labor of certain immigrants
for whom he translated, arranged jobs
collected wages and provided bad housing
while taking a large percentage of what they earned.
Eventually one man protested
and roused up the others
so the labor broker fired the troublemaker.
But before he left, the broker
slipped money into his pocket
and then had him arrested for theft.
As the court needed a translator
one of Herschel's brothers was asked.
The broker went to Herschel's father
and appealed to him as a fellow Jew
to order his son to falsify the accused's story
during the trial. Herschel's father refused
saying *this*
is a matter of justice.
But later when the laborer was acquitted
and the broker himself charged,
Herschel's father would permit no word
to be translated against him.
After all, he said, he *is* a Jew.

And isn't this the idea of a family?
You don't want any member to cause harm to somebody else

Photo 20: Students of Jewish National Radical School, Montréal, c. 1920.

but at the same time you don't want one of us hurt.

On the other side of my life
it was a similar pattern to get to North America.
My mother's mother, Margaret Matusov
was born near Vitebsk about 1870
and eventually married a carpenter.
They left Russia together
spent six months in Berlin
and arrived in England about 1895
settling in Newcastle
until 1910, when Joseph left for Canada.
His wife and, by now, four children
went to Liverpool to wait
while he earned the passage money
lost it gambling, and by 1912 had it again
and the whole family arrived in Toronto.

At every stage of these journeys: life
and death. Margaret's sister
a woman whose name no one I talked to recalls
was with the family as it waited in Liverpool
and met and married a man named Bailey, *Uncle Mushka*
and stayed. Herschel identifies
an old photograph as one of his brothers
dead of T.B. in northern Ontario before the First World War.

So many people have become
just a name on a chart I made
or at most a few anecdotes and odd facts.
An important date in a life
shrinks from being a particular incident
on a certain day in one of the months
— a moment during which someone
was probably even aware of the weather —
to being just a reference to some hazy
approximate year.

And the family is dwindling: couples now mostly have
one or two children
moving apart on the map, and in their lives.

But is it only the words of a priest, or lines
on a form from the State, or the birth of a child
that can make a family? Over the decades
people have also tried religion and class
race and the tribe. Myself
I think we have come to another kind of family.
Perhaps now it is just ourselves and our friends
— some of whom we like a lot, and others
we see as little as possible of like any unpleasant relative.

One list I have of my friends
includes a nurse, a seaman, a clerk
a builder, a printer, a logger, a teacher
and so on. But this doesn't explain who they are
any more than if I wrote down their names:
each with its own family
that can also be traced across this continent to where
it leaps backward over an ocean into another world.

I meet so many people, enjoy them
live with them or around them for years
and then some turn into words on paper
in a letter, or on a chart.

I believe all these people form a family.
And now I've said that
I think it is up to someone else to worry about
which of them are Jews.

J. I. Segal

A Jew

My comrades are all such travellers
buzzing around in planes,
with one look they take the measure
of the wide bend of the sky.

If they have breakfast in Montreal
they drink coffee in New York,
of course that's all very grand,
even wonderful — but also queer.

Theirs are pleasures I renounce
especially on rainy days
when I can sit down beside the window
and think about an old wayside inn;

And how a cart full of Hasidim
drove up there late one night
and changed the simple little inn
to a beautiful palace;

And how the small band of faithful
sat around the wooden table
as radiant as if they were gathered
in the corridors of heaven.

Photo 21: Hyman's Book Store, Spadina Ave., Toronto, 1925.

Later I couldn't even remember
the Torahs and Haggadahs
but my heart is still full
of sweet worshipful longing.

It's no use my turning east
and it's no use my praying west,
I'm forever on the road, in transit,
dragging my baggage of exile.

That world is all gone now,
there's no monument to mark it,
and the only leaf left from the deluge
is a page in a Yiddish book.

So what is the leaf's green message
what stories does it bring?
only that a tree stood on the road
lighted by a single star.

The tree is still standing there
with the little star on its branch,
and it shines so strangely on the road
and the tree too has grown strange;

But it survives, my Jewish tree,
like a talisman of homecoming
and it longs to gather all us Jews
from our spaceless boundaries of loss.

Translated from the Yiddish, 1984,
by Miriam Waddington

Glossary

Aliyoth	Going up to read from the Torah in the synagogue.
Am K'shai Oref	A "stiff-necked" or tenacious group of people. A Biblical description of the Jews.
Ba'al Shem Tov	1700-1760 "Master of a Good Name". Founder and first leader of the Chassidic movement in modern times. Famous as a miracle worker.
Belial (Belia'al)	Demon in Jewish mysticism. Also a name applied to Satan.
Bibelforscher	(Ger.) Bible researcher. (Used ironically in *The Second Scroll.)*
Boruch Hashem	"Blessed be the name" (of G-d). Hebrew benediction, usually said in gratitude for a happy event.
Boychik	"Little Boy"; affectionate greeting or description of a young man or boy.
Derech-Eretz	Hebrew term meaning good manners and proper behaviour.
Diaspora	Exile. The dispersion of Jews throughout the world; Jewish communities in countries outside of Israel.
Farbrengen	A gathering of Chassidic Jews to meet with their "Rebbe" (Rabbi).
Ferdeleh	"Little Horse"; affectionate Yiddish term for a horse.
Fiel	Yiddish term for "much".

Gaberdines Type of material from which traditional Jewish men's coats were made.

Goy, Goyim, Goyische ''Nations''. Sometimes used as a term describing non-Jews.

Gymnasium The German term for a secondary school which prepares students for University.

Hagba Raising the Torah before and after its reading in the synagogue.

Haggadah Literally, ''telling''. The book used during the Passover Seder which outlines the order of the service and recounts the Exodus from Egypt.

Hakofos Circling the bima (platform) of the synagogue during certain holidays.

Halachah The part of the Talmud which contains the legal discussion.

Hassid A member of a Jewish sect founded in Poland around 1750 in opposition to religious rationalism and scholarly elitism.

Juif French for Jew; sometimes used in a derogatory sense.

Kaddish A prayer in Jewish ritual. One type of ''Kaddish'' is a mourner's prayer usually said by the son of the deceased.

Kike As offensive slang word for Jew.

Kliene (Klein) Yiddish word for ''little''.

Kol Nidrei ''All Our Vows'' - The opening words of a prayer in the Yom Kippur eve service.

L'Chayim	"To life"; Hebrew toast to health.
Litvak	A Lithuanian Jew.
Milah Banquet	The meal celebrating a Jewish circumcision ceremony.
Mensch	"A Person"; Yiddish word meaning a decent, worthy human being.
Oy Gevalt	"Oh, no!" ; Yiddish exclamation of dismay.
Pogrom	An organized massacre of people, originally of Jews, in Russian or Poland in the last two centuries.
Rachmoness	A Yiddish word derived from Hebrew, meaning pity.
Rashi-Solomon Bar Isaac	(1040-1105) Jewish Scholar, born in France; author of commentaries on the Pentateuch and Talmud.
Reb	Yiddish term used when addressing a respected person.
Rebonoh Shel Olem	"Master of the Universe!" Hebrew exclamation, with reference to G-d.
Shabus	Sabbath; the Jewish day of rest.
Schnorrer	Yiddish word for a beggar. One who wheedles others into supplying his wants.
Seit Gesund	Be well; Yiddish blessing.
Sestina	Thirty-six line lyrical verse form.
Shiksa (Shikse)	A non-Jewish girl. Often used disparagingly. (Male form is Shaygetz)

Shma-Yisroel — ''Hear, O Israel''. Hebrew prayer proclaiming the unity of G-d.

Shofar — The ram's horn blown during the Jewish New Year service and at the conclusion of Yom Kippur.

Shtetl — Yiddish; a Jewish town or village formerly found in Eastern Europe.

Shul — Literally ''school''; the Yiddish word for synagogue.

Tau-Aleph — 'From ''Z'' to ''A'''. The last and first letters of the Hebrew alphabet.

T'fillin — Phylacteries; small leather boxes containing prayers worn by Jewish men on the left arm and forehead during morning weekday prayers.

Torah — The body of all Jewish wisdom and law. Also refers to the actual scrolls of the Law (the five books of Moses).

Yeshiva — A higher school for Talmudic study; A rabbinical seminary.

Yisgadal V'Yiskadash — ''Magnified and Sanctified''. First two words of the Hebrew Kaddish prayer. (See there)

Yoisher — Yiddish term for rectitude or honesty.

Zigeuner — (Ger.) ''Deceptive, lying people''; also: Gypsies.

Biographies

Allan, Ted, *(1916-   ). Lies My Father Told Me.* Ted Allan was born in Montreal to second generation parents. His background was the basis for the short story "Lies My Father Told Me". He later turned it into a screen play for a movie which was nominated for an Academy Award. He has written other books, both fiction and non-fiction, short stories, various radio, TV and movie scripts and numerous theatrical plays which have been produced in London as well as Toronto. Two of his better-known works include the novel: **This Time a Better Earth** and a biography of Dr. Norman Bethune entitled **The Scalpel; the Sword,** which he co-authored.

Bronstein, Elliott, *(1952-   ). The Ritual Hour.* Elliott Bronstein grew up in Winnipeg, Manitoba. He was part of the late '60's generation, which in Winnipeg occurred in the early '70's. Since 1972 he has lived in Greece and Ireland, crossed Europe twice by bicycle, and traveled for a year in the Andean countries of South America. He has worked as counselor, teacher, chimney-sweep, furniture stripper, and senior center director. Bronstein lives in the United States, but still makes a yearly pilgrimage to Winnipeg, which remains the setting for most of his short stories.

Cohen, Leonard, *(1934-). Story of Isaac; Hitler; All There is to Know About Adolf Eichmann; The Genius;* Excerpts from **The Favourite Game;** *Out of the Land of Heaven.* Leonard Cohen grew up in the wealthy upper-class area of Westmount, complete with a chauffeur and governess. He was rebellious and quite unconventional. He barely graduated from McGill and made a short-lived attempt at graduate studies in Columbia University, leaving after three weeks. Returning to Montreal, he published his first book of poetry, **Let Us Compare Mythologies.** In it he explored the powerful and sometimes conflicting images of Christian and Jewish cultures. He began reading his poetry in coffee houses and began a first novel which was never published.

He was also drawn into his family's clothing business but left it and Montreal when he was awarded a Canada Council grant to travel to England and pursue his writing. During this time **The Favorite Game** was written and published. From England he went to Hydra, a small island in Greece, where he stayed for the next ten years. In Greece he composed both poetry such as the collection, **Flowers for Hitler,** and another novel, **Beautiful Losers.** By the time he returned to North America permanently he had become popular not only as a writer and poet but was more widely known as a singer and composer with songs like **Suzanne, The Story of Isaac** and **Bird on a Wire.** He was doing as many concerts as poetry readings and his first two record albums, **Leonard Cohen** and **Songs From a Room** were compared to Bob Dylan's works both in their appeal to the youth of the sixties and their powerful and disturbing images. More recent works include **Death of a Ladies' Man** and **Book of Mercy.**

Cohen, Matt, *(1942-). The Universal Miracle.* Matt Cohen was born in Kingston, Ontario which became the setting for many of his works. He moved to Ottawa and then graduated from the University of Toronto. He taught for a short while and now lives and writes on a farm near Godfrey, Ontario. He has published a series of connected novels as well as a book of short stories, **Columbus and the Fat Lady,** and a recent novel entitled **The Spanish Doctor.**

Cooperman, Stanley, *(1929-1976). Masada.* Stanley Cooperman was born in New York and taught in various universities in the United States and Canada. He eventually settled in Vancouver. He has a number of books of poetry published as well as critical essays. He has published over 300 poems in eighty different magazines.

Goldenberg, Murray, *(1949-   ). Kol Nidrei.* Murray Goldenberg was born in Winnipeg and attended the University of Manitoba, where he graduated in 1972. Since that time, he has worked as an English and Geography teacher, community worker, freelance writer and educational consultant, and in an assortment of jobs as farm labourer, construction worker, and youth leader. After stays of various lengths in Israel, Sri Lanka, and British Columbia, he settled in a small farmhouse in rural Manitoba, where he currently languishes. He has published poetry and prose in various prairie anthologies and journals.

Gotlieb, Phyllis, *(1926-   ). Kaddish; A Ceremonial.* Phyllis Gotlieb was born and raised in Toronto, a third generation Canadian. She is married to a university professor and a mother of three. Besides poetry she is also known for science fiction short stories, novels and radio dramas. One of her novels, **Why Should I Have All the Grief?** is about a holocaust survivor of Auschwitz. Other works include: the novels **O Master Caliban!** and **A Judgment of Dragons,** and a poetry collection entitled **The Works.**

Gotlieb, Sondra, *(1936-   ). The Wrongies.* (Excerpt from **True Confections).** Sondra Gotlieb grew up in Winnipeg's North End during the forties and fifties. She is now a magazine journalist in Ottawa and a contributing editor to **Maclean's** and **Chatelaine.** She has published two cookbooks, **The Gourmet's Canada** and **Cross Canada Cooking,** and a novel entitled **First Lady, Last Lady.**

Kleiman, Ed, *(1932-   ). The Handicap.* Ed Kleiman grew up in Winnipeg's North End and graduated from the University of Manitoba. He then took his M.A. at the University of Toronto and taught in London, England, for two years. **The Immortals,** his first collection of short stories, was written during a sabbatical in Massachusetts in 1974. He is now an associate professor of English at the University of Manitoba and is currently completing a second collection of short stories.

Klein, A. M., *(1909-1972). The Second Scroll; And in that Drowning Instant; Beggars I Have Known; Portraits of a Minyan.* A. M. Klein was born to an Orthodox family four years after its arrival in Montreal, in flight from Russian persecution. He was one of two male twins but his brother died in his first year. Klein grew up fluent in five languages and was a brilliant student. He had intended to become a rabbi but then chose law and was called to the bar in 1933. He was also deeply involved in writing and his culture. He became editor of the **Canadian Jewish Chronicle** in 1939 and in 1940 published his first book of poetry, **Hath Not a Jew.** By 1945 his poetry had received so much recognition that he became a visiting lecturer in poetry at McGill University. In 1948 he was awarded the Governor General's Award for Poetry for **The Rocking Chair and Other Poems.** His most famous novel, **The Second Scroll,** received international critical acclaim. In 1955 he was struck by a severe illness and lived in seclusion until his death in 1972.

Korn, Rachel, (1898-). My Mother Often Wept. Rachel Korn, who was born in Poland, lived in Russia and Sweden during and after World War II, and immigrated to Canada in 1948. She writes in Yiddish, but has been translated into many other languages; **Paper Roses, Selected Poems of Rachel Korn** has recently been translated into English by poet Seymour Levitan.

Kreisel, Henry, (1922-). Chassidic Song. Henry Kreisel was born in Vienna and escaped the Nazis in 1940. He was considered an ''enemy alien'' by the English government and interned in a special camp in Canada. When some of his writing was smuggled out his true circumstances were recognized and he was freed from the camp. He is best known for two novels, **The Rich Man** (1948) and **The Betrayal** (1964). **The Almost Meeting & Other Stories** is a collection of short stories including *Chassidic Song* and represents twenty-five years of writing. He is presently a professor of Comparative Literature and Drama at the University of Alberta in Calgary.

Layton, Irving, (1912-). The Real Values; Synagogue in West Palm Beach; Das Wahre Ich; Post Crematoria; For My Two Sons, Max and David. Layton is a controversial and aggressive figure in Canadian poetry. He is outspoken in his attitudes towards his own Jewishness as well in his ideas about his ideas about love, power, education and many social issues. His parents emigrated from Rumania when he was a baby and he grew up in Montreal. There he first studied agriculture and then economics. He eventually taught at a parochial boys' school. He is now a professor of English at York University. He has published about twenty-five books of poetry since 1954, including **A Red Carpet for the Sun,** which received a Governor General's Award for Poetry. He has published short stories, edited books of poetry and is also a commentator on public affairs. Some of his works include: **Collected Poems, Engagements, The Prose of Irving Layton, For My Brother Jesus,** and **Droppings from Heaven.**

Levine, Norman, (1924-   ). Lower Town, Ottawa. Norman Levine was raised in Lower Town, Ottawa, which, like Mordecai Richler's St. Urbain Street in Montreal, was what he called "a lower class, near slum neighbourhood". His family's religious orthodoxy also tended to isolate him from the rest of Ottawa. He joined the RCAF during World War II and after university in Montreal moved to a village in Cornwall, England, where he lived for more than thirty years. He returned to Canada in 1980. He is best known for his short stories and has published many books including **Thin Ice, Canada Made Me** and **I Don't Want to Know Anyone Too Well.**

Ludwig, Jack, (1922-   ). Requiem For Bibul. Jack Ludwig was born and raised in Winnipeg and attended the University of Manitoba and the University of California. He presently teaches at the State University of New York. He has published two novels, **Confusions** and **Above Ground,** and many short stories.

Malus, Avrum, (1943-   ). I Am A Modern Jew. Avrum Malus, who was born in Montreal, teaches literature at the Université de Sherbrooke. He has published a book of poetry entitled **I Set The Fire Which Destroyed Our Home.**

Mandel, Eli, (1922-   ). Rabbi Berner's Farm; Day of Atonement: Standing; Psalm 24. Eli Mandel was born in Estevan, Saskatchewan. In 1943 he went overseas with the Army Medical Corp. He returned after the war and received his M.A. He has now completed a PhD. and is a professor in the Fine Arts and Humanities departments at York University. His first poems were published in 1954 and he has received many awards for his works including a Governor General's Award for **Idiot Joy.** Other works include **Out of Place** and a more recent collection entitled **Dreaming Backwards.** He is also known as an editor and a literary critic.

Maynard, Fredelle Bruser, *(1922-). From Yon Far Country; The Okay Store:* excerpts from **Raisins and Almonds.** Ms. Fredelle Maynard was born in Foam Lake, Saskatchewan, and moved extensively as a child, as her writings express. She has a PhD. from Radcliffe and writes on a free lance basis. She has taught creative writing and divides her time between Toronto and New Hampshire, where her husband teaches university.

Mayne, Seymour, *(1944-). Zalman.* Seymour Mayne divides his time between Jerusalem and his native Montreal. His parents were immigrants who lost most of their families in the Holocaust. He is a professor of English at the University of Ottawa and has edited as well as translated numerous books. He has published over 700 poems, some of which are collected in two books, **Name** and **The Impossible Promised Land: Poems New and Selected.**

Richler, Mordecai, *(1913-). The Street; Pinky's Squealer; This Year at the Arabian Nights Hotel; The Holocaust and After.* Richler was born a third generation Canadian in a working class area in Montreal. He worked his way through Sir George Williams University with a series of jobs, including bill collector, bartender, waiter, factory hand and journalist, and then attended art school for a short time. He finally turned to fiction writing. After a year in Europe, mainly in Spain, he finished his first novel, **The Acrobats,** at the age of twenty-two. At 28 he moved to London where he stayed on and off for two decades working as a novelist and screen writer. However, many of his settings and characters remain distinctly Canadian and after eight novels and many essays, articles and short stories he is considered one of Canada's finest writers. He has been criticized and praised for his irreverent and outrageous depictions of Jewish characters. His work includes **The Apprenticeship of Duddy Kravitz** which is also a successful movie, **St. Urbain's Horsemen, Joshua Then and Now,** and a children's story, **Jacob Two Two and the Hooded Fang.** He has now returned to Montreal where he lives with his wife and five children.

Segal, Jakov-Itzchok, *(1896-1954). Late Autumn in Montreal; A Jew; Aunt Dvorah; Scenario; A Song About My Son.* At fifteen, J. I. Segal immigrated from the Ukraine to Montreal, where he was to live for the rest of his life.

He became a tailor and later a teacher in the Jewish Day schools. Although he wrote some early poetry in Hebrew and Russian, most of his works are in Yiddish. Poetry collections include **Fun Mayn Velt, Sefer Yiddish.**

Sherman, Joseph, *(1945-). Notes Towards a Jewish Poem; Commentary on the Jewish Problem; The Only Game in Town.* Joseph Sherman was born in Bridgewater, Nova Scotia and grew up in Cape Breton. He has several collections of his poetry in print, including **Birthday** and **Chaim the Slaughterer.** He is presently teaching in New Brunswick.

Sherman, Ken, *(1950-). Alien.* Ken Sherman, Toronto born, received his B.A. from York University and M.A. in English literature from the University of Toronto. He has written for various periodicals and was the co-founder and editor of **Waves.** After extensive travel, he began teaching in various community colleges in Ontario. His collections of poetry include **The Cost of Living, Snake Music,** and **Words for Elephant Man.**

Torgov, Morley, *(1928-). Queen Street,* from **A Good Place to Come From.** Morley Torgov's childhood in Sault Ste. Marie is the subject of his book **A Good Place to Come From,** which won the Leacock Award for humour. He now lives and writes in Toronto and has published two novels, **The Abramsky Variations** and **The Outside Chance of Maximilian Glick.**

Usiskin, Michael, *(1876-1950). How Come Jews Want to be Farmers?* Michael Usiskin was a Jewish intellectual and farmer who was born in London. Arriving at Edenbridge Farm Colony in east-central Saskatchewan in 1911, he lived there for most of his life. In later years he retired to Winnipeg, where he died. His best-known work was a Yiddish-language book of memoirs entitled **Oksen Un Motoren,** which was published originally in 1945, and has recently been translated under the title of **Uncle Mike's Edenbridge** by his niece, Marcia Usiskin Basman.

Waddington, Miriam, *(1917-). Second Generation; A Place of Witches; Unquiet World; Traffic Lights at Passover.* Miriam Waddington was born in Winnipeg to Russian immigrant parents. She attended the Peretz Shule there. Later, she attended an Ottawa high school and graduated as a social worker from the University of Toronto. She worked in clinics, hospitals, prisons and various agencies and then taught social work at

McGill University. After giving up professional work to raise her children, she became more involved in poetry, publishing **Green World** in 1945. Ms. Waddington is now a professor of English and Canadian Literature at York University in Toronto and has published eleven books of poetry, dozens of critical articles, short stories, reviews and translations of Russian and German poetry. Her own work has been translated and published in the Soviet Union and Rumania, and has won many important awards in Canada. Some of her collections of poetry include **Green World, The Second Silence, Driving Home, The Price of Gold, The Visitants,** and **Summer at Lonely Beach and Other Stories.**

Wayman, Tom, *(1945-). Where I Come From: Grandfather; Jews.* Tom Wayman was born in a small town in Ontario and then moved with his parents to Prince Rupert, B.C. He graduated from the University of British Columbia and then travelled and studied in California. Returning to Vancouver at twenty-four, he spent the next six years working in factories and construction crews. His poetry reflects his respect and understanding of common working people and is seldom concerned with Jewish identity. Collections include **Waiting for Wayman, Money and Rain: Tom Wayman Live!** and **Living on the Ground: Tom Wayman Country.**

Weintraub, William, *(1926-). Sport in the Old Testament.* William Weintraub was born in Montreal, where he still lives. He graduated from McGill University to become a journalist and copy editor. He has since written for radio and television as well as written and produced documentary films. His own award-winning screenplay of his book,**Why Rock the Boat?,** was made into a film in 1974. He has also written a novel called **The Underdogs.**

Wiseman, Adele, *(1928-). The Sacrifice.* Adele Wiseman was born in Winnipeg and graduated from the University of Manitoba. She travelled extensively, working as a teacher in Italy, an editor in England and crossing the Pacific to China in a coal-laden cargo boat. Her most famous novel, **The Sacrifice,** published when she was twenty-eight, is set in Winnipeg's North End during the period of large-scale immigration from Eastern Europe. It won the Governor-General's Award for Fiction. Other works include a play entitled *Testimonial,* the novel, **Crackpot,** and **Old Woman at Play,** a biography. She now lives in Toronto.

Acknowledgements

Allen, Ted. *Lies My Father Told Me;* from **Northern Lights.** C.E. Nelson, Ed: Doubleday, 1960.

Bronstein, Elliot. *The Ritual Hour;* Reprinted by permission of the author.

Cohen, Leonard. *The Genius, Story of Isaac;* from **Selected Poems, 1956-1968.** *Out of the Land of Heaven;* from **The Spicebox of Earth** (1961). *Hitler, All There is to Know about Adolph Eichmann;* from **Flowers for Hitler** (1964). *Palais D'Or, Mother, The Park;* from **The Favourite Game** (1970). All selections reprinted by permission of McClelland & Stewart, Toronto.

Cohen, Matt. *The Universal Miracle;* from **Night Flights.** Reprinted by permission of Doubleday & Co. Inc., 1978.

Cooperman, Stanley. *Masada;* from **Cannibals:** Oberon Press, Ottawa.

Goldenberg, Murray. *Kol Nidrei;* from **Chautauqua Review,** Winnipeg, 1983.

Gotlieb, Phyllis. *A Ceremonial, Kaddish;* from **Zodiac,** Brian Meeson, Ed.: by permission of the Canadian Council of Teachers of English.

Gotlieb, Sondra. *The Wrongies;* from **True Confections: or How My Family Arranged My Marriage.** Reprinted by permission of Musson Book Company, Toronto, 1978.

Kleiman, Ed. *The Handicap;* from **The Immortals:** NeWest Publishers Ltd., Edmonton, 1980.

Klein, A.M. *Beggars I Have Known;* from **The Canadian Forum,** Toronto, Ont. *Portraits of a Minyan, And in that Drowning Instant;* from **Collected Poems of A.M. Klein (1974).** Reprinted by permission of McGraw-Hill Ryerson Ltd. *The Second Scroll;* from **The Second Scroll:** McClelland & Stewart, Toronto, 1961.

Korn, Rachel. *My Mother Often Wept;* from **Jewish Dialogue**. Translated from the Yiddish by Seymour Levitan.

Kreisel, Henry. *Chassidic Song;* from **The Almost Meeting & Other Stories:** NeWest Publishers Ltd., Edmonton, Alberta, 1981.

Layton, Irving. *Synagogue in West Palm Beach;* from **Droppings from Heaven** (1979). *The Real Values, Das Wahre Ich, For My Two Sons, Max and David, Post Crematoria* from **The Unwavering Eye: Selected Poems, 1969-1975:** All reprinted by permission of McClelland & Stewart Ltd., Toronto.

Levine, Norman. *Lower Town, Ottawa;* from **Canada Made Me.** Reprinted by permission of the Bodley Head Ltd., for Putnam & Co., 1958.

Ludwig, Jack. *Requiem for Bibul;* from **Atlantic Magazine.**

Malus, Avrum. *I Am a Modern Jew;* from **I Set the Fire Which Destroyed Our House.** Reprinted by permission of the author.

Mandel, Eli. *Day of Atonement: Standing; Psalm 24;* from **Crusoe: Poems Selected and New:** House of Anansi Press, Toronto, 1973. Reprinted by permission. *Rabbi Berner's Farm;* from **Out of Place:** Press Porcépic, Victoria & Toronto, 1977.

Maynard, Fredelle Bruser. *The O-Kay Store; From Yon Far Country;* from **Raisins and Almonds:** by permission of Doubleday & Co. Inc. 1972.

Mayne, Seymour. *Zalman;* from **The Impossible Promised Land:** Mosaic Press, Valley Edition, Oakville, Ontario, 1981.

Richler, Mordecai. *This Year at the Arabian Nights Hotel;* Reprinted by permission of the author. *The Street; Pinky's Squealer;* from **The Street** (1969). *The Holocaust and After;* from **Shovelling Trouble** (1972). All reprinted by permission of McClelland & Stewart, Toronto.

Segal, J.I. *Scenario;* from **Soifer Yiddish;** *Aunt Dvorah; Late Autumn in Montreal; A Jew;* translated and adapted from the Yiddish by Miriam Waddington © 1984. *A Song About My Son;* English translation © by Seymour Levitan.

Sherman, Joe. *Commentary on the Jewish Problem;* from **Birthday:** New Brunswick Chapbooks; University of New Brunswick Press, Fredericton, New Brunswick, 1969. *The Only Game in Town;* from **Chaim the Slaughterer:** Oberon Press, Ottawa, Ontario, 1974. *Notes Towards a Jewish Poem;* Reprinted by permission of the author.

Sherman, Ken. *Alien;* from **Snake Music:** Mosaic Press, Oakville, Ont., 1978.

Torgov, Morley. *Queen Street;* from **A Good Place to Come From:** Lester & Orpen Dennys Publishers Ltd. Tor., 1974.

Usiskin, Michael. *How Come Jews want to be Farmers?;* from **Uncle Mike's Edenbridge,** translated by Marcia Usiskin Basman: Peguis Publishers Ltd. Winnipeg, Manitoba, 1983.

Waddington, Miriam. *A Place of Witches;* from **Summer at Lonely Beach and Other Stories:** Mosaic Valley Editors, Oakville, 1982. *Second Generation;* from **The Glass Trumpet:** Oxford University Press, Toronto, 1966. *Traffic Lights at Passover;* from **The Season's Lovers:** Ryerson Press, Toronto, 1958; 1984 © Miriam Waddington. *Unquiet World;* from **Green World:** First Statement Press, Montreal, 1945; © 1984 by Miriam Waddington.

Wayman, Tom. *Where I Come From: Grandfather;* Reprinted by permission of the author. *Jews;* from **Free Time: Industrial Poems:** MacMillan of Canada, a Division of Gage Publishers Ltd., 1977. Reprinted by permission of the author.

Weintraub, W. *Sport in the Old Testament;* from **Why Rock the Boat?:** Reprinted by permission of McClelland & Stewart, Toronto.

Wiseman, Adele. *The Sacrifice;* from **The Sacrifice:** MacMillan of Canada, a Division of Gage Publishing Ltd., 1968.

Every reasonable effort has been taken to trace ownership of copyright material. Information that will enable the publishers to rectify any omission in future editions will be appreciated. Unless otherwise stated, copyright remains with the authors.

Photo Acknowledgements

(1) From **Toronto Jewish Congress/Canadian Jewish Congress Ontario Region Archives:**
The Atlantic Fur Co., Toronto, early 1940's.
Jewish immigrants from Europe arriving at Halifax, c. 1949.
Prospectors' Store, Timmins, Ont., 1912.
Hyman's Book Store, Spadina Ave., Toronto, 1925.
Ryerson School basketball team, Toronto, 1915.
Zionist Youth Camp, Grimsby, Ont., 1946

(2) From **Canadian Jewish Congress National Archives, Montréal:**
First religious service for Canadian Jewish servicemen in Germany, March, 1945.
German Jewish refugees presents Torah to Canadian Jewish Congress, c. 1949.
Jewish refugees arriving in Canada from Europe, c. 1947.
Highland regiment parading through St. Urbain, Montréal.

(3) From **Jewish Historical Society of Western Canada, Winnipeg:**
Store and home of Zebulon Frank, Vancouver, 1916.
Jewish farm, Lipton, Sask., 1916.
Balfour Day Parade, Winnipeg, 1918.
Reverend Charloff ("Mohel") performing circumcision ceremony, 1972.
Blowing of the Shofar for High Holiday services.
Reading from the Torah at Beth Jacob Synagogue, Winnipeg, 1930's.
Jewish Holocaust victims during evacuation of a ghetto, c. 1943.
Cast of Yiddish play at Queen's Theatre, Winnipeg, 1918.
Jewish firemen, Victoria, B.C., c. 1870.

(4) From the **Jewish Public Library, Montréal:**
Hasidic youth studying Gemara, Montréal, 1960's.
Students of Jewish National Radical School, Montréal, c. 1920.